A Sense of *Community*

A Sense of *Community*

Essays on the Television Series and Its Fandom

Edited by
ANN-GEE LEE

McFarland & Company, Inc., Publishers
Jefferson, North Carolina

LIBRARY OF CONGRESS CATALOGUING-IN-PUBLICATION DATA

A sense of Community : essays on the television series and its fandom / edited by Ann-Gee Lee.
    p.   cm.
Includes bibliographical references and index.

ISBN 978-0-7864-7590-2 (softcover : acid free paper) ∞
ISBN 978-1-4766-1571-4 (ebook)

1. Community (Television program)   I. Lee, Ann-Gee, 1977–

PN1992.77.C64S46 2014
791.45'72—dc23   2014011331

BRITISH LIBRARY CATALOGUING DATA ARE AVAILABLE

© 2014 Ann-Gee Lee. All rights reserved

No part of this book may be reproduced or transmitted in any form or by any means, electronic or mechanical, including photocopying or recording, or by any information storage and retrieval system, without permission in writing from the publisher.

Cover image: Cast of *Community*, Season 2, 2010-2011 (Photofest)

Printed in the United States of America

McFarland & Company, Inc., Publishers
  Box 611, Jefferson, North Carolina 28640
    www.mcfarlandpub.com

For all the *Community* fans out there
and all the writers who inspire us.

Table of Contents

Preface	1
Introduction	3

Part I: Taking Things Literarily

Adventures in Time, Space and Community College: Narrative Structure and Thematic Depth — MINA HALLING	7
Modern Heroism — AMANDA RITER	24
Greendale Hyperreality — NETTIE BROCK	36
The Greendale Trickster: The Rise and Fall of Ben Chang — ANN-GEE LEE and NOAH E. SCHMIDT	51

Part II: The Political Playground

Inculcating Victorian Masculinities at "Loser College": Jeff Winger's Male Poses — LINDSY LAWRENCE	65
Feminist and Postfeminist Discourses: Reading the Britta Problem — JESSICA FORD	82
Creating a Colorblind Community: Dean Pelton and the Greendale Human Beings — MELISSA VOSEN CALLENS	98
Parody as Civic Discourse in "Basic Lupine Urology": The *Law and Order* Episode — JEREMY W. COOK and ROBIN M. MURPHY	111

Part III: Pop Culture Across the Curriculum

My Dinner with Abed: Postmodernism, Pastiche and Metaxy in "Critical Film Studies" — ELIZABETH FLEITZ KUECHENMEISTER	125

"That's So Meta!" Allusions for the Media-Literate Audience
  in *Community* (and Beyond) — BRIDGET JULIE HANNA   138

My Dinner with Andre/Our Dinner with Abed: Genre and
  the Audience — SALLIE MAREE PRITCHARD   152

Advanced Introduction to Liminality: *Community* on the Fringe
  — LISA K. PERDIGAO   167

Part IV: Extracurricular Activities

Community's Communities: Bringing the Fan to the (Study)
  Table — JOSEPH S. WALKER   181

"Cool, Cool, Cool": New Media Rhetorics of *Community*
  — G. BRET BOWERS   197

"Six seasons and a movie!" *Community*, Creative Processes and
  Being Meta — LAURA TANSLEY   211

About the Contributors   225
Index   227

Preface

Being a part of the growing population of internet-television viewers, I encountered *Community* on Hulu. As a rhetorician, when I watch television, I often garner material that can be implemented in my composition or rhetoric courses, particularly to show rhetorical aspects or to use humor as mnemonic devices. Besides looking for possible course material, my favorite reason for watching a particular show and devoting myself to it would be the fact that I may write about it academically. The idea for this edited collection germinated in such a way.

After watching the first season of *Community* through Hulu and also buying multiple copies of the Season 1 DVD to convert friends into faithful fans, I thought to myself, "I really want to write about *Community*." Often, I respond to calls for papers about television shows that interest me, so I decided that I did not want to just write one essay and be done with it; I wanted an entire collection about *Community*. However, the idea stayed dormant for a couple of years. I decided to take the initiative and write my own call for papers, focusing on *Community*. First and foremost, I wanted to know how other *Community* fans around the world felt about the show — and now I know. Along with colleagues past and present, I have encountered new acquaintances who share the same passion I have for the show. Through this project, we have created our own community, an academic network.

Being an academic, I enjoy the show because it is about college: I pay close attention to the professors — their eccentric behaviors and teaching practices; how the students are learning, if at all; and the most enjoyable part, how the names of the episodes sound like a class or they focus on a specific course the members of our favorite study group are taking. There is always a lesson to be learned by the characters and the audience. At times, it seems the audience is allowed to participate in the madness; the characters are often being deceived, and as the audience, we are included in the deception. I think that is one reason that makes the show so much fun to watch besides the fact that some of us get to flash back to our own days of being in college and can at times relate to their situations.

Since the show started, there have been numerous fans of *Community* who were devising their own theories about the show in public domains. Therefore, this book is not just for teachers or academics. Readers of this collection will be happy to see that our topics and theories in the more qualitative fields of literature, politics, and popular culture are quite accessible. While study of popular culture may not be valued as much as empirical and/or quantitative studies, television episodes are multimodal texts that are much more complex. Those unfamiliar with our theories have an opportunity to broaden their horizons while those familiar with the show will be able to understand the show more in depth through application of what we consider practical knowledge.

Overall, I thank the contributors for their enthusiasm, for taking their time out of their own classes and occupations to write thoughtful and focused essays and for their patience in waiting for my responses. For whoever said "Two heads are better than one," I see it more as strength in numbers, which clearly shows in our collection. Each contributor is such a character in him or herself, and I have enjoyed getting to know each one, especially through his or her writing styles and thoughts on the show.

Many of the contributors agree that we have grown much from writing from this collection. We have improved as writers, as thinkers, as fans of the show that dare to take risks. Of course, we are far from being experts on the show since the show's writers are always taking things in different directions. That is what makes the show and its development so exciting.

Introduction

Community centers on the shenanigans of a diverse study group who are in a Spanish class together. The study group consists of a mix of traditional and non-traditional students — their leader, Jeff Winger, a former lawyer; Britta Perry, a political feminist; Abed Nadir, a popular culture enthusiast; Shirley Bennett, a mother; Troy Barnes, a former jock and Abed's partner in crime; Annie Edison, a naïve overachiever; and Pierce Hawthorne, a racist and sexist old man. There are also Benjamin Chang, their maniacal first Spanish teacher, and Craig Pelton, the eccentric dean of Greendale Community College, along with other well-known guest stars who play troublemaking students, nutty professors, or frightening administrators. Besides interesting characterization, the show abounds with pop-culture pastiche and delights viewers with its hilarity, brilliance, and complexity.

Community debuted in fall 2009 and was nominated for the 36th People's Choice Awards. The year after, the show was picked up for a second season and was hailed as the best new comedy of the year by critics nationwide. In 2010 and 2011, the show received numerous nominations at the 41st and 42nd NAACP Image Awards, Teen Choice Awards, *Entertainment Weekly*'s 3rd Ewwy Awards, 37th People's Choice Awards, the Comedy Awards, 1st Critics Choice Television Awards (won an award), TCA Awards, and Satellite Awards, among many others. The show won the 2012 *TV Guide* Magazine Fan Favorites Awards, and in February 2012, according to Hulu, "With the help of its Twitter-happy cast and a tireless fanbase, *Community* took down AMC's force of a zombie show, *The Walking Dead*, by more than 11,000 votes to win Hulu's 2012 Best in Show competition." Finally, at the 2nd Critics Choice Television Awards in 2013, *Community* won Best Comedy series. When fans heard that the show was about to be canceled, perhaps due to tension on the set, they reacted creatively and quickly. With their help, *Community* is going to make it to its fifth season, and fans hope for many more to come — perhaps six seasons and a movie, which is one of the show's inside jokes.

In this book, Part I will familiarize readers with several of the most popular episodes in different ways, Part II will focus on particular characters and specific episodes, Part III will cover the behind-the-scenes aspects such as screenwriting and television techniques, and Part IV will address audience participation and fandom, which have contributed to the show's survival.

Part I, "Taking Things Literally," contains four essays pertaining to literary theory. To begin, Mina Halling, in "Adventures in Time, Space and Community College: Narrative Structure and Thematic Depth," covers the narrative structure and thematic depth in various episodes. Halling considers narration and theme to be the key to the success of the show; by using these narrative structures as a means for thematic commentary, rather than as an end in-and-of-themselves, *Community* is advancing the way sitcom genre creates stories. In "Modern Heroism," Amanda Riter notes how *Community* creator Dan Harmon has been influenced by Joseph Campbell's concept of the hero. In the show, each character's role changes due to their unconscious desires. This opportunity to move and to embrace a new aspect of their character allows viewers to examine the group's roles and relationships in entirely new ways. Nettie Brock explores "Greendale Hyperreality" and analyzes the ideas of realness and falseness through the show's use of flashbacks. Brock argues that the flashbacks do not feature, as per the convention, events, or encounters previously experienced by the audience. Instead, these are new events in the audience's eyes, thereby expanding the reality of the characters, by contributing to their back-stories. The show also introduces an interesting thought: how much of this world (*Community*'s) is real? Next, in "The Greendale Trickster: The Rise and Fall of Ben Chang," Ann-Gee Lee and Noah E. Schmidt tease out Chang's trickster tendencies as he utilizes a rhetoric of fear to prevent others from getting to know him and disclosing his secrets. Chang's deception of the Greendale community and the viewer sets him up as possibly the most important character and leads to some of the show's funniest moments.

Part II, "The Political Playground," contains four essays which focus on gender, race, and law. Lindsy Lawrence focuses on the study group's leader in "Inculcating Victorian Masculinities at 'Loser College': Jeff Winger's Male Poses." She highlights *Community* as a modern-day campus narrative and compares Jeff to Thomas Hughes' title character in *Tom Brown at Oxford*, a campus narrative from the 19th century. Lawrence discusses masculinity in Victorian and modern times, particularly in the roles of various types of male college students. Jessica Ford, in "Feminist and Postfeminist Discourses: Reading the Britta Problem," focuses on one particular character, Britta Perry, who may appear at first as self-aware and pop-culturally educated as Abed, or even the show itself. Ford demonstrates how Britta is a product of third-wave feminist pop culture. However, in Britta's interactions with the other females, her assumptions about herself and the world are challenged. In "Creating a Colorblind Community: Dean Pelton and the Greendale Human Beings," Melissa Vosen Callens focuses on the antics of the dean in his preoccupation with race. Callens argues that by his acts of overly focusing on race, his colorblindness is actually detrimental to the school's understanding of race. By focusing on the dean's outlandish and over-the-top behavior, the show demonstrates how ludicrous it is to suggest that race and racism are nonexistent. Jeremy W. Cook and Robin M. Murphy dissect a specific episode in "Parody as Civic Discourse in 'Basic Lupine Urology': The *Law and Order* Episode." The episode follows the formula of *Law and Order* so closely that it bests the original series and results in bricolage, giving *Community* a new, more critical identity. Cook and Murphy apply John Locke's theory of civic (rhetorical) discourse, which centers on the idea that communication should be for the benefit of the audience and for the public good.

Part III, "Popular Culture Across the Curriculum," begins with "My Dinner with Abed: Postmodernism, Pastiche and Metaxy in 'Critical Film Studies.'" Elizabeth Fleitz Kuechenmeister focuses on a specific episode, "Critical Film Studies," claiming *Community*'s use of pastiche, in combination with its use of intertextuality and self-referentiality, effectively develops the plot as well as the character of Abed, who is unable to understand real-world situations without popular culture. Kuechenmeister studies viewer reactions to this use of intertextuality, considering this episode the most highly complex in the series. Bridget Julie Hanna, in "'That's So Meta!' Allusions for the Media-Literate Audience in *Community* (and Beyond)," also focuses on the episode "Critical Film Studies." Hanna claims that *Community* sets up two types of jokes to produce laughter from two different audiences: slapstick and situation comedy for the not-so-media-conscious, and parody with an added level of meaning for the media-literate. Hanna illustrates how the reappropriation of genres within *Community* opens a discussion between texts, creator, and audience. Sallie Maree Pritchard, in "*My Dinner with Andre*/Our Dinner with Abed: Genre and the Audience," provides another perspective on the episode "Critical Film Studies," which she considers a game in which the characters and the audience are invited to play. However, while Jeff and the rest of the study group lose the game, the audience is encouraged to win. In "Advanced Introduction to Liminality: *Community* on the Fringe," Lisa K. Perdigao shows how throughout its four seasons, *Community* has experimented with the form and structure of network television. With an inaugural episode that showcases the evolution of television and a final episode that ends with the promise of alternate storylines, seemingly infinite possibilities, the fourth season of *Community* can be read as a study of its own liminality.

Part IV, "Extracurricular Activities," examines *Community* as an entity and its extensions (webisodes, video games, actors' Twitter pages, and so on) as well as fan contributions to its survival. Joseph S. Walker explores the fun of audience participation in "*Community*'s Communities: Bringing the Fan to the (Study) Table." Walker explains how the show has evolved into a complex, fully realized satire of the traditional sitcom, of traditional relationships between a media text and fans. *Community* is acknowledging its place in a new media landscape where the partnership with the viewer is more intense and more important than ever. In "'Cool, Cool, Cool': New Media Rhetorics of *Community*," G. Bret Bowers shows how the internet has served as a space for *Community*'s popularity to grow and spread as the show's primary way of generating fandom and increasing its popularity. Bowers examines the rhetorical activities and devices that the cast and writers of *Community* participate in and which are behind *Community*'s internet popularity through application of the "rhetoric of cool" and three relative terms, chora, appropriation, and commutation. To end the collection, Laura Tansley, in "'Six seasons and a movie!' *Community*, Creative Processes and Being Meta," explores the metatextuality of the show and Abed's metacommentary. Various episodes take on additional metatextual significance, connecting with fans about its future and were used as campaign slogans to encourage the NBC network to renew the show for a fourth season.

The contributors have invested a large amount of time and energy into this collection (though not nearly as much as the writers of the show). We are proud of contributions to the growing body of knowledge that is theory and look forward to future seasons of *Community* to inspire us further.

PART I:
TAKING THINGS LITERARILY

Adventures in Time, Space and Community College: Narrative Structure and Thematic Depth
Mina Halling

The 1990s and 2000s saw an explosion in narrative complexity in all forms of TV, especially sitcom. In the last 20 years, sitcoms have expanded narrative potential by introducing and popularizing complex narrative devices such as nested flashbacks and mockumentary. *Community* uses these narrative tools to craft comedy and stories in unexpected ways, but it also integrates these narrative structures into the thematic content of the show. Using these devices, the show comments on popular culture and its role in contemporary society, the kinds of stories being told and the nature of storytelling itself, the issues the characters face, and the development of the characters themselves. By using these narrative structures for thematic commentary, *Community* is advancing the way the sitcom genre creates stories. By analyzing the devices used in some of the most complex episodes, one can clearly see the themes those devices enhance and the connection between the stories the episodes are telling and the way they are being told.

"Modern Warfare" (Episode 1.23)

In this episode, everyone on campus is given paintball guns. The game spins wildly out of control while the characters experience Greendale versions of classic scenes from action movies like *The Warriors* (1979), *Die Hard* (1988), and *28 Days Later...* (2002). This style of genre parody episode has become a signature of the show. These episodes have the freedom to range far and wide on the generic spectrum because, as John Frow explains, "no text is unique; we would not recognize it if it were. All texts are relevantly similar to some texts and relevantly dissimilar to others.... All texts are shaped by the repetition and the transformation of other textual structures" (47). Genre blending and jumping is easy for audiences to follow because all texts exist in a relationship with other texts — no genre is completely unrelated to other genres. He also points out, "The genre is not a *property* of a text but is a function of reading. Genre is a category that we *impute* to texts, and under different circumstances this imputation may change. Think of the way different productions of a play, each involving the staging of an interpretation, may substantially alter the relevant genre framework" (102). Genres are created by readers through the act of reading, which makes the act of switching from one to another simpler than it would initially seem; the episode simply needs to include generic cues to indicate the category.

The ease with which modern audiences can respond to generic cues is an advantage in creating these episodes, but it also adds to their complexity. For instance, it is possible, given that all genres are imputed to existing texts, that as we watch "Modern Warfare" the *characters* are living a regular day within their community college genre which happens to have paintball in it, while the *audience* experiences a direct reference to *Die Hard* through generic cues embedded at the diegetic level and in the stylistic choices. In this scenario, the characters do not experience the shift in genre; the audience does. This could serve to extend the audience's suspension of disbelief and allow the show to create more extreme circumstances — if the audience believes the characters do not experience the shift in genre, then those shifts can be more extreme without the audience requiring a reaction from the characters. There is one other key observation Frow makes about the nature of genre that puts this idea: that the characters are living a generically neutral day which the audience experiences as generically unique in tension.

Frow emphasizes that although genres are overlapping (easy to mix) and created by the reader (easy to cue to the audience), they are far from simple: "This is where the real complexity of texts lies; if we are to read well, we cannot but attend to those embedded assumptions and understandings which are structured by the frameworks of genre and from which we work inferentially to the full range of textual meaning" (101). Though generic structures are deceptively easy to move through, putting old characters in new genres changes the relevant "textual meanings" (motivations, behaviors, and speech patterns). Having them live out an action movie without responding to those tropes is inherently false, especially on a show set in modern America where it would be natural for characters to be as genre savvy as their audience is. The characters *must* be affected by the generic shift for that shift to mean anything.

Community approaches this inherent shift, in this and other genre-parody episodes, by allowing the new genre to influence significant character moments in addition to creating fun, over-the-top escapades. This episode's action-heavy exploits are grounded in Jeff Winger and Britta Perry's sexual tension. At the end of the game, the two directly address the new generic conventions into which they have been thrust: "The group would be thrilled. The wounded soldier fantasy means we're moments from doing it, right?" Then they end up having sex on the study room table, agreeing not to tell anyone. The episode ends with a significant character moment which is both compliant with ongoing characterization and explicitly affected by the shift in the episode's genre.

Ultimately, these characteristics of genre switching make the episode both more realistic and more complicated. By grounding character motivations in their feelings about ongoing relationships, the episode offsets the absurdity of the parody, making the action more realistic within the established (somewhat absurd) reality of Greendale. By combining character events with audience cues, the show ensures the genre shift remains relevant to the audience's reading of a situation and the character's reaction to that situation. This interplay allows the show to turn ambitious, large-scale genre experiments into simultaneous small-scale character studies.

"Intermediate Documentary Filmmaking" (Episode 2.16) and "Documentary Filmmaking: Redux" (Episode 3.8)

With these two episodes, the show investigates the popular "mockumentary" structure used in modern sitcoms, such as *The Office* (2005–), *Parks and Recreation* (2008–), and *Modern Family* (2009–). The first depicts Pierce Hawthorne in the hospital, telling the group he is dying and bequeathing them gifts as Abed films the proceedings. The second finds Abed creating a *Hearts of Darkness* (1991) style making-of documentary of Dean Pelton's attempt to film a new commercial for Greendale. The commercial spins out of control when Pelton brings in famous Greendale alum, Luis Guzmán, and dedicates himself to creating a piece of true art. Both episodes focus on character development. The first investigates Pierce's discomfort in trusting the group to love him as he is; the second shows Pelton learning to accept Greendale in spite of its flaws. However, each also takes the audience wholly and deeply into documentary format, with the first aiming at the narrative style of modern mockumentary sitcoms and the second interrogating the role of the filmmaker in more traditional documentary.

Ethan Thompson investigates the development of mockumentary from genuine parody to something more complex: an accepted style of TV narrative neither dependent on nor completely separate from its documentary roots. On mockumentary style shows, characters directly address the camera in "talking head" segments but are rarely affected by camera presence. He states, "What initially may appear to be a visual strategy of fakery or "mocking" the documentary can more importantly play a role in affecting ... narrative complexity" (68). The style is complex in its attempt to portray "reality" as it pertains to these characters — sitcom characters who will behave in silly ways in crazy situations, but who will do so in a far more visually "realistic" (what we have learned to recognize as realistic) manner than a traditional three-camera sitcom. Thompson describes changes in mockumentary over time as shift in audience viewpoint: "This borrowing of documentary style is about finding not just a mode of production but a method of reading as well: ... this is 'real' — at least relative to other television" (71). The claim to some form of truth or higher reality leads to a complex relationship between audience and character behavior. Use of talking heads gives audience insight into the characters not possible in other formats and maintains this "reality claim" to an extent, but the way characters ignore the camera makes them seem more like traditional TV characters. It is a complex balancing act which completely shifts the way shows can tell stories; they can jump into surprising or unlikely character motivations by having characters explain them directly to camera, thereby taking advantage of the style's inherent reality claim as pointed out by Thompson.

The first episode, "Intermediate Documentary Filmmaking," takes aim at this inherent narrative shortcut by using the narrative tools of mockumentary to comment on the nature of storytelling. It pokes fun at the style as Abed explains his decision to film: "I'm excited about the narrative facility of the documentary format. It's easier to tell a complex story when you can just cut to people explaining things to the camera." Abed addresses these advantages from a thematic perspective in his final commentary: "Fortunately, if in the end your documentary is turning out just as messy as real life, you can always wrap it up with a series of random shots which, when cut together under a generic voice-over, suggest a profound thematic connection. I'm not knocking it. It works." The episode deconstructs the narrative and thematic advantages inherent to documentary format by first reinforcing the utility of the reality claim by using talking heads, then downgrading the importance of the reality claim by pointing out the control Abed retains over the proceedings as editor. Thus, the episode uses its unique structure to comment on structure itself.

The second episode focuses more on documentaries and less on sitcoms, encouraging the audience to question the filmmaker's role in the events they record by portraying Abed Nadir as morally ambiguous. As the Dean goes deeper into his insane vision for Greendale's new commercial, Abed tells the other characters that he knows something terrible is going to happen and the group is horrified he will not do anything about it:

> ABED: The Dean is going insane and taking all of you with him.
> TROY: If you know that, then do something!
> ABED: I'm doing everything I can. I only have so many cameras.

Abed claims that as a filmmaker he is supposed to be a "fly on the wall," not affecting the action as it unfolds in any way, and the tension between Abed-as-filmmaker and Abed-as-Greendale-Student will ultimately be the thematic core of the episode.

The question of the role of the filmmaker in documentary has been pondered ever since documentary made the shift from didactic (telling how things are) to mimetic (showing how things are). We are led to believe that modern-day documentarians are flies on walls, presenting only mimetic narratives. Bill Nichols points out the inevitable effect that the identity of the filmmaker has on audience: "The difference follows the distinction between the documentary practice of observational filmmakers whose lack of identity facilitates their function as a surrogate audience ... and the narrative practice of sharing the point of view of an individuated character" (11). The episode melds the two ideas: Abed wants to be and spends the majority of the episode behaving like an identity-less observational filmmaker, but no matter what he does, he remains Abed, an individuated, familiar character. By interrogating these two competing paradigms, the episode encourages the audience to contemplate the role of the filmmaker in documenting real-life.

Vivian Sobchack articulates this tension between art and ethics: "The concern for getting a clear and unobstructed image, and the belief that it is possible to strip that image, that representation, of human bias and perspective and ethicality so that it is "objective," indelibly marks the inscriptions of the professional gaze with their own problematic ethical perspective" (qtd. in Nichols 14). There is no doubt the episode pursues these issues by placing Abed-the-student and Abed-the-filmmaker at odds. Ultimately, Abed decides he cares too much about his school to let it fall apart, re-editing a new commercial for Greendale and telling the Dean, "some flies are too awesome for the wall."

These episodes significantly shift the way the show tells stories, and in doing so they create deeper character development and new opportunities for humor. *Community* also takes the opportunity to interrogate the "realism" of documentary style itself, first by deconstructing the effects of the reality claim by explicitly revealing where it succeeds and where it fails, and then by encouraging the audience to consider the relationship between the storyteller and the stories he tells by putting Greendale's fate in Abed's reluctant hands.

"Advanced Dungeons and Dragons" (Episode 2.14)

This episode adopts the tone and style of an epic fantasy adventure. An expositional voiceover introduces "Fat Neil," a background character who has developed depression after years of taunting. Jeff arranges a game of Dungeons and Dragons (D&D) to cheer him up. Pierce feels excluded and attempts to derail the game, but his interjections ultimately save Neil's life. Despite the grand nature of the opening narration, what seems to be another large-scale genre parody quickly mutates into a small-scale bottle episode; the epic fantasy journey takes place in the characters' heads. We experience their journey as they do, with sound effects, musical cues, character descriptions, and occasional narration helping us understand the story within the story.

The episode employs an impressive framing method to tell the story, allowing the study group to create a new and unique story world existing only in their own minds. It is sometimes difficult to apply narrative terms conceived with literature in mind to more visual narrative modes. Is, for instance, a narrative that the characters construct but the audience does not visually experience truly a framed narrative? By using a definition provided by Marie-Laure Ryan, "A narrative territory frames another territory when its verbal representation both precedes and follows the verbal representation of the framed territory" (876), we can safely conclude that the narrative of the study group spending the day playing D&D (the "Study Room" narrative) frames the narrative of the D&D game being played (The "Cavern of Draconis" narrative). This same relationship can also be expressed, according to Mieke Bal and Eve Tavor, as the Cavern of Draconis narrative being "embedded" in the Study Room narrative.

The use of narration in the episode, which first appears to be strictly part of the fantasy parody, introduces another layer to the proceedings. By opening with, "Gather close that ye might hearken the story of Fat Neil," the show establishes a primary narrator who relates the Study Room narrative in which the Cavern of Draconis narrative is, in turn, created. This ultimately creates three levels: the primary narrator in the first (the "Fat Neil" narrative), which is understood as outside or beyond Greendale in some way due to the narrator's omniscience; the study group in the second, which is Greendale as we have come to understand it; and the characters being played by the study group in the Cavern of Draconis in the third, a world accessible only through the characters' imaginations.

By using Bal and Tavor's framework for understanding embedding—for the purposes of deconstructing embedding in television as opposed to literature—we can gain a deeper understanding of each narrative layer. According to them,

> Within its own proper limits, narrative communication presents a narrative subject called the *narrator* who proffers sentences, the direct content of which is a vision.

This vision or presentation is the act of another subject who is *contained* related to the first subject (the narrator), and this second subject is the focalizer.... This focalizer presents a history or diegesis. This history is the act of another subject, usually plural, which is the agent of the events which compose the history and whom we call the actor [44–45].

To reduce these roles to their most basic definitions: the narrator tells, the focalizer sees, and the actor does. The difficulty in applying these categories to TV or film is immediately obvious: outside of explicit first-person narration, it is rare that audiences can identify the narrator (who is telling the story) and even rarer that they can identify the focalizer (who is seeing the story) especially given how often the two roles overlap.

If we can simplify these roles, we can gain a better understanding of the difference in the three story-levels at play. At the innermost level, the Cavern of Draconis level, Abed (narrator) tells the study group (focalizers) what to imagine their characters (actors) doing: "You've been shot by an arrow. Yeah, it hurts." At this level, the three roles are easy to identify, but explicitly pointing them out establishes where the action is actually taking place (the imagined world of the game), which is significant given the few cues the audience is given to remind them of that world. At the middle level, the Study Room level, the Narrator (likewise the narrator) describes what the study group members (focalizers) do as they play the game: "And so it was that the group began to describe themselves walking. And as they described themselves walking, so did Abed confirm they walked." The roles are harder to identify because the study group is acting as both focalizers and actors, but this level takes place at the same narrative level as the rest of the series, which makes it the audience's status quo.

At the outermost level, the Fat Neil level, the Narrator narrates and Neil acts, but the key to understanding this newly established Fat Neil level is in the narrator's fourth-wall breaking style of address. I would argue that at this level, the audience acts as the focalizers. The Narrator has omniscient knowledge about Neil's actions, implying that we are not seeing him through the eyes of regular characters, and addresses the audience directly, acknowledging their presence. This use of audience makes it clear that the narrator exists outside of the world of Greendale (the world in which the Study Group narrative exists). For the first time in the show's run, the audience is hearing dialogue not explicitly directed at someone in the Study Group narrative (or in a narrative within), which means there must be a narrative level outside the one in which the show usually moves.

Creating this new outer layer provides the show with several opportunities — it is a new, quick way to deliver exposition, it strengthens the genre parody, and it provides new avenues for humor. Most importantly, it gives the show the opportunity to develop Pierce, who was in the midst of a villainous arc at this point, without losing the ambiguity of the character's journey. We can assume (based on the show's style) that Neil will be saved, so the real question is whether Pierce will help or hinder the group's efforts to do so. The episode, to preserve Pierce's characterization as a somewhat-loveable jerk, gives Pierce an instrumental role in Neil's recovery without claiming that he does any of it deliberately. It uses the extra layer of narration to make Pierce's role in the story explicit: "And so it was that Pierce Hawthorne saved the life of Fat Neil, while learning very, very little"—in a way that avoids tipping his characterization too far in either direction. The use of narration appears to be a simple part of the fantasy parody, but the show could not tell this story (at least nowhere near as effectively) without the narration providing an external narrative level from which to comment on Pierce's behavior.

Another concept from Ryan that applies to the embedded structures of the episode is contamination: "Aside from the changes effected in the narrator and narratee, the events of the upper level have no influence on the events of the lower level" (890). In uncontaminated embedding, the embedded narrative does not influence the narrative in which it is embedded. If this were to hold true, the Cavern of Draconis narrative could have no effect on the Study Room narrative. However, the purpose of the Cavern of Draconis narrative is to keep Neil from hurting himself. The embedded level is explicitly designed to influence the outer level; the two narratives bleed into each other constantly.

The conversations in the Study Room affect the world of the Cavern of Draconis, which affects relationships and interplay of the characters in the Study Room. Pierce's emotions lead him to create a character who ruins things; this angers the study group, who commit to the game for reasons other than helping Neil, which causes them to treat him with more respect and humanity. Neil's newfound confidence allows him to defeat Pierce's character (in the Cavern of Draconis) by talking to Pierce outside the game (in the Study Room). Due to the complex interplay between two story worlds, understanding the effect each has on the other is integral to understanding the episode. This contamination makes the episode more complicated at a basic structural level, but also serves to complicate character motivation and interaction more than they would have had the Cavern world remained separate from the Study Room world.

As always, the complex narrative devices do not exist simply for complexity's sake. The interplay between the two story worlds is key to the emotional arcs Neil and Pierce experience: although Pierce learns very little, it would have been impossible for Neil to find a valued place in the group without Pierce's in-game (Cavern) behavior distracting them from their unhelpful out-of-game (Study Room) pity for Neil.

"Abed's Uncontrollable Christmas" (Episode 2.11)

This episode differs from the rest of the series in an immediate and remarkable way, done entirely in stop motion. Abed explains that the world is stop-motion because it is "the most important Christmas in the history of the universe!" Unfortunately Abed is the only one who can see the stop-motion world around him. The episode takes us through Abed's delusion-induced dream world as he undergoes therapeutic hypnosis. The study group helps Abed find the meaning of Christmas by searching the "Planet Abed" he has created in his mind.

In approaching this episode, we should reexamine Ryan's definition of a framed narrative in a new context: "A narrative territory frames another territory when its verbal representation both precedes and follows the verbal representation of the framed territory" (876). Abed's adventures on Planet Abed function in a similar way to the study group's adventure in the Cavern of Draconis, but since the constructed narrative of the episode presents only the embedded narrative (the world as Abed sees it), one cannot apply basic embedded narrative theory to it. However, as Ryan points out later in the same article, "The frame diagram should model the narrative in its logical deep structure, which in this case inverts the surface structure specified by the temporal order of presentation" (878). Although we are not explicitly shown Planet Abed's status as an embedded narrative, we are told through subtle cues in the deep structure of the narrative that it is, in fact, a fictional world created by Abed.

The episode presents reality as Abed perceives it, but it also firmly holds onto reality as the rest of the study group experiences it. To understand how the episode provides the audience with insight into both story-worlds, we turn to another essay by Ryan, who points out a key binary in narrative theory: "A diegetic narration is the verbal storytelling act of a narrator.... A mimetic narration is an act of showing" (*Narrative Across Media* 13). This dichotomy is especially relevant in the context of TV narrative because TV shows almost always use mimetic narration. However, by embedding story-worlds (as seen in the previous episode) and complicating things further by making one character fully aware of that story-world, the episode necessitates the use of diegetic narration to inform the audience about both story-worlds. By inviting the audience into the embedded narrative and leaving most characters outside it, the episode subverts expectations by making the audience work to remember the narrative level on which the show actually takes place. This subversion allows the show to make observations about that narrative level through the embedded level by allowing us to see these characters acting separately from their usual narrative level. Presenting the Planet Abed level, and only the Planet Abed level, invites the audience to question the significance of these dueling realities — Abed needs the

Planet Abed delusion to cope with the reality of his situation, so to truly understand his situation, we must also see the delusion.

Obviously, the other significant narrative tool used here is the shift in medium. Ryan presents two common perspectives on the historical relationship between media and narrative. One is to view media as a technical means of expression, like the way clay or watercolors can act as physical outlets for expressive ideas. The other is to view media as a channel of information or entertainment. According to Ryan, "Media filter different aspects of narrative meaning. Far from being completely undone at the end of the journey ... the shape imposed on the message by the configuration of the pipeline affects in a crucial way the construction of the receiver's message" (*Narrative Across Media* 17). In simpler terms, narratives have a basic nucleus which remains the same from medium to medium—*Lord of the Rings* is still *Lord of the Rings*, as film or book—but when the narrative shifts from one medium to another, it will *inevitably* experience a shift in the way it is being told, by nature of the new "pipeline" it is being fitted into.

This "pipeline" concept means that although this story is basically stable, choosing to tell it in such an atypical way inevitably affects the narrative itself. The episode differs from a more "normal" episode in that the stop-motion style provides the show with more freedom when it comes to humor, especially in constructing visual gags. However, it also gives *Community* the opportunity to drop characters into completely unrealistic situations and test how they react.

More than anything, the new medium gives insight into Abed's mind, allowing the show to present Abed's worldview as he sees it, a rare opportunity for a non-mockumentary, non-narrated show. To return to Ryan's binary, the show can present Abed's unique paradigm through mimetic narration instead of the audience's diegetic viewpoint. This shift to mimetic narration allows the episode to give the audience a unique perspective on a familiar character. The most obvious example comes when Abed assigns his fellow study group members "Christmas Identities," revealing how Abed really sees them. For example, Britta becomes Britta-Bot because Abed is concerned that she is too disconnected from the people in her life. If the episode had remained live-action, we would have seen descriptions of Britta as she might appear in Abed's imagination, similar to descriptions employed in the D&D episode, but the shift in media gives us the opportunity to see with him, which absolutely "affects in a crucial way the construction of the receiver's message" (Ryan, *Narrative Across Media* 17). Without the media shift, we would be receiving a significantly different message.

The entire episode works to give insight into Abed and the extent to which he must use pop culture—in this case, Christmas clichés—to relate to the world around him. It is a concept the show explored before and would use again, but always in terms of how Abed relates to Jeff, the study group, or the school as a whole. By shifting the medium in which they tell the story, *Community* delves into Abed's personal paradigm in a way it never could have in live-action.

"Paradigms of Human Memory" (Episode 2.21)

In this episode, the study group has gathered to create a diorama of their study room. As they are working, they find a pile of mementos and reminisce about the school year in flashback clips or "analeptic anachronies," shifts of time-frame set in the past. Unlike a traditional clip show, it becomes clear to any dedicated audience member that these are not familiar clips. The episode moves from new clips of previous episodes to clips from totally unfamiliar premises, giving the audience brief glimpses of everything from a haunted house to a wig-cutting class.

By understanding how each flashback works at a technical level, using definitions from Gerard Genette, we can properly articulate what makes them different from a classic clip show. The first task is to define the main narrative of the episode — the time the group spends in the study room reminiscing. In Genette's terms, this would be called the dispatching narrative because "it is always necessary to come back to that position, which is central" (47). Although the flashbacks are not always broken up with a return to the study room, they almost always rely on introductions from the study room scene in order to occur, making the designation of the "Study Room Diorama" scene as the dispatching narrative ultimately accurate, if imperfect.

The other broad term that can be ascribed to the Study Room Diorama scene is the concept of "first narrative." According to Genette, "We will henceforth call the temporal level of narrative with respect to which anachrony is defined as such, 'first narrative'" (48). The first narrative refers to the period of time covered by the primary "storyline." If we view something as a flashback, it must be happening before the first narrative, so in this case, it makes sense to view the Study Room Diorama scene as the first narrative.

The flashbacks (or analepses) have a myriad number of possible defining characteristics in Genette's view, but I will focus on their extent, their reach, and their type. On the subject of extent, Genette explains: "I will name this type of retrospection, which ends on an ellipsis [temporal jump] without rejoining the first narrative, simply *partial* analepsis" (62). All the flashbacks in the episode are partial analepsis; they never catch up to and rejoin the Study Room Diorama scene. This is also the case for the flashbacks in the average clip-show — they reflect on past episodes that are separated from, and never rejoin, the first narrative.

Defining an anachrony's reach, Genette reveals, "[It] can reach into the past or future, either more or less far from the "present" moment (that is, from the moment in the story when the narrative was interrupted to make room for the anachrony): this temporal distance we will name the anachrony's reach" (48). With the exception of those flashbacks that refer to specific dates (Halloween, Christmas, and St. Patrick's Day) the reach of each analepsis in the episode is left intentionally vague. We know that each of these things took place in the same school year as the dispatching narrative, but that is all. This is markedly different from the average sitcom clip-show, wherein the audience has some idea of the reach of the clips because they refer to events the audience is familiar with since they took place in past episodes.

The last way Genette categorizes flashbacks is by type: "Which I will call *completing* analepses, or "returns," comprises the retrospective sections that fill in, after the event, an earlier gap in the narrative" (51). Almost every analepsis in the episode is a return; it brings the audience back in time to an event they never saw. In contrast, the classic clip-show uses "recall" to bring the audience back in time to an event they were shown in the same manner. To summarize, the analepses in the episode resemble average clip-show clips in their extent (they never rejoin the first narrative) but diverge from average clip-show clips in their reach (we are rarely given an explicit time frame for them) and their type (they are almost all "returns" to situations the audience has never seen before).

By using the time-worn clip-show structure to deliver completely new scenarios and interactions, the episode gives the audience (and characters) the opportunity to re-examine central relationships in a broader way, revealing unhealthy patterns. Clips from earlier episodes could have been used to illustrate similar points in a more typical clip-show, but the innovative "new-flashback" format allows the show to make connections without rehashing old material, allowing the audience to make connections between familiar situations and new, less defined ones on their own. In creating a "new clip" clip-show, the episode uses a familiar structure to introduce the audience to a new side of the narrative they have been experiencing all season long.

Almost all the flashbacks in the episode are different from the average clip-show in the ways previously described, but the episode also includes two large experimental flashback structures. Although these anachronies can be defined in Genette's terms, their inherent complexity and visual nature make it difficult to gain a deeper understanding using just these terms. In the first of these two experiments, the group members confront their internal toxicity by remembering previous fights. First, Abed reminds the study group of their fight during a camping trip. The audience is shown the camping trip, where Abed reminds the group of the fight they had while painting Shirley's nursery. Once the audience is shown the nursery scene, we see Abed remind the group about the time they fought during Caesar Salad Day. On Caesar Salad Day, Troy becomes so overwhelmed with the fighting that he begins to scream. As he screams, the audience flashes to "Shirley's Nursery Troy," who is also screaming, then to "Camping Trip Troy," who is screaming, and the audience finally returns to see "Study Room Diorama Troy" screaming, in a levels-upon-levels structure that defies simple categorization.

In Genette's terms, these Troy freak-out scenes all have the same extent (partial, as they never meet up with the first narrative), reach (defined only in relation to each other) and type (they all return to scenarios the audience has not seen). However, the "nested" structure of the analepsis, in which one moment is always being remembered *within* another, turns each flashback into the dispatching narrative for the subsequent flashback, which is completely different from the rest of the clips in the episode. This nested structure serves to restate and emphasize several themes at play — the toxicity of the group's friendship especially — but it also specifically interrogates Troy's role as the group's most innocent member. By using each new flashback as a dispatching narrative, this scene emphasizes the snowball effect the group's fighting has on Troy's psyche in a way that would be far less effective (if not impossible) if the scene had relied on the Study Room Diorama scene as its dispatching narrative.

The second large scale experiment occurs when Jeff tries to end their reminiscing and fighting with a final "Jeff speech," an in-show trope in which Jeff solves problems with a rousing speech to set minds at ease. We see Jeff begin his speech in the study room: "We've known each other for two years now." The scene transports to another Jeff speech: "And yeah, in that time, I've given a lot of speeches." As the speech in the study room continues normally, the audience is taken through ten different past scenarios with ten different Jeff speeches, creating a nonsensical mishmash of messages ultimately becoming the archetypal Jeff speech.

This moment is also defined in basic terms from Genette — each clip's extent is partial, its reach is completely undefined, and all are returns to new scenarios. However, two interesting things are going on in the nature of those returns and the dispatching narrative. Each scene is introduced as a return to a new scenario, but as the speech goes on, the audience is brought back to each scenario; each of the ten situations covered by the speech functions first as return and then as recall. This speech is also notable for being the first time the dispatching narrative breaks down in the episode. Jeff refers to past speeches in the Study Room Diorama scene, but we do not know if he is directly referring to scenarios we see. We do not know if the characters are seeing what we are, a distinct shift from the way the rest of the flashbacks are dispatched. Ultimately, these subtle but important changes allow the episode to undermine audience expectation (that they will see a certain kind of clip, that they will be dispatched to that clip from the first narrative), leaving the show free to directly interrogate Jeff's role in the group and the show in a way that is impossible within the regular confines of audience assumptions.

The question of Jeff's role beyond the deceptively simple "center" of the group would be a big theme for Season 3, but this seems to be when the show first explores it in greater detail, encouraging the audience to consider Jeff as both a character in a TV show and a real person. Since it has already stripped away several layers of audience expectation, the episode can deconstruct and recreate the show's own tropes by presenting the Jeff speech in the most ridiculous way possible, interrogating the purpose of this obviously televisual device. Jeff makes experience-summarizing-speeches in later episodes, but pushing back against the character's most television-like behavior allows the show to push him to more interesting places. By making us laugh at his tendency to fix everything in a single speech, the show weakens his ability to do so, revealing that his role in the group dynamic is (or should be) more complex than assumed.

Interpreting this episode is complex due to the many analeptic levels, but by using Genette's defining characteristics, we can clearly see how this episode diverges from similar clip-shows and how that divergence affects the audience's experience. The episode also uses innovative and deconstructive anachronies to investigate the group as a whole, Troy's role in it, and Jeff's identity as both a television character and a human being.

"Remedial Chaos Theory" (Episode 3.3)

This episode follows the deceptively simple story of one night. The total amount of time that passes in the characters' lives is probably less than ten minutes. As usual, the way they tell this simple story elevates the material beyond the kind of storytelling historically common in sitcoms. The evening is shown seven different times — once for each study group member — and in each "timeline," the audience sees what happens when each person briefly leaves Troy and Abed's new apartment to retrieve a pizza from downstairs.

These alternate timelines are not, despite their name, a temporal shift that can be accurately described using Genette's terms. They are not previous events the audience has failed to see, but rather imaginary events that the audience sees as real. We are not being returned to fill in the gaps of unnarrated events — we are being shown different events entirely.

Gerald Prince provides us with the definition for this: "The category ... that I will call *disnarrated* covers all the events that *do not* happen though they could have and are nonetheless referred to (in a negative or hypothetical mode) by the narrative text" (30). Each of the first six timelines is a disnarrated narrative event, showing what might have happened, not what did happen. Although the term is most commonly used at a smaller scale (applied to hypothetical situations that arise from dialogue, not whole scenes) the timelines explored here certainly qualify as disnarrated.

Prince points out that the disnarrated is not reliant on internal cues: "The disnarrated ... is disnarrated only relative to a given diegesis, and only if it designates in that diegesis a possibility that remains unrealized" (34). An event can only be disnarrated in relationship to the narrative the audience sees. Here, the disnarrated is explicitly created within the real or "prime" narrative. Each time Jeff goes to roll a die and decide who has to leave to retrieve the pizza, Abed points out that, as he sees it, Jeff is now creating six different timelines. The act of wondering about the timelines ultimately creates them.

The most important thing the episode does with the timeline structure is investigate each character's role in the group, a function laid out by Prince: "Since it depicts what is not but might be and is often linked to carelessness, ignorance, or limitations ... it can function as a characterization device" (35). The simple act of removing a member of the study group from the room for a few minutes, one by one, delivers insight into each character and how they function in the group. When Abed leaves, the group devolves into emotional turmoil with hurt feelings and accidentally shared secrets, whereas Troy's absence leads to a complete breakdown as well as an apartment fire and gun-shot wounds.

Prince also explains that the use of the disnarrated can emphasize the significance of a particular narrative event: "When it relates to a character's vision, it underlines the quality of the narrated itself rather than the value of its construction: 'This narrative is worth narrating because *it* could have been otherwise, because *it* usually is otherwise, because *it* was *not* otherwise'" (36). In the context of this episode, the disnarrated demonstrates to the audience that the usual seven-person study group story is worth narrating because the study group *could* be this study group, the one without Troy, or Abed, or Pierce. However, the study group could not exist at all without Jeff, so what happens when he is the one removed?

In a telling move, both for his character and the group dynamic, Jeff's absence in what is ultimately the "real" version leads to the happiest timeline. Without Jeff there to reject Britta's enthusiastic "Roxanne" sing-a-long as he had in every other timeline, the remaining group members have an exuberant dance party. In explaining the relationship between the disnarrated and the thematic points of a narrative, Prince contributes to our understanding of this group interaction: "Furthermore, it plays a part in thematic designation, in the individualization of themes, since it signals that certain of their manifestations are abandoned for the sake of certain others, that certain possible articulations are not selected" (38). The results of the "real" timeline are being repeatedly underlined as the episode presents all the options that are not selected. Thus, we can conclude that the most important characterization is Jeff's.

The show continues to investigate Jeff's role in the group throughout Season 3, establishing him as a somewhat negative influence and encouraging the audience to consider what it means to be the "center" of a community. Jeff's role has been peacemaker, a reasonable task both in terms of his characterization and the practical concerns of making an ensemble television show. Jeff pulls them back down to reality, settles their disputes, and denies interest in wild adventures. Once the group has been together for two years and made a genuine commitment to be in one another's lives, what does the role of peacemaker really mean? By showing all the versions of the study group that were not selected, and ultimately demonstrating that the Jeff-less version is not what one would expect, the episode investigates Jeff's changing role as the group evolves and reveals that his influence is not necessarily always positive.

The multiple timeline structure of the episode allows the show to isolate each character's influence in a very specific and explicit way — by giving each of them their own disnarrated, un-selected timeline and making it easier to examine their interplay with other characters. This reveals new things about each member of the study group, but as the character removed from what is ultimately the "real" timeline, Jeff is the one we learn the most about. This structure may seem like simply a cool and exciting way to tell a story, but at a deeper level it is an opportunity to interrogate the very function of the central character.

Conclusion

Community has demonstrated that it can use its characters to tell any story. These episodes provide a glimpse of innovative, complex storytelling the show engages in regularly. However, these episodes offer investigation of the relationship between storytelling style and thematic depth. Each episode investigates the role of genre in storytelling, advantages and disadvantages of documentary format, the effect of embedded story layers, the unique perspective inherent in a new medium, complexity of time in narrative, and relevance of the stories that might have happened, while retaining strong characters and unique comedic voice.

Works Cited

"Abed's Uncontrollable Christmas." *Community*. NBC. 9 December 2010.
"Advanced Dungeons and Dragons." *Community*. NBC. 3 February 2011.

Bal, Mieke, and Eve Tavor. "Notes on Narrative Embedding." *Poetics Today* 2.2 (1981): 41–59. *JSTOR.* Web. 15 February 2012.
"Documentary Filmmaking: Redux." *Community.* NBC. 17 November 2011.
Frow, John. *Genre.* London: Routledge, 2006.
Genette, Gerard. "Order." *Narrative Discourse: An Essay in Method.* Ithaca: Cornell University Press, 1980.
"Intermediate Documentary Filmmaking." *Community.* NBC. 17 February 2011.
"Modern Warfare." *Community.* NBC. 6 May 2010.
Nichols, Bill. "History, Myth, and Narrative in Documentary." *Film Quarterly* 41.1 (1987): 9–20. *JSTOR.* Web. 15 February 2012.
"Paradigms of Human Memory." *Community.* NBC. 21 April 2011.
Prince, Gerald. "The Disnarrated." *Narrative as Theme: Studies in French Fiction.* Lincoln: University of Nebraska Press, 1992. *EBSCOhost EBook Collection.* Web. 23 February 2012.
"Remedial Chaos Theory." *Community.* NBC. 13 October 2011.
Ryan, Marie-Laure. *Narrative Across Media: The Languages of Storytelling.* Lincoln: University of Nebraska Press, 2004.
____. "Stacks, Frames and Boundaries, or Narrative as Computer Language." *Poetics Today* 11.4 (1990): 873–899. *JSTOR.* Web. 15 February 2012.
Thompson, Ethan. "Comedy Verité? The Observational Documentary Meets the Televisual Sitcom." *The Velvet Light Trap* 60 (2007): 63–72. *Project Muse.* Web. 15 February 2012.

Modern Heroism
Amanda Riter

> You know what makes humans different from other animals? We're the only species on Earth that observes Shark Week. Sharks don't even observe Shark Week, but we do. For the same reason I can pick up this pencil, tell you its name is Steve, and go like this *[snaps pencil]* and part of you dies, just a little bit on the inside. Because people can connect with anything.—JEFF WINGER, "Pilot" (Episode 1.1)

> I can tell life from TV, Jeff. TV has structure, logic, rules, and likeable leading men. In life, we have this. We have you.—ABED NADIR, "Anthropology 101" (Episode 2.1)

According to *Community* creator Dan Harmon, "All life, including the human mind and the communities we create, [march] to the same, very specific beat" ("Story Structure 102"). The first three seasons of *Community*, as written, produced, and run by Harmon, are founded on this principle of structure. For Harmon, heroic journeys follow the same basic pattern: sending the hero on a quest through his or her own unconscious, finding truths buried there, and bringing them back to implement in the hero's life and world. However, Harmon breaks with the traditional confines of a set, singular hero, and instead chooses to also create these heroic journeys through the unconscious for supporting characters.

In traditional narratives, there is a singular protagonist who is usually considered the hero of the work. Though there is some variation across genres and mediums, this guideline of one story, one main hero, usually holds true. This pattern has been apparent in stories for as long as stories have existed, but it was explicitly and famously laid down by Joseph Campbell. With Campbell's ideas as a foundation, Dan Harmon takes this pattern and uses it as the foundational structure for his own stories. To Harmon, the right pattern is the essential trait to make a story resonate with its audience. That resonance plunges the audience into the unconscious mind along with the hero and is what makes a story successful. Because of this belief in the supreme importance of structure, Harmon allows characters who are not traditionally the hero of *Community* to rise to the occasion and have episodes in which they become the hero and whom the audience can follow through the unconscious.

Joseph Campbell laid out this traditional approach to the hero in its most explicit terms. As a comparative mythologist, Campbell spent his career crafting a unified theory of the hero, also known as the monomyth. This theory espouses the idea that all of the world's heroes of myth, legend, and religion follow the same basic pattern. This pattern consists of "a separation from the world, a penetration to some source of power, and a life-enhancing return" (Campbell 28). This circular structure forces every hero beyond the bounds of his or her known world and into the unknown. While away, the hero confronts the mythological beings that dwell in these foreign places. Through the confrontation, the hero finds his or her way to the knowledge that the hero can bring back to bless their society. To Campbell, this structure illuminates the path of all heroes and is the framework for a deeper journey that every hero must traverse.

According to Campbell, the unknown world that each hero must successfully navigate is one of the unconscious mind. Whatever tangible trials the hero might face over the course of the story, that road is merely representative of the dark things lurking within the unconscious. It is the hero's role to leave the world behind and go "to those causal zones of the psyche where the difficulties really reside" and come back from the adventure with "something forgotten not only by ourselves but by our whole generation or our entire civilization" (12).

Buried deep within the unconscious are truths that contain the power to regenerate society and free it from its ills. In order to find those truths, Campbell argues that the hero must fight his or her way through the dark urges that dwell within the unconscious and then bring back the inspiration he or she found buried underneath the layers of "vapors, odd beings, terrors, and deluding images" that exist there (5). For Campbell, the hero's journey is a matter of venturing into the unconscious world to find the gems that are buried within. The hero is not defined by his or her traits or by the physical perils that he or she faces but by the steps he or she walks to make his or her way through the unconscious.

To Harmon, this pattern of an individual venturing into the unknown in order to find truths and bring them back to society is the basic pattern of all stories. Without this pattern, Harmon contends that there is no story. This circular structure speaks to a pattern of death and rebirth, order and chaos, which all people and societies abide by. Harmon asks, "Why this ritual of descent and return? Why does a story have to contain elements, in a certain order, before the audience will even recognize it as a story? Because our society, each human mind within it and all of life itself has a rhythm, and when you play in that rhythm, it resonates" ("Story Structure 102").

This pattern is universal because all peoples and societies must undergo the process of descent and return, and be renewed by the journey. It is the role of heroes — and has been since myths and legends were first created — to venture into the unconscious and bring back the truths that are hidden there. Since this is a universally shared experience amongst all peoples and individuals, stories that follow this pattern of descent and return resonate with their audience. When a story resonates, the audience connects to the hero's journey, going along with the hero into the realm of the unconscious. No matter the hero, the pattern of descent and return speaks to every individual's own need to confront the perils of the unconscious.

As creator and head writer of *Community*, Harmon draws on the pattern of Campbell's monomyth to guide the narrative structure of *Community*. Harmon has developed a cycle that closely follows Campbell's heroic journey, distilling down Campbell's mythic focus into something more applicable to storytelling. Harmon's cycle encompasses eight steps that he deems critical to any successful story. Each of these steps takes up its own spot on a circle that contains the whole of any and every plotline on *Community*.

Harmon refers to these circles as "embryos" as "they contain all the elements needed for a satisfying story" (qtd. in Raftery). When a story is truly satisfying to the audience, "it will resonate. It will send your audience's ego on a brief trip to the unconscious and back" ("Story Structure 102"). However, when a story lacks the elements of this embryo, it will break down and fail to carry the audience into the unconscious. With this cycle in place, Harmon is able to craft stories that provide the audience with a hero who can carry them through the steps of the journey into the unconscious and back out the other side.

Harmon lays out eight specific steps that each hero must undergo in order for their journey into the unconscious to resonate with the audience. These steps encompass the pattern that a hero must follow in order to leave their place of comfort, venture into the unconscious, and return to society with what they have learned. Harmon's eight steps are as follows:

1. A character is in a zone of comfort;
2. But they want something;
3. They enter an unfamiliar situation;
4. Adapt to it;
5. Get what they wanted;
6. Pay a heavy price for it;
7. Then return to their familiar situation;
8. Having changed [qtd. in Raftery].

These steps focus on the progression of the story's hero. As the hero goes, the audience follows.

The character begins in a place that they know and understand, but "something is off balance in the universe"; thus, the hero cannot go on with things as they have been ("Story Structure 104"). The lack of balance leads the hero to Step 2: wanting something in his or her world to be different. The character will then venture away from the world he or she knows, entering the unknown world that represents the unconscious. A hero cannot simply be granted the knowledge that he or she seeks, however, so the hero must find a way to adapt to the unconscious world and traverse all its perils. In the very heart of the unconscious world, the hero will find the knowledge that he or she went to seek, but there is a price to be paid for that knowledge, and at this point the hero gains "full control over [their] destiny" and truly becomes a hero ("Story Structure 104"). From here, the hero must return to the world he or she left behind and share with his or her society what he or she has learned from the journey to the unconscious world. The audience mirrors each step taken by the hero. When the hero ventures into the realm of the unconscious, the audience goes with them, and as individuals, the audience is able to face their own unconscious at the same time. This pattern is what resonates with the audience and carries the audience into the realm of the unconscious alongside the hero.

In this narrative cycle, Harmon also focuses on the need for individuals to venture into the unknown and confront what lurks there. Harmon is practical about the need for a heroic cycle. As the hero of a story ventures into the unknown, he or she takes the audience along, allowing the audience to experience the same journey and learn the same things through the process. By traveling with the hero, the audience confronts the unconscious in their own minds without having to actually leave home. To explain this process, Harmon likens an individual's mind to a house

> with an upstairs and a downstairs. Upstairs, in your consciousness, things are well-lit and regularly swept. Friends visit. Scrabble is played, hot cocoa is brewing. It is a pleasant, familiar place. Downstairs, it is older, darker and much, much freakier. We call this basement the unconscious mind. The unconscious is exactly what it sounds like: It's the stuff you don't, won't, and/or can't think about. [...] And even though it contains life-sustaining energies (like the fuse box and water heater), it's a primitive, stinky, scary place and it's no wonder that, given the choice, we don't hang out down there ["Story Structure 102"].

Harmon operates with the same belief as Campbell: that all individuals have a divide in their minds between conscious and unconscious. This divide is a problem for all individuals, not just the heroes of stories. However, because all individuals have this unconscious lurking in the back of their minds, any hero venturing into the unconscious will resonate with everyone.

It is not enough, however, that all individuals have this divide between conscious and unconscious. According to Harmon, it is important that individuals face their own unconscious. The unconscious contains those elements that keep individuals and society moving forward. However, people prefer not to indulge in the dark impulses that dwell in their unconscious minds. Therefore, when the unconscious and all its disreputable elements are ignored for too long, it rears up and demands to be noticed. Individuals want to ignore the unconscious, but as Harmon believes,

> your pleasure, your sanity and even your life depend on occasional round trips [to the basement]. You've got to change the fuses, grab the Christmas ornaments, clean the litter box. To the extent that we keep the basement door sealed, the entire home becomes unstable. The creatures downstairs get louder and the guy upstairs (your ego) tries to cover the noise with neurotic behavior. For some, eventually, the basement door can come right off its hinges and the slimy, primal denizens of the deep can become Scrabble partners. The point is: Occasional ventures by the ego into the unconscious, through therapy, meditation, confession, sex, violence, or a good story, keep the consciousness in working order ["Story Structure 102"].

Harmon again shares the same basic belief as Campbell that it is necessary for all individuals to take this trip into the unconscious and face what lurks there, or the unconscious will find its own way out. In order to prevent the unconscious from bursting out of the basement, every individual must venture into his or her own unconscious mind. According to Harmon, one of the many ways that a person can face the unknown is through the stories, by connecting with a hero and going with them into the unconscious and coming back refreshed.

The main vehicle of this connection in *Community* is a character named Jeff Winger. From almost the beginning of the pilot episode, Jeff strides onto the screen and becomes the hero that the audience follows into the unconscious. According to Harmon, "[t]he pilot episode of a TV show usually tells the story of a person entering a new situation" and for *Community* that new situation is Jeff coming to Greendale Community College for the first time ("Story Structure 105"). The audience discovers that Jeff has been disbarred for faking an undergraduate degree and cheating on his Law School Admission Test. The local Bar Association has required that Jeff obtain a legitimate bachelor's degree before he can be reinstated to the practice of law. The audience is introduced to Jeff near the beginning of his first semester at Greendale, coming to understand that he is struggling in his Spanish 101 class and has a crush on a fellow classmate, Britta Perry. In his effort to get closer to Britta, Jeff pretends to be a Spanish tutor and inadvertently creates a study group ("Pilot," Episode 1.1).

The members of this study group become the supporting characters in Jeff's story throughout the seasons of *Community*. Along the way Jeff, becomes almost a mentor to Abed Nadir and Troy Barnes, while also developing a romantic attachment towards Annie Edison, becoming best friends with Shirley Bennett, and dealing with Pierce Hawthorne, who vacillates between friend and occasional villain. Over the four seasons, the audience becomes acquainted with each of these supporting characters, but it is clear from the very first episode that Jeff is meant to be the hero of *Community*; it is his weekly journey into the unknown that the audience is meant to be following. These supporting characters are designed to be just that — support for Jeff along his path as the hero.

Jeff steps into the unknown when he enters Greendale, and his journey through the unconscious is the basis for the arc of the entire series of *Community*. Jeff begins his time at Greendale furious that he has to be there and determined to get out as quickly as possible so that he can go back to the life he had before. However, heroes are meant to venture into the unconscious world and come back changed, so by the intended end of the series, Jeff's priorities are different.

Although the majority of *Community*'s episodes contain two to three plotlines, the main plot almost always revolves around Jeff and his journeys into the unconscious. These journeys allow him to grow from the self-centered lawyer he is at the beginning of the series to a man who concentrates on helping his friends. In the show, Jeff begins with no concern for anything beyond getting his life back to the way it was. He ardently believes that "if I [talk] long enough I [can] make anything right or wrong" ("Pilot," Episode 1.1).

However, throughout the series, Jeff ventures into the unconscious and learns about himself in the process, bringing back knowledge from these journeys that help him change. By the middle of the first season, Jeff has progressed enough to mock how he was before and admit that he missed his study group friends over the winter break in "Investigative Journalism" (Episode 1.13). In "Introduction to Finality" (Episode 3.22), at the end of the third season (thought to be Harmon's last episode) Jeff is able to give a speech about how he has learned to "stop thinking about what's good for [himself] and start thinking about what's good for someone else." As the hero of the vast majority of *Community*'s episodes, Jeff ventures into the unconscious almost every week, which gives him the chance to learn about himself and use that knowledge to improve his own world. Even with episodes that contain a single hero and bring the group together in a singular plotline, Jeff is usually the hero.

However, several of *Community*'s episodes put aside the standard format of main plot and multiple subplots to instead bring together all the characters into one shared quest. In these episodes, the supporting characters rally behind a singular hero to help them on their journey through the unconscious. The first of these singular plotline/hero episodes is "Modern Warfare" (Episode 1.23) from *Community*'s first season.

The plot of this episode revolves around a campus-wide paintball game for the prize of priority registration. Jeff is the hero of the episode, guiding the audience into the unconscious world of the game through various trials and in pursuit of what he believes to be his goal. However, in the unconscious mind, Jeff confronts his own self-serving tendencies and realizes that it might be better to serve his fellow students than to win the coveted prize for himself which may accelerate his chances of graduation. When Jeff leaves the unconscious world of the game, he turns over his prize to Shirley to help with her family rather than keep said prize. Here, Jeff is the hero, not only of the entire show, but also of this specific episode. Jeff continues in his role as hero in this singular plotline/hero episode, leading the audience on an action-oriented adventure and winning the day in a way that makes it difficult to deny his status as hero. However, it is not the content of the journey that has made Jeff a hero; it is the structure of his journey into the unconscious and back again.

In "Cooperative Calligraphy" (Episode 2.8), Jeff is still clearly the hero of the singular plotline/hero episode, despite its calmer plot. While "Modern Warfare" is an action-oriented story, "Cooperative Calligraphy" is a largely character-driven bottle episode in which the study group attempts to find Annie's missing purple pen. The study group spends the entire episode within the bounds of their study room, each of them growing increasingly erratic as they search the room, then their bags, then rip apart the room, then search one another in their underwear, and then finally cut open Pierce's leg casts in pursuit of the missing pen.

As the episode progresses, the study group grows more and more distrustful of one another, their bond fracturing under the belief that one of them would steal the pen and subject the rest of the group to this circumstance just because they were unwilling to confess. For Jeff, the distrust is his journey into the unconscious because it is something he has rarely experienced when dealing with the study group. As the hero, Jeff eventually finds the knowledge that he has gone into the unconscious to seek, allowing him to trust the group again. Jeff shares this knowledge with the study group and convinces them that it is more probable that something imaginary — such as the ghost Troy had proposed — might have stolen the pen rather than believing a member of their group would have put them through such an ordeal. Jeff never accomplishes the task of finding the pen, which he has assumed was the point of entering the unconscious world. Instead, Jeff enters the unconscious and confronts his own doubts to guide the rest of the study group back out with him. Although Jeff's journey into the unconscious is less action-oriented in this episode than it was in "Modern Warfare," he still follows the pattern of descent and return that is followed by every hero.

Despite Jeff's status as the undisputed hero of the entire series and of most of the episodes of *Community*, on occasion there are singular plotline/hero episodes in which another character rises up to take the spotlight. According to Harmon's own structure, a story succeeds when it can take the audience on a journey into their own unconscious and bring them back refreshed. It is not enough for stories to be unique or exciting; they must have this pattern. This also means that it does not matter what kind of character becomes the hero so long as the hero can guide the audience through this process. Harmon argues that it is easy to connect an audience to a hero because all the audience has to do is show one. He says that people would have to "go out of [their] ways to keep the audience from imprinting on them" ("Story Structure 104"). With this pattern in place and a hero introduced, Harmon believes that the story has everything it needs to succeed. With this presumption in the value of structure firmly in place, Harmon makes the occasional shift away from Jeff as the hero and gives other characters the chance to go through their own journeys.

Abed is one of the first characters that Harmon allows to be the hero of a singular plotline/hero episode. In "Abed's Uncontrollable Christmas" (Episode 2.11), Abed takes the study group and the audience with him into the unconscious. Abed does so by creating and bringing all into a world of stop-motion animation in a quest to discover the true meaning of Christmas. However, since his study group cannot see the animation, their quest is to figure out what has gone wrong to make Abed see the world this way.

In pursuit of their respective goals, the group joins Abed in a therapy session, and together they venture to "Planet Abed" in their quest to find the North Pole and the true meaning of Christmas at Santa's Workshop. Abed takes the group along with him, literally into his unconscious mind. Planet Abed is a representation of what dwells in Abed's unconscious. Although Abed and the study group have different stated goals to be achieved through this journey, what they find in Abed's unconscious is the same and fulfills all of their needs. Together, they discover that it actually does not matter what had happened to Abed. Moreover, it does not matter what the meaning of Christmas was supposed to be: Christmas has whatever meaning one assigns to it. Though they go through the unconscious for different reasons, the journey is enough to enlighten both parties: the study group and the audience. Even though Abed is not the usual hero of *Community*, in this episode he clearly rises up to the challenge and fulfills the cycle that Harmon says makes a character a hero. With Abed guiding the path, the study group successfully navigates his unconscious, and the audience does as well.

In another episode, "Regional Holiday Music" (Episode 3.10), Abed rises up to the challenge of being the hero once again. This time, while taking the audience and the study group into the unconscious, he brings them into a musical. After Abed strives to create some holiday magic with the group and is rejected, he is then persuaded to join the glee club for a Christmas pageant.

This is the moment when Abed enters the unconscious world with his quest as bringing his study group along with him into the glee club, so they can experience some Christmas spirit together. Although Abed is not typically the character who functions as *Community*'s hero, he proves that he is capable of doing so. Not only does he take the study group into the unknown, but he takes the audience with him once again. Abed's quest for joy during the holidays is something that most viewers can relate to, and he provides the viewers with a story that resonates. Though Abed was Harmon's first foray into allowing another character the chance to stand as the hero and guide the audience and the study group into their unconscious, he accomplishes the task, and he is not the last.

In addition to Abed, multiple supporting characters from the study group are given their own singular plotline/hero episodes in which they rise up to the role of hero. By granting Abed the opportunity to be a hero, even if just for an episode, something in *Community* changes. Other characters are given their own chances to become the hero who guides the audience into the unconscious and back out again. In "Epidemiology" (Episode 2.6) Troy is the hero, in "Virtual Systems Analysis" (Episode 3.16) Annie is the hero, and in "Digital Estate Planning" (Episode 3.20) Pierce is the hero. There are also times when characters outside the study group become the hero of the story, such as in "Documentary Filmmaking: Redux" (Episode 3.8) in which Dean Pelton is the hero, and in "Advanced Dungeons and Dragons" (Episode 2.14) in which fellow student Neil is the hero. Harmon branches out to make other characters the hero in these singular plotline/hero episodes and even embraces characters outside the group for such a role. When each of these characters becomes the hero for an episode, this gives them a chance to venture into their own unconscious and to give the audience a chance to connect with a different character as they follow the pattern of the hero.

On a rare occasion, Troy is given the opportunity to play the hero. In "Epidemiology" (Episode 2.6), the study group attends Greendale's Halloween party, only to eat some contaminated food and transform into zombies. Though the study group shares this journey, it is Troy's own journey and self-discovery that makes him the hero of the episode. Troy begins the episode in matching *Aliens* movie theme costumes with Abed, only to put aside his costume when he believes it makes him too nerdy. Though the plot of the episode appears to be traversing the unconscious world of zombies, it is actually about Troy venturing into his own unconscious to deal with his self-confidence. At the climax of the story, Troy decides to accept himself for who he is, nerdiness and all. It is this acceptance that drives Troy to re-enter Greendale after he has escaped and so that he might save the other students. To Troy, it may be the nerdy thing to do, but being true to himself is what allows him to save them all. Here, Troy becomes the hero of both his own story and the singular plotline/hero episode, and he was only able to be the hero because he faced what dwelt in his own unconscious.

In "Virtual Systems Analysis" (Episode 3.16), Annie becomes the hero. This episode revolves around Annie joining Abed in his Dreamatorium. Abed inadvertently insults Annie during their simulation, and in return he overhears Annie declare, "people bend over backwards to cater to him." Abed takes this statement to heart, and the episode consists of Annie traveling through Abed's Dreamatorium simulation to reach the root of his problem and fix it. The contents of the simulation are all creations of Abed's mind, placing the whole journey in Abed's unconscious. In the depths of Abed's unconscious — symbolized by Abed being trapped in a locker like students used to do to him in junior high — there lies Abed's fear that eventually everyone will grow tired of him. At the same time that Annie is trying to get to the root of Abed's problem, Abed accesses the root of Annie's own unconscious. Abed believes that Annie is in love with Jeff and wants to be with him, yet when Abed confronts her about this, Annie faces her own unconscious and realizes that it is not so much Jeff she loves, as the thought of being able to make a man like Jeff love her. After Annie has reached an understanding of her own unconscious, she still must pull Abed back to the conscious world with her. Annie confronts Abed about his fear that his friends will eventually cast him aside. She deals with this fear by comforting Abed, "You're afraid you don't fit in. You're afraid you'll be alone. Great news, you share that with all of us, so you'll never be alone and you'll always fit in." Here, Annie simultaneously confronts the troubles in her own unconscious and the troubles in Abed's. She manages to guide Abed, the audience, and herself through his unconscious, like any good hero.

In "Digital Estate Planning" (Episode 3.20), Pierce becomes an unlikely hero. In this episode, Pierce and his friends in the study group are forced to compete in a computer game so that Pierce can receive his inheritance. The unconscious realm begins when the group enters the video game. Pierce travels through the comically unfamiliar game world in order to face his father, who is the boss at the end, or the villain. However, the truth that Pierce must uncover and face in the unconscious is not his father, but that his father had an illegitimate child. For most of the episode, Pierce's newfound brother, Gilbert, is the antagonist, struggling to keep Pierce from his inheritance. Pierce finds the truth for which he has gone into the unconscious to seek when he realizes that his brother has spent his life being mistreated by their father. Therefore, Pierce decides to support his brother rather than support himself. This is rare because for most of the series, Pierce is self-serving, putting aside the concerns of others, including his own friends in the study group, in order to further his own agenda. By giving Pierce the chance to be the hero, the writers show that he is able to put aside the concerns that so often plague him throughout the series. Instead,

Pierce is able to confront his own unconscious and come away with the knowledge that he can do right, at least by his brother.

In "Documentary Filmmaking: Redux" (Episode 3.8), *Community* ventures outside the study group for the hero. The plot of this episode revolves around Dean Pelton attempting to create a commercial for Greendale Community College. As the production of the commercial progresses, Pelton slowly descends into dictatorial behavior and is eventually abandoned by all the students due to his behavior. Pelton argues that he simply wants to make the best commercial possible, but through the process of entering the unconscious world of creating the commercial, he comes to realize he is motivated by something else. Pelton discovers that everything he has done for Greendale has been because he believes that Greendale is insufficient compared to the school he attended as an undergraduate. When he comes to understand this motivation, Pelton is able to release that prejudice and understand the value of Greendale in a way in which he never has been able to understand before. Hence, his journey through the unconscious as the hero of the episode allows him to release his expectations and fully embrace Greendale for what it is.

In "Advanced Dungeons and Dragons" (Episode 2.14), the hero is one step further removed than the Dean and is found in a fellow classmate they call "Fat Neil." In this episode, Jeff arranges a game of Dungeons and Dragons, involving the study group and Neil. Jeff discovers that Neil has been contemplating suicide due to something Jeff might have said; therefore, he gathers the group so that Neil can feel camaraderie and have a chance to feel like his life is worthwhile. Despite Jeff being the organizer of the game, Neil takes this journey through the unconscious, and that is what makes him the hero. Neil is struggling with a belief in his own value, and his journey into the unconscious deals with that. Neil enters the unconscious world when he begins the game, and he must struggle against his own doubt and the heckling of Pierce before he can find the knowledge that he seeks.

At the climax of the narrative, when Neil has lost everything he had worked for in the game, he realizes that that losing does not affect who he is as a person. Pierce has defeated the study group and revealed to Neil that Jeff was the person who had coined the nickname "Fat Neil," so everyone has been calling him that. This name-calling has plagued Neil throughout his time at Greendale Community College. Despite being at his lowest point, Neil achieves his knowledge by extending forgiveness to Pierce. The audience may acknowledge forgiveness being a difficult and noble act, thereby granting Neil power. With this newfound power, Neil realizes that despite not having a weapon in the game, he still has enough control over his own life, to control how he reacts to a bully like Pierce. That realization frees him from his concerns with how he is treated. Despite being a seldom-used character in *Community*, Neil is still able to follow the pattern laid out by Harmon and carry the audience through the unconscious as the episode's hero.

Harmon adheres to a strict story structure that he believes will provide the kind of catharsis and resonance that carries the audience into their own unconscious. To Harmon, the structure of the story is enough to let the audience engage, and he shows that belief by allowing multiple supporting characters to become the hero of an episode. *Community* is known for its innovation in nearly all aspects of its storytelling, and creating this new perspective about which character can be the hero is an extension of that. Dan Harmon's certainty in the value of structure is enough that it opens the door to a new kind of narrative structure that allows for multiple characters to assume the role of singular hero rather than television's traditional notion of one or two clearly defined heroes, or perhaps no clear hero at all. All these examples demonstrate the fluidity to *Community* that has created a new space for the old constraints of how heroes are approached.

Works Cited

"Abed's Uncontrollable Christmas." *Community*. NBC. 9 December 2010.
"Advanced Dungeons and Dragons." *Community*. NBC. 3 February 2011.
"Anthropology 101." *Community*. NBC. 23 September 2010.
Campbell, Joseph. *The Hero with a Thousand Faces*. 3rd ed. Novato, CA: New World Library, 2008.
"Cooperative Calligraphy." *Community*. NBC. 11 November 2010.
"Digital Estate Planning." *Community*. NBC. 17 May 2012.
"Documentary Filmmaking: Redux." *Community*. NBC. 17 November 2011.
"Epidemiology." *Community*. NBC. 28 October 2010.
Harmon, Dan. "Story Structure 102: Pure, Boring Theory." *Wikia.com*. Wikia, Inc., n.d. Web. 13 November 2012.
____. "Story Structure 104: The Juicy Details." *Wikia.com*. Wikia, Inc., n.d. Web. 13 November 2012.
____. "Story Structure 105: How TV is Different." *Wikia.com*. Wikia, Inc., n.d. Web. 13 November 2012.
"Introduction to Finality." *Community*. NBC. 17 May 2012.
"Investigative Journalism." *Community*. NBC. 14 January 2010.
"Modern Warfare." *Community*. NBC. 6 May 2010.
"Pilot." *Community*. NBC. 17 September 2009.
Raftery, Brian. "How Dan Harmon Drives Himself Crazy Making *Community*." *Wired*. Condé Nast, 22 September 2011. Web. 13 November 2012.
"Regional Holiday Music." *Community*. NBC. 8 December 2011.
"Virtual Systems Analysis." *Community*. NBC. 19 April 2012.

Greendale Hyperreality
Nettie Brock

> So, maybe we are caught in an endless cycle of screw-ups and hurt feelings. But I choose to believe it's just the Universe's way of molding us into some kind of super-group ... prepared for any insane adventure life throws our way. And I don't know about you, but I'm looking forward to every one of them. —JEFF WINGER, "Paradigms of Human Memory" (Episode 2.21)

Since its beginning, *Community* has featured a myriad of televisual and filmic tropes and conventions. The show and showrunners delight in turning these tropes on their heads and subverting them in new and interesting ways. One such trope that has been featured twice in the first three years of the show's run is that of the clip show flashback.

In the two episodes featuring this type of flashback — "Paradigms of Human Memory" (Episode 2.21) and "Curriculum Unavailable" (Episode 3.19) — the clips do not feature, as per the convention, events or encounters previously experienced by the audience. Instead, these are new events in the audience's eyes, thereby expanding the reality of the characters, by allowing the audience to learn of their back-stories. However, in "Curriculum Unavailable," the idea is suggested that all of Greendale Community College is a manifestation of the collective imagination of the study group, who are, in fact, in an insane asylum. The group briefly ruminates on this idea and a "flashback" ensues for which they are shown in the asylum, reenacting various events from the show. Through these flashbacks, *Community* works to expand not the reality of Greendale, but the hyperreality — the simulacrum. This essay intends to explore the hyperreality of *Community*, through a few episodes — "Paradigms of Human Memory," "Curriculum Unavailable," as well as the alternate realities presented in "Remedial Chaos Theory" (Episode 3.3). In doing so, I hope to expose the simulacrum of Greendale Community College and the impact *Community* has on "conventional" sitcoms in order to look to the future of Greendale-esque sitcom-simulacra, focusing specifically on *Cougar Town*.

By presenting the idea that the events we have seen are false, the show introduces an interesting thought: how much of this world is real? To explore this question, readers need to think about "hyperreality," which Umberto Eco would define as "the absolute fake" (31). Greendale Community College presents all the attributes of a "real" sitcom college in that the students clearly attend classes and complete assignments. It is, however, difficult to equate *Community* with other sitcoms set at universities, as it does not, in fact, display the classic traits of a college sitcom. The Journal of Higher Education argues that none of the popular college sitcoms, which are few and far between, portray any semblance of an actual university:

> *Community* does not capture the real community college — as if there were one. But neither do *M*A*S*H*, *Scrubs*, or *The Office* capture actual institutions. Comedy exaggerates, romanticizes, and deconstructs. *Community* plays off stereotypes and clichés, reinforcing and puncturing them at the same time. Another college show currently airing, *Greek*, about sororities and fraternities, is just as absurd, with elegant houses, formal flirting lessons, and "unhappy face" cupcakes sent to decline invitations. It enacts the same myth as *Community* [Bauman].

Greek (2007–2011) and *Blue Mountain State,* another college sitcom that ran from 2010–2011 on Spike TV, engaged in raucous, frat-boy-esque hijinks and humor. *Community* deviates far from this norm, proving instead to be a wackier version of *Friends* (1994–2004) or even a 21st century *Seinfeld* (1989–1998), in the author's opinion. *Community* is an ensemble show about little or nothing beyond the lives of the seven members of the study group, yet these seven characters are fully realized, sometimes even reaching beyond the stereotypes from which they originated. They each have full stories, as seen on screen, and relationships that have been built naturally over the course of the show. The point of this essay, however, is not necessarily to equate *Community* with other college sitcoms or with other sitcoms in general, but instead to compare it to the "real world": the world in which the audience exists.

At this point, it is easy to point to all television as being a simulacrum of reality, realizing that *Community* is not unique in this. However, in this situation the difference is that the show is not just aping reality but is simulating the sitcom genre without quite being a sitcom. Because of the fluctuating nature of *Community*'s episodes, the show is constantly wavering between serious sitcom and sitcom parody. In other words, it switches between sitcom reality and sitcom simulacrum.

First of all, *Community* is not a series that is easily summarized. The Internet Movie Database defines it thusly: "A smarmy lawyer, whose education is deemed void by the bar, is forced to attend a local community college with an extremely eclectic staff and student body" ("Community [2009–]"). However, to someone who has seen the show that does not quite seem sufficient. In the episode that forms the basis of our argument, "Curriculum Unavailable" (Episode 3.19), the series is described by their psychiatrist as "this fantastical community college where everything that happens is unbelievably ridiculous and it all revolves around [the study] group." Both of these descriptions include similar words, primarily, "eclectic" and "ridiculous." These words are essential to understanding the series.

The key to understanding *Community* is to understand the disparate types of episodes featured on the show. Tully Barnett and Ben Kooyman break down the types for us:

> The show deliberately alternates between what we might call "straight" episodes dealing with traditional sitcom premises (albeit in meta-fictional ways) and more ambitious, unconventional episodes featuring outlandish premises, often infused with recognizable tropes of Science Fiction, Fantasy genres and fan cultures [110].

To demonstrate what Barnett and Kooyman mean, I would like to point out that the more straight episodes can be those such as the Season 1 finale, "Pascal's Triangle Revisited" (Episode 1.25). The plot summary of the episode, as provided by the Internet Movie Database is as follows: "Jealousy runs rampant at Greendale as Britta and Professor Slater fight for the affection of Jeff. Meanwhile, Troy is confused when his best friend, Abed, doesn't invite him to move into his dorm room." As the reader can see, this is a typical sitcom plot, consisting of a love triangle and conflicts between best friends.

On the other hand, we can also examine the descriptions for the two-part finale of Season 2, "A Fistful of Paintballs" (Episode 2.23). According to the episode summary on the Internet Movie Database, "In a 'spaghetti western' parody, Pierce tries to get revenge on the rest of the study group during this year's paintball tournament." And here is the synopsis for the episode that follows it, "For a Few Paintballs More" (Episode 2.24): "When the study group learns that there's a sinister plot behind the paintball tournament, they unite the remaining players to defeat the enemy." From these descriptions, it is apparent that the first parodies Sergio Leone's *A Fistful of Dollars* (1964) and the second, although its title derives from *For A Few Dollars More* (1965), it is a direct homage of *Star Wars* (1977) through vocal affirmation by Abed as well as direct cinematic correlations. These two episodes are indicative of the "unconventional" episodes.

By combining the straight and the "unconventional" episodes, creator Dan Harmon and the writers create the everyday world of the series. However, the reality is not actually real, nor is it "absolute unreality" (Eco 7). As the series vacillates between straight and unconventional episodes, the world of Greendale

Community College wavers between reality and a world that is miles from the real but apes the conventions typically associated with this type of sitcom reality convincingly with hyperreality.

Rather than being a perfect copy of the real, non-televisual world, however, Greendale Community College is more akin to Disneyland and Eco's analysis therein, being "at once absolutely realistic and absolutely fantastic" (43). We are presented with this ethereal world called "Greendale." This world, which is only ever identified as being Greendale Community College and takes place in no discernible city or state (even though, according to the fictional school website, it is purported to be Greendale, Colorado, a place which looks to be more Southern California than anywhere in Colorado), is a perfect replica of the real world with a little bit of extra fantasy thrown in.

However, if we are approaching *Community* from a postmodern perspective, we realize that inherent in an exploration of the simulacrum is the idea that place is irrelevant. In other words, where something takes place is secondary to the issues that rise in that place and how they are dealt with (Dalton and Linder 262). How else can we equate Greendale and Disneyland? Like Disneyland, where dreams come true, Greendale is a place of whimsy. Early in the second season, when Jeff asks "Is this campus getting more cartoony every day?" he is not wrong. In every day or episode in the second season, the show creeps closer and closer to the simulacrum. Do not forget the second season ends with the western/science fiction homage paintball war. Additionally, Greendale, like Disneyland, is a world where the boundaries between reality and imagination lie. It is here, in this equivalency that we find the connection to Eco: there is no clear real and fake. Greendale is a real world that cannot possibly exist in the real world; the boundaries are not clearly defined; thus, it is hyperrealistic.

In his philosophical treatise, *Simulacra and Simulation* (1981), Jean Baudrillard lays out the "successive phases of the image" as it becomes simulacrum:

> [I]t is the reflection of a profound reality;
> it masks and denatures a profound reality;
> it masks the absence of a profound reality;
> it has no relation to any reality whatsoever;
> it is its own pure simulacrum [4].

In other words, the image begins as simply a reflection and slowly shifts into a mask, which overtakes and overpowers the original image. The simulacrum, the reflection of the image, becomes an image itself that has lost semblance of the original image.

If we apply Baudrillard's phases to *Community*, we would discover that it follows the progression almost exactly. The pilot appears to be a tale of a community college with a few quirky characters, but it is also in line with a typical sitcom structure, reflecting reality. We have a handsome leading man who aims to sleep with the beautiful leading lady; a series of obstacles are placed in the way of that relationship; and then a group of supporting players is introduced, who act as foils for the couple and the means of progressing the plot over the subsequent seasons. Additionally, the other basic definitions of the sitcom apply to *Community*: the half-hour length, the domestic setting (which, in this case, is the study room, which functions as the "home" for the characters), the stereotypes that the characters initially fall into, and so on (Mills 49).

Over the course of the first season, the show introduces sequences that border on the bizarre, thereby masking reality. Once the show arrives near the end of the first season in "Contemporary American Poultry" (Episode 1.21), any resemblance to reality or even the stereotypical sitcom has clearly disappeared. The episode is a blatant *Goodfellas* (1990) parody in which, instead of raising through the ranks of the mob, the study group is ascending the hierarchy of the cafeteria; instead of peddling cocaine, they become corrupt only to acquire and supply chicken fingers. The show maintains this phase of Baudrillard's progression for most of the series — constantly wavering between reality and hyperreality. This is most likely for audience ratings because a show which has completely abandoned any semblance of reality but which still totes itself as a reality-based sitcom is a difficult concept to successfully market to a popular audience.

However, a few episodes have abandoned reality all together and taken a far more drastic track into the hyperreal, and perhaps even beyond. For example, in Season 2, "Abed's Uncontrollable Christmas" is completely done in claymation or clay animation (Episode 2.11). In Season 3, "Pillows and Blankets" (Episode 3.14) is a Ken Burns-esque documentary spoof; Burns is famous for his documentaries on the Civil War. A couple episodes after, "Virtual Systems Analysis" (Episode 3.16) is told completely within a simulation of the series in a *Star Trek: The Next Generation* (1987–1994) Holodeck-type room, all borne from Abed's imagination. And "Digital Estate Planning" (Episode 3.20) finds our favorite study group in 8-bit video game form. By the end of Season 3, any modicum of belief the audience has that Greendale Community College and the world in which it exists is a part of reality or any typical sitcom has completely evaporated. These episodes demonstrate the malleability of the sitcom form and its ability to delve into and beyond the realms of the hyperreal. Further, these episodes help the audience determine how *Community* functions as a simulacrum. This simulacrum can be explored by examining how the reality of *Community* was established in the first place through common television tropes such as the clip show episodes.

"Paradigms of Human Memory" (Episode 2.21)

This episode in Season 2 is the first of two clip show episodes in the series. Clip show episodes are a form of the flashback television trope. TV Tropes lists twelve types:

1. Flashback Cut: [a] very brief flashback.
2. Flash Back Echo: ...[T]he past events in the flashback parallel what [is] occurring in the present.
3. Happy Flashback: A flashback to a happy time may segue into a Troubled Backstory Flashback (see next page).
4. How We Got Here: The episode opens In Medias Res [Latin for "in the middle of things"; the episode begins in the middle of the action then flashback to explain how they have reached this point]; then the events leading up to the episode's beginning are explained via flashback.
5. Mid-Battle Flashback: The character is losing in a fight and flashes back to [his or her] training to retrieve the knowledge to win.
6. Pensieve Flashback: The present-day version of the character shows up inside [his or her] own memories of the past ... to provide snarky commentary or to inexplicably interact with the past.
7. [*Rashomon*] Style: [m]ultiple flashbacks depicting one event from several different perspectives. [This is based on the 1950 film by Akira Kurosawa that looks at a single event, a rape, from the perspective of each of the witnesses in turn.]
8. Self-Serving Memory: A character flashes back to an event, only for the flashback to be quite different from what actually happened, usually to make that character look better.
9. Separate Scene Storytelling: [i]f the flashback is being recounted.
10. Troubled Backstory Flashback: A character with a Dark and Troubled Past flashes back to a happy memory that transforms into a bloodbath.
11. Whole Episode Flashback: A flashback that takes up the whole episode. (In literary works, this would be an example of a "frame story.")
12. Flashback within a Flashback: [This] occurs when a character recounts an event in which he [or] she also flashbacks into ANOTHER event within the first flashback.

Upon inspecting this list, the episodes we are discussing fall into the "Whole Episode Flashback," especially since under this category, we find the "Clip Show" trope. These episodes were very popular in the days before "reruns, syndication, and videotapes/DVDs" (TV Tropes, "Clip Show") on shows such as *Friends* (1994–2004) and *The Golden Girls* (1985–1992). The initial purpose of a clip show is frequently to save on money by simply having the characters sitting around reminiscing and having those memories appear on the screen as the clips.

This is how "Paradigms of Human Memory" begins, with the group making their twentieth diorama. Then it quickly subverts the trope by portraying moments we, as the audience, have never seen, but that are said to have taken place during the continuity of the show. These moments include, but are not limited to the following: showing a trip the group took to a Wild West town, the group taking over for the glee club, the group going a St. Patrick's Day "adventure," and the group wearing straightjackets when they are locked in a padded room. The flashbacks additionally transcend the "Whole Episode Flashback" trope and are, at times, in the "Flashback within a Flashback" trope. The group remembers itself remembering another moment when they remember another moment.

There are also brief glimpses of heretofore — unseen scenes from episodes during the seasons: a scene during the Halloween episode, "Epidemiology" (Episode 2.6), in which Abed observes Britta and Jeff sneaking into a closet and a scene of the group indulging Abed's claymation fantasy in "Abed's Uncontrollable Christmas" (Episode 2.11). According to series reviewer, Alan Sepinwall, these moments were not filmed at the same time as the episode in which they are supposed to have taken place; the set for Halloween episode had to be fully reconstructed.

On the other hand, these moments work to expand the universe of the show. Through these scenes, the audience is shown proof that the characters have existed beyond the times they have been on screen. Along this line, Baudrillard says in regards to history, "We require a visible past, a visible continuum, a visible myth of origin, which reassures us about our end" (7). Additionally, according to Eco, a cult object, such as *Community*, "must provide a completely furnished world so that its fans can quote characters and episodes as if they were aspects of the fan's private sectarian world" (198). This first clip episode works towards these collective goals: to create a full history in order to expand the fan base.

The episode does not try to show us any episodes that could not exist within the *Community* that we know of; it does not attempt to defy or subvert the reality as already established by the show. Each of the escapades that the study group remembers is a perfectly plausible situation. The moments might seem bizarre, but they are all done within the confines of the show and just barely border on the hyperreal. Each of the flashbacks is linked to the others by a common thread. At the end of the episode, the group has gone through its usual motions: they start remembering, they begin to argue, they are on the cusp of dissolving the group, then Jeff gives a rousing speech to unite them all once again (the speech, which occurs in nearly every episode, is commonly referred to as a "Winger" speech). The flashbacks each reflect these events taking place, actually becoming a third type of flashback trope: the Flashback Echo. There is no deviation from the norm in these episodes.

Finally, the title of the episode, "Paradigms of Human Memory" (Episode 2.21), carries significance. Typically, with *Community* episodes, the title is based upon a class that would appear on a college course list, which also reflects the events occurring in the episode. For example, "Debate 109" is the ninth episode of Season 1 and prominently features a debate. "Paradigms of Human Memory" fits into this "basic paradigm" yet this word, "paradigm," sheds an interesting light upon the episode, not because of what it is saying, but because of what it is not saying. Paradigms are usually discussed in terms of the change they are undergoing: i.e. Kuhn's paradigm shift. Therefore, one could say that Dan Harmon is establishing the paradigm for the show in this episode simply so that he can begin the shift. From this point forward, every episode delves just a little bit further into the hyperreal.

"Curriculum Unavailable" (Episode 3.19)

This is the episode that is emblematic of the paradigm shift. This particular episode begins the same as "Paradigms of Human Memory," with the study group having a series of flashbacks, but then it subverts both its very nature as a clip show and the entire pseudo-reality of the show. Then the paradigm shifts.

This episode begins with Abed, who is having trouble adjusting after being expelled from Greendale, arrested, and sent to a psychiatrist — along with the whole study group. Because Abed refuses to go to any doctor alone, the group has accompanied him. The session commences with the series of flashback/clips, in a more organized fashion than "Paradigms of Human Memory." They begin with clips of Abed as increasingly unstable, proceed to the others in the group being equally crazy, continue to the general insanity of Greendale itself, and end with scenes of the good memories of Greendale. Unlike "Paradigms of Human Memory," these flashbacks do enter into the world of the simulacrum by their bizarre nature. The flashbacks include another paintball tournament (this one shot as a film noir homage), Annie acting out "Troy and Abed and Annie in the Morning" (based upon "Troy and Abed in the Morning" a completely fake morning show), Shirley finding the cut out of a gun in a library book, Abed narrating Pierce's actions, and so on. While none of these, by themselves, are un-real, they are outside the ordinary actions of a typical sitcom. Then the episode takes a turn.

As the group is preparing to leave, the psychiatrist proclaims that Greendale Community College does not actually exist — it is a shared psychosis amongst the group, who are then shown to be inmates at Greendale Asylum. The group members then lapse into a flashback. This time, however, the flashback clips acted out by the "inmates" in the "asylum" are, in fact, moments previously seen on the show. These moments range from the various paintball episodes to "Regional Holiday Music" (Episode 3.10) in which the study group again takes over for the glee club, even to "Paradigms of Human Memory," and beyond.

These alleged hallucinations are previously conceived of as *real* moments to the audience. Thus, reality itself is presented as an alternative reality, displacing and undermining the possibility of an original or "true" reality. The simulacrum is complete. Any semblance to reality has completely disappeared; hence, hyperreality has taken over. Furthermore, the audience no longer needs to distinguish between fantasy and reality in order to understand the plot, as both are equally valid states for hyperreal environments.

To this end, the psychiatrist even points out just how absurd the idea of Greendale is: "This fantastical community college where everything that happens is unbelievably ridiculous, and it all revolves around you as a group.... And you've attended Greendale for three years but don't community colleges end after two?" He vocalizes the comments of the audience, particularly those wondering why the study group members have not yet graduated. Because of this one moment, which is very quickly dismissed by Jeff as not being true, everything the audience thought they knew about the show is suddenly undermined.

This episode parallels an episode of Joss Whedon's acclaimed fantasy series *Buffy the Vampire Slayer* entitled "Normal Again" (Episode 6.17). Here, after she is stung by a demon, vampire-slayer Buffy "wakes up" in an asylum in Los Angeles. She is told that she has been having an extended delusion in which she believes she is a vampire slayer. The episode revolves around her trying to decide which world is "real" and which reality is "better." In an essay discussing the episode, Len Geller argues,

> It raises the real possibility of a permanent subversion of the text not just a temporary one. It calls into question not just portions of the text but the entire text. The postmodern resonance of the episode is not confined to this destabilizing effect; it also implies an antirealist epistemology that runs counter to the dominant realist assumptions of the show [2].

The statement applies to "Curriculum Unavailable" as well and nicely sums up the way that subversion exposes the simulacrum and demonstrates the instability of mediated realities. Again, the title of the episode basically provides no real title for the episode. If the paradigm is that episode titles are reflective of the "curriculum" or events contained within the episode, having the title as "Curriculum Unavailable" suggests a nothingness to the episode. The simulacrum has completely overrun the entire show; hence, the paradigm has shifted.

"Remedial Chaos Theory" (Episode 3.3)

One final episode can be discussed in conjuncture with this subversion. This episode occurs at Troy and Abed's new apartment and is in the same vein as the *Rashomon* flashback previously listed: "[m]ultiple flashbacks depicting one event from several different perspectives" (TV Tropes, "Flashback"). Seven different alternate realities are posited in this episode, each one based on a different member of the group leaving the apartment for a short period of time. The "real" timeline is positioned as the one for which Jeff leaves and returns to find the study group happily dancing to The Police's song, "Roxanne." The worst timeline is that in which Troy leaves and returns to find the house on fire, Pierce shot in the leg, and a long-nosed troll statue flying towards his face. At the end scene of the episode, the characters are back in the ludicrous timeline: Pierce has died, Annie has been committed, Shirley has become an alcoholic, Jeff has lost an arm, and Troy has lost his voice box. Abed decides that this is the most evil timeline and it creates felt goatees for all of them, à la *Star Trek*'s "Mirror, Mirror" (Episode 2.33) alternate reality episode in which the most obvious distinguishing characteristic of the evil reality is Spock's beard. The timelines of the other *Community* characters fall between these two on the scale of chaos to calm.

The significance of this episode of *Community* is in the idea that Jeff's timeline is assumed, but it is never explicitly stated as being the "real" timeline, as he functions as the main character. Therefore, from that point forward in the series, the audience is able to retain a degree of doubt regarding in which character's reality the story continues. In these alternate realities, "all these worlds belong to the same universe and constitute modifications of the same story" (Deleuze, *Cinema 2* 132). In fact, even into the current fourth season, a modicum of doubt remains in Abed. By the end of the third season, his "darkest timeline" doppelganger (Abed with the evil–Spock goatee) takes control of Abed and attempts to bring the darkest reality into the current reality. A Winger speech brings the normal Abed back. In the season 4 Christmas episode, "Intro to Knots," Abed again wonders about the darkest timeline. The situation he imagines is ludicrous (Evil Jeff gets Evil Annie freed from imprisonment, then declares their intent to take over the "Prime Timeline"), and yet it suggests a uniting of the timelines. Where the show is headed, we can only hypothesize about, but we know that among the Prime Timeline and the Darkest Timeline exist five other realities. Therefore, the show itself could exist in any of them.

Adding to this doubt, the events of "Curriculum Unavailable," as well as the events in the show in general further build *Community's* simulacrum. In *Sophist*, Plato defines the simulacrum, if not in so many words by presenting two types of images. The first is "the art of likeness-making;—generally a likeness of anything is made by producing a copy which is executed according to the proportions of the original, similar in length and breadth and depth, each thing receiving also its appropriate color" (qtd. in Jowett 114). The second type of image is what is created in order to make the object depicted look realistic, but is, in fact, altered to create the appearance of reality. Plato adds, "[T]hey give up the truth in their images and make only the proportions which appear to be beautiful, disregarding the real ones" (qtd. in Jowett 114–115). He labels this second type, "phantastic" art, an "appearance" but not a true "likeness" (qtd. in Jowett 114–115). Therefore, this phantastic art is the simulacrum.

In terms of *Community*, the first type of image would be the episodes like the pilot—episodes that perfectly mimic other sitcoms. The second type of image is, of course, the simulacrum. And yet it is not the truly outlandish episodes such as "A Fistful of Paintballs" (Episode 2.23) but is, instead, episodes such as "Cooperative Calligraphy" (Episode 2.8), episodes which present the appearance of a "real" world but which are tinged with the absurd. "Cooperative Calligraphy" is the series' bottle episode—an episode of a sitcom which takes place entirely within one location where the characters never leave and no new characters enter—a fact that Abed repeatedly reminds the characters of by saying "this is starting to feel like a bottle episode" and other such things. What we can understand from this is that the simulacrum of *Community* is not the world of the continual homage to films and movies, but those episodes that are homages (and even parodies) of sitcom tropes. The film homages do not come close to resembling a traditional sitcom, but the slightly offbeat episodes: those episodes that are simply tinged with the absurd. These are the episodes that show the simulacrum. One could say that the series wears homage-tinted glasses, that each episode is paying homage to something and by changing the rules they are paying homage to, it has completely subverted the homage. Therefore, the simulacrum has taken its place.

Gilles Deleuze overturns Plato's criticism of the more "beautiful" simulacrum in order to deny "the primacy of original over copy, of model over image; [and instead] glorifying the reign of simulacra and reflections" (*Difference and Repetition* 66). What this may mean is that once the audience members relinquish the reigns of realism, they can more fully engage with the narrative of *Community*. Rather than following Plato's beliefs on hyperreality, the audience must, according to Deleuze, glorify the simulacrum over the original. Once the audience stops believing they are watching a sitcom and realizes that they have entered a whole new sitcom-world, then the spectatorial engagement will be heightened.

Community and the Sitcom

One has to ask: when does a sitcom stop being considered a sitcom? At what point do we acknowledge that *Community* has gone beyond the sitcom and into the simulacrum of a sitcom? The answer is as follows: at the moment when that simulacrum is exposed and the reality looks in on itself, transcending the boundary between hyperreal and self-reflexive. The hyperreal is intended to eclipse the tropes of the sitcom while any self-reflection purposes to inspect those conventions and expound upon them. Eco tells us, "the public is meant to admire the perfection of the fake and its obedience to the program" (44). Along this line, again to look to Eco, Greendale "not only produces illusion, but in confessing it — stimulates the desire for it" (44). When *Community* divulges its simulacrum to the audience, the importance of that illusion is heightened; as a result, the rest of the sitcom world takes note.

The show upon which *Community* has had the most influence is *Cougar Town* (2009–). This show started as an ordinary sitcom but rapidly obeyed Baudrillard's succession of the image and descended into an original, hyperreal sitcom simulacrum. The show, which began at ABC, was cancelled and was then given a second life on TBS. There, it may be given the opportunity to descend further, not being hampered by broadcast network restraints in regards to audience ratings. However, the biggest influence that the two shows have on each other are not in regards to the hyperreality of *Cougar Town* but of *Community*'s and how *Cougar Town* is a part of that hyperreality.

On *Community*, *Cougar Town* is exactly what it is in our real world — a TV sitcom. The only difference is that the Greendale version of *Cougar Town* is based on a British series, *Cougarton Abbey* (playing on the popular British drama, *Downton Abbey* [2010–]). We know that *Cougar Town* is Abed's favorite show, as he frequently makes reference to it. More important is his reaction when the show has gone on hiatus — he goes catatonic. At this point, he switches to *Cougarton Abbey* only to discover that it only lasted six episodes and that all the characters committed suicide at the end. He switches again to *Inspector Spacetime*, which viewers can figure out is a *Doctor Who* (1963–1989, 2005–) parody.

What makes the connection between these two sitcoms so interesting is how Abed's obsession with *Cougar Town* is, in fact, reflected on *Cougar Town*. He appears on the series as an extra. To be clear, it is not actor Danny Pudi who is featured in the background of a scene in Season 2, Episode 21 of *Cougar Town* — it is the character of Abed Nadir. He acts and reacts like Abed. When the reverse is true and two of the actors, Dan Byrd and Busy Phillips, from *Cougar Town* appear as extras in the second season finale of *Community*, "For a Few Paintballs More" (Episode 2.24), there is no indication that Travis Cobb and Laurie Keller (the characters they play on *Cougar Town*) are visiting Greendale. However, *Community* is a TV show in the *Cougar Town* universe; Travis and Laurie frequently mention watching it. And yet the exchange between the shows is not equivalent. While *Community* is said to be just a TV show on *Cougar Town*, there are indications that *Community* is "real." The first, of course, is Abed's appearance on the show; during the opening credits, *Community* is obliquely referenced twice. In "Contemporary Impressionists" (Episode 3.11), Abed is directly quoted as saying "I didn't know it was back on either," and in the following episode, the title of the series has been altered to "Cougarton Abbey." *Cougar Town* frequently alters its name, mocking the fact that the name no longer resembles the premise of the series, which began as the adventures of an older woman dating a series of younger men, but has changed to being, like *Community*, a show about a group of friends having adventures in their everyday lives. Clearly, this example can demonstrate that the lines between ordinary sitcom and *Community* are becoming blurred. Granted, both *Community* and *Cougar Town* have roots that began with *Scrubs* (2001–2010) and much of the wackiness and unconventional story telling can be traced through that. *Scrubs*, also created by Bill Lawrence, is again, about an everyday scenario, in this case a hospital, and the occurrences there. However, much of the series is told through the lead character, John Dorian, played by Zach Braff, and his fantasies. However, that does not preclude the importance of the sitcom simulacrum. Deleuze tells us:

> Everything has become simulacrum, for by simulacrum we should not understand a simple imitation but rather the act by which the very idea of a model or privileged position is challenged and overturned. The simulacrum is the instance which includes a difference within itself, such as (at least) two divergent series on which it plays, all resemblance abolished so that one can no longer point to the existence of an original and a copy [*Difference and Repetition* 69].

Through application of Deleuze's idea, if we see that the sitcom is beginning to be overturned in two disparate series (on two disparate networks) that work together to disrupt the reality, all while simultaneously existing in each other's worlds but not in the same universe, the idea is that the simulacrum is not unidirectional and is beginning to make an impact on televisual paradigms on a broader scale. The series, *Community*, watches the sitcom genre, which is watching reality, which is watching the sitcom genre, which is watching *Community*. The layers are intricate, but they are affecting one another. *Community* is exposing its simulacrum, and thus, the simulacrum begins to bleed into the sitcom reality.

The sitcom genre is paying attention, as evidenced by shows such as *Cougar Town*, and the audiences are also paying attention despite the fact neither of these series has garnered huge audiences. The Season 3 finale of *Community* was viewed by 2.48 million people (Bibel, "Thursday Final Ratings), while the finale of *Cougar Town* was viewed by 3.5 million (Bibel, "TV Ratings Tuesday"). In comparison, the highest rated broadcast sitcom is *The Big Bang Theory*, which had 6.9 million viewers on November 29 (Kondolojoy). On cable, original sitcoms are not nearly as frequent, and when they are shown, they rarely top 1 million viewers. However, on November 15, *It's Always Sunny in Philadelphia* only had 0.7 million viewers (Bibel, "Thursday Cable Ratings"). Clearly, this proves that in contrast to *It's Always Sunny in Philadelphia*, shows such as *Community* and *Cougar Town* do have large followings. After *Community* was put on hiatus in 2011, the backlash on Twitter was so extreme that *Time* magazine reporter James Poniewozik said that there was a "10-to-1 greater ratio of Community fans than the actual TV viewership." These viewers are paying attention, as proved by the series 4 premiere, which was pushed from October 16, 2012 to February 7, 2013, which brought in nearly 4 million viewers.

Conclusion

The simulacrum of *Community* has been exposed. The series has presented moments in which the audience began to question everything they believed about the series and by doing so, the door was opened to notice the dissonance between *Community* and other sitcoms and where that dissonance leads. We could discuss any number of avenues, making certain assumptions about televisual audiences. Instead of doing so, however, let us simply say that as more audiences, which include the genre itself, begin to question the reality of the sitcom and accept the simulacrum of *Community*, more series in the same strain will appear. At that moment, specific terminology needs to be considered. We also need to find answers to certain questions: If it is just the simulacrum of a sitcom, can it still actually be called a sitcom? What if it is not a sitcom at all and is only the simulacrum? Is it still a sitcom? Some may call it "neo-classical"; readers can just call it a "sitcom simulacrum" or something different altogether. What we can be sure about is the fact that the paradigm is shifting. The sitcom reality is becoming aware of itself and elevating into hyperreality. It began at Greendale Community College. And this is only the beginning.

Works Cited

"Abed's Uncontrollable Christmas." *Community*. NBC. 9 December 2010.
Barnett, Tully, and Ben Kooyman. "Repackaging Popular Culture: Commentary and Critique in Community." *Networking Knowledge* 5.2 (2012): 109–134.
Baudrillard, Jean, and Sheila Glaser Faria. *Simulacrum and Simulation*. Ann Arbor: University of Michigan Press, 2010.

Bauman, M. Garrett. "Community College, With a Laugh Track." *Chronicle of Higher Education* 56.15 (2009): B12–B13.

Bibel, Sara. "Thursday Cable Ratings: 'Thursday Night Football' Wins Night, 'Jersey Shore,' 'Burn Notice,' 'It's Always Sunny in Philadelphia,' 'Project Runway All Stars' and More." *TV by the Numbers*. 30 November 2012. Web. 6 December 2012.

____. "Thursday Final Ratings: 'American Idol,' 'Grey's Anatomy,' '30 Rock' Adjusted Up; 'Touch,' 'Scandal' Adjusted Down." *TV by the Numbers*. 18 May 2012. Web. 6 December 2012.

____. "TV Ratings Tuesday: 'Cougar Town' Finale Up, 'America's Got Talent' Rises." *TV by the Numbers*. 30 May 2012. Web. 6 December 2012.

"Community (2009–)." *Internet Movie Database*. IMDB.com, Inc., 1990–2013. Web. 6 December 2012.

"Community Pulled from NBC's Schedule: The Backlash." *The Week*. The Week Publications. 16 November 2011. Web. 19 November 2012.

"Contemporary American Poultry." *Community*. NBC. 22 April 2010.

"Contemporary Impressionists." *Community*. NBC. 22 March 2012.

"Cooperative Calligraphy." *Community*. NBC. 11 November 2010.

"Curriculum Unavailable." *Community*. NBC. 10 May 2012.

Dalton, Mary M., and Laura R. Linder. *Sitcom Reader: America Viewed and Skewed*. Albany: State University of New York Press, 2005.

"Debate 109." *Community*. NBC. 12 November 2009.

Deleuze, Gilles. *Difference and Repetition*. New York: Columbia University Press, 1994.

"Digital Estate Planning." *Community*. NBC. 17 May 2012.

Eco, Umberto. *Travels in Hyperreality: Essays*. San Diego: Harcourt Brace Jovanovich, 1986.

"Epidemiology." *Community*. NBC. 28 October 2010.

"A Fistful of Paintballs." *Community*. NBC. 5 May 2011.

"For a Few Paintballs More." *Community*. NBC. 12 May 2011.

Geller, Len. "'Normal Again' and 'The Harvest': The Subversion and Triumph of Realism in Buffy." *Slayage* Online. 2011. Web. 6 December 2012.

Hibberd, James. "'Community' Surprise: Ratings Up." *Entertainment Weekly*. Entertainment Weekly, 8 February 2013. Web. 14 February 2013.

"Intro to Knots." *Community*. NBC. 18 April 2013.

Kondolojy, Amanda. "Broadcast TV Show Ratings — Weekly Top 25 TV Ratings Broadcast Top 25: Sunday Night Football Tops Week 10 Viewing Among Adults 18–49 and is Number 1 With Total Viewers." *TV by the Numbers*.4 December 2012. Web. 6 December 2012.

Mills, Brett. *Sitcom*. Edinburgh: Edinburgh University Press, 2009.

"Paradigms of Human Memory." *Community*. NBC. 21 April 2011.

"Pascal's Triangle Revisited." *Community*. NBC. 20 May 2010.

"Pillows and Blankets." *Community*. NBC. 5 April 2012.

Plato, and Benjamin Jowett. *Sophist*. Gloucester: Dodo, 2009.

Poniewozik, James. "Intermediate Suspended Animation: NBC's Midseason Slate Puts Community on Hold." *TIME*. Time, 15 November 2011. Web. 6 December 2012.

"Remedial Chaos Theory." *Community*. NBC. 13 October 2011.

Sepinwall, Alan. "Review: 'Community'–'Paradigms of Human Memory': Remember the Time?" *Hitfix*. 21 April 2011. Web. 7 November 2012.

"Virtual Systems Analysis." *Community*. NBC. 19 April 2012.

The Greendale Trickster: The Rise and Fall of Ben Chang

Ann-Gee Lee and Noah E. Schmidt

> I first met Chang when I hired him as a Spanish teacher at Greendale. Then he became a disgraced student, a psychopathic music major, a homeless vent dweller, a security guard, keytarist, power-hungry war lord, and, now, Kevin. It's sad to see him like this. Well, it's mixed. He was pretty terrible before.—DEAN PELTON, "Advanced Documentary Filmmaking" (Episode 4.6).

Tricksters flourish in the form of clever or foolish animals in folklore, real-life con artists who conjure up false credentials or identities, or as comedic characters on television. Since ancient times, the trickster has appeared in mythology of widespread cultures. Native American folklore specialist Larry Ellis notes how difficult the trickster is to pinpoint: he is "the scorned outsider and the culture-hero, the mythic transformer and the buffoon" who "may assume an array of contradictory personae in the course of a single narrative, moving from one to the other with the skill of a practiced shape-shifter while tripping on his tail at every turn." The trickster "creates through destruction and succeeds through failure" (Ellis). For example, in Native American stories, Coyote plays the role of both the creator and the trickster; as trickster, he creates chaos, and as creator, he tries to restore the order. In the Deep South, the slaves had stories about Br'er Rabbit, who is always trying to outwit the other animals in the stories, not always the hero. Br'er Rabbit is thought to have originated from West African mythology in which Anansi the spider is an important character who used his cleverness to outwit others and get himself out of scrapes.

In *Community*, both benevolent and sinister tricksters abound. Jeff Winger can be seen as a reformed trickster: he faked a degree to become a lawyer and must return to school for a real degree; sometimes, he resorts back to his selfish lawyer-like ways by trying to manipulate others, but feels guilty and does the right thing in the end. Troy Barnes and Abed Nadir can also be taken as tricksters — they are always subverting the audience's expectations. For example, they have their own morning show without a camera filming them. Moreover, they are both childlike. Abed lives in his own world, populated by his imagination and his own skewed concept of how "normal" people interact. He may manipulate people, but this manipulation is in the service of making the world more understandable to him through TV or movie analogies. At the end of "Accounting for Lawyers" (Episode 2.2), Troy sees Abed as a cartoon speaking to him from a tunnel painted on the wall. Cartoon Abed tells Troy, "Nothing's impossible here. Animals can talk. Your heart is shaped like a heart. And the smell of pie can make you float. You have to believe, Troy." Troy prepares to enter the tunnel. As Real-Life Abed pops out from behind a garbage can to tell him not to believe, Troy replies, disappointed, "I didn't ... I didn't." Abed responds as Troy leaves, "I may have done some damage there." This does indicate self-awareness to Abed as a trickster.

The show's most prominent trickster, however, Benjamin Franklin Chang, is unapologetic regarding his deceptions. Chang, the study group's initial Spanish teacher at Greendale Community College, is possibly the show's most interesting character. Blogger Kevin Hilke states, "During the first season, Chang, as the teacher of Spanish 101, the course that united *Community*'s cast into a study group, was explicitly necessary for the show's existence." As Greendale's most notorious trickster, Chang serves as the impetus for the study group, yet he belongs nowhere and is constantly trying to find a place for himself. The one consistent trait he carries is his deceptive nature.

Before discussing how Chang was able to fool his students and colleagues, a definition of the trickster archetype is needed. Father of analytical psychology Carl G. Jung came up with the term, "trickster," in relation to dreams; this archetype resides in the unconscious psyche. Jung considers the trickster to be similar to the Roman god, Mercury (Greek god, Hermes) because he changes his form and has a dual nature (qtd. in Viljoen and Van Der Merwe 39). *TV Tropes* provides more basic characteristics of the archetype:

> A trickster is a character who plays tricks or otherwise disobeys normal rules and conventional behavior ... openly questions and mocks authority, encourages impulse and enthusiasm, seeks out new ideas and experiences, destroys convention and complacency, and promotes chaos and unrest. At the same time, the trickster brings new knowledge, wisdom and many [a]n Aesop['s fable]. Even when punished horribly for his effrontery, his indomitable spirit [or plain sheer foolishness] keeps him coming back for more.

This definition of the trickster archetype touches on various characteristics of Chang. He is not a typical college professor: he wields race as a weapon and a shield, his personality and psyche are unstable, he abuses his power regularly on and off campus, and he uses manipulation and deception to protect himself or achieve his goals. Moreover, it is sometimes confusing or difficult to define his role in the story due to his trickster tendencies.

One reading of Chang in the first season propagates from Amy Chua's controversial tiger archetype. In *The Battle Hymn of the Tiger Mother*, Chua opens her book by describing the symbolism of a tiger: "the living symbol of strength and power, generally [inspiring] fear and respect" (2). Chang is a "tiger teacher" not just because his nickname is *El Tigre Chino*; he signifies intimidation and at most times confusion. He is able to succeed for some time by establishing a rhetoric of fear. He even incorporates somewhat viable pedagogy, yet with further investigation, his shortcomings become obvious. Later, as his power disintegrates, he becomes a paper tiger, or ineffective reactionary. However, when he rises to power as a dictator, Chang is vanquished. It is entertaining for the viewers to watch him climb up the authority ladder only to fall back down and climb back up again.

Lest we think that ridiculous behavior like Chang's is limited to the realm of fiction, there are many notable examples of tricksters in popular media. Chang's motivations in many ways mirror theirs. Recently in the news, Secretary of State John Kerry and Senator John McCain cited Dr. Elizabeth O'Bagy as their expert on Syrian affairs. Journalists, who wanted to know more about the attractive and ubiquitous young woman, discovered she is only 26 and does not actually have a doctorate. While O'Bagy claims that she will be defending her dissertation soon, people have been unable to locate the school where she has been studying. It was discovered that as an intern for the Institute for the Study of War, she had only begun researching Syria for 20 months (Newton-Small). Like Chang, O'Bagy took advantage of a situation and misrepresented her credentials for personal gain. Similarly, Michael Geeser from Las Vegas Channel 8 news provides another example of one gentleman fabricating a Ph.D. to obtain a teaching position at a local community college, which would increase his salary by $20,000. The benefits of purposefully fabricating a Ph.D. are apparent: more money, respect, and increased social status. What these tricksters and Chang fail to appreciate are the mental gymnastics required to maintain the deception. In the case of Chang, maintaining his deception requires alienating anyone who might get close enough to know him to be a fraud. For Chang, alienation of others leads to loneliness for himself.

The obituary of Val Patterson of Salt Lake City hints at a similar real-life dilemma. Having inadvertently received a fraudulent Ph.D., Patterson lived decades deceiving even those close to him. In his self-penned obituary, he posthumously confesses to his crimes:

> I really am NOT a PhD. What happened was that the day I went to pay off my college student loan at the U of U, the girl working there put my receipt into the wrong stack, and two weeks later, a PhD diploma came in the mail. I didn't even graduate, I only had about 3 years of college credit. In fact, I never did even learn what the letters "PhD" even stood for [Ritz].

This confession shows awareness of his wrongdoings and an attempt to mitigate damage to his reputation. In other parts of the letter, he apologizes for unrelated incidents: for stealing a safe from a hotel, for plugging up Old Faithful, and for causing trouble at amusement parks. To soften the deception, he tells his co-workers that he did contribute good ideas and made them laugh. Chang exhibits similar contrition when his deception was uncovered. To win the study group's forgiveness, in part because he realizes that his previous attempts at alienation had worked too well, he goes out of his way to try to make amends. The study group is reluctant to forgive him and even seem to take revenge in the form of their own manipulations. Despite his efforts, he still ends up with no friends, no job, and no prospects.

Online reaction to Patterson's obituary is similar to the study group's reaction when Jeff receives Chang's confession. Most of the responses are negative, stating Patterson deserved to go to jail. But for viewers of *Community* and readers of the obituary, the experience can be cathartic. One reader exclaims, "It made me laugh, it made me cry, and it made me appreciate my life and all the opportunity that it offers a bit more.... Thank you" (Ritz). By leaving behind his legacy, or rather a self-written confession-style obituary, Patterson's mischievous spirit lives on through cyberspace, and his shame becomes a lesson for all. There is no denying that Chang's awful behavior and the ignominy of his downfall is entertaining.

While Chang's motivation is the same as O'Bagy and Patterson, his means of maintaining his deception are different. For Chang, fear and the confusion caused by fear are weapons in his arsenal. In turn, Chang is controlled by his fear of being found unqualified. Aristotle's definition of fear as "...a pain or disturbance due to a mental picture of some destructive or painful evil in the future" captures Chang's belligerent anxiety. He uses fear to discourage others from delving into his qualifications and is driven by fear of discovery. Chang is afraid that if his deception is discovered, he may lose his job, which has been secure for six years.

Week 1 in his Spanish class would be a trial for even the most dauntless student. In "Spanish 101" (Episode 1.2), Chang begins the day with a defensive bombardment of Asian stereotypes that he clearly does not fit: "Every once in a while, a student will come up to me and ask, 'Señor Chang, why do you teach Spanish?'" He laughs a little and then continues to say disdainfully, "They say it just like that—'Why do *you* teach Spanish?' 'Why *you*? Why not math? Why not photography? Why not martial arts?'" He continues, "I mean surely it must be in my nature to instruct you in something that's ancient and secret, like, oh, building a wall that you can see from outer space." He then tells them why he teaches Spanish: "It is none of your business ... I don't wanna have any conversations about what a mysterious, inscrutable man I am." He erupts in a fit of laughter, pauses, and then bellows: "I am a Spanish Genius! In *español,* my nickname is *'El Tigre Chino!*'" and commences to pretend he is biting Shirley Bennett in the neck, "'Cause my knowledge will bite her face off! So, don't question Señor Chang or you'll get bit. Ya bit! Ya bit!" The students look horrified and say nothing.

Kevin Hilke points out, "Chang's introduction to his Spanish 101 students in the series' [second] episode is a study in preemptive overcompensation for a dearth of self-confidence. He declares himself 'a Spanish genius' and promises that his superior knowledge will 'bite [the] face off' all who dare to question him." However, this may not be due to lack of self-confidence but may be done deliberately to dissuade students from looking into his lack of qualifications. Despite the content of his rant, his purpose is not anti-racist; his purpose is to make students uncomfortable and prevent them from questioning him. The viewers are acutely aware of the students' discomfort and flinch at the thought of having to navigate this semester-long minefield. Thus, viewers find out early in the series the need for a Spanish study group. Moreover, viewers who think they have Chang figured out in Season 1 would be horribly mistaken and challenged in the seasons to come. Nothing that Chang does can really be taken at face value.

One ironic aspect of Chang's monologue is the fact that in later episodes, he "cries wolf" numerous times in terms of race. This is his way of instilling confusion in those around him; he lacks consistency, and people do not know how to react to him. In "Celebrity Pharmacology" (Episode 2.13), he asks Shirley, "Are you ignoring me because I'm Korean?" She replies, "You're Chinese." His response is, "Oh, there's a difference?" This statement taken with his previous oversensitivity to race further confounds Shirley and the viewer. Chang continues to use racial sensitivity as a weapon in "Epidemiology" (Episode 2.6) when donning a female ice-skating outfit for Halloween, he dares people to guess who he is. Britta guesses Michelle Kwan. Jeff guesses Kristi Yamaguchi. Chang gleefully replies, "Peggy Fleming. You're racist! Just been proven racist by the racist-prover." Taken alone, his "racist-proving" could indicate that Chang is a zealous anti-racist crusader, but in other episodes, he exhibits outright racism. In "Advanced Criminal Law" (Episode 1.5), in trying to find out who cheated during a test, he goes around the room, guessing. He looks at Annie and says, "Mary Ann." He looks at Pierce and says, "Grandpa." He looks at Shirley and calls her "Jackée." And when he reaches Abed, he refers to him as "Kumar."

This blatant display of racism conflicts with his previous racial oversensitivity, which creates confusion. Furthermore, with someone who is so defensive or unpleasant, it is difficult to establish any type of rapport—but this is deliberate. As the trickster, he is able to occupy two opposing roles, as a "racist-prover" and as a racist. Rather than undermine his character, this reinforces the duality often seen in tricksters. This duality is purposeful: to discourage others from getting to know the real Chang, whoever that may be.

Besides his racial sensitivity and empty threats, Chang hides behind his tiger façade through his pedagogy. As the show progresses and we see how he treats his students, most viewers of *Community* would immediately dismiss him as a horrible teacher. On the other hand, if they also had horrible language-learning experiences, they can relate to the study group's difficulties. However, compared to the other courses the study group takes from Seasons 1 to 4, his course most resembles an actual college class. The writers provide Chang with typical foreign-language teaching practices to keep the class busy and as a red herring for viewers. Although his teaching style is unorthodox, Chang's methodologies are basically viable and mirror acceptable forms of language pedagogy. Curriculum-wise, Chang's class appears to be a typical college class. He spends time lecturing, utilizing the grammar-translation method (when we look at the blackboard, the left side has the Spanish words while the right side has the English ones) and giving them quizzes and tests. And because it is a language course, he incorporates communicative activities. One of their first assignments is to write conversations with a partner. When Jeff and Pierce have gone overboard in their presentation, Chang does provide somewhat constructive feedback: "Why are there costumes? These are supposed to be short conversations." However, he fails them both for the assignment with an F and an F-. This is their first semester of Spanish, possibly the first assignment, and he fails them.

To mask his lack of qualifications, he implements strictness. Education experts Tom V. Savage and Marsha K. Savage state, "some teachers ... believe that psychological intimidation is an important tool in maintaining order in the classroom" (53). This is just one of Chang's ways to control his students. In "Environmental Science" (Episode 1.10), after Annie has not put down her pen after he calls time during an exam, he tells them, "I want you all to write a one page essay in *español* entitled "Annie's Mistake." When Pierce protests, "Why doesn't Annie have to write it?" Chang replies, "Okay, two pages entitled "The Consequences of Questioning Authority." Shirley becomes worried and says, "Uh ... this is Spanish 101. I know how to say hello, tomorrow, and that tables are female. That's the only Spanish you taught us." Chang is annoyed by her effrontery: "Oh? Six pages on ignorance!" And then after Britta tries to calm everyone day and says, "Guys! Put your hands down. Señor Chang, please continue. We respect your authority," Chang responds, "Thank you, Britta. 20 pages on ass-kissing! Due on Monday." We do not really know if any members of the study group had attempted to write the punishment essay. However, we do know that he is abusing his power. Instead of acknowledging that he has made class too difficult, he is annoyed that they have not learned from him. This sequence further serves to alienate Chang from his students.

It is ironic that a liar such as Chang so overtly rails against dishonesty. In "Advanced Criminal Law" (Episode 1.5), when he discovers that someone had cheated on the test, he declares: "There's one Asian stereotype that does apply to me. Whoever did this insulted my honor and they've got 24 hours to come forward, or Mr. Miyagi here will wax off everyone's score, and the whole class gets a zero." Besides referring to a stereotype, Mr. Miyagi from the *Karate Kid* movies, Chang has just employed the traditional Chinese punishment: kill the chicken to scare the monkeys. He will not listen to reason or take the time to find out why someone even resorted to cheating. He will simply punish everyone until the secret is out. The irony here stems from an insistence on academic honesty from a thoroughly dishonest person. It is likely that Chang is casting blame upon them to prevent accusations regarding his inadequacy.

There are even rare instances when Chang is flexible. He seems pleased when they take their learning beyond the classroom in "Introduction to Statistics" (Episode 1.7) when Annie convinces him to let them do a *Día de los Muertos* event for extra credit. In the webisodes, he has students create videos for a grade. At the end of the second Spanish webisode, he dislikes the video that Abed and Alex (whom we know as Star-Burns) made but allows them to redo their video for a higher grade ("Star-Burns El Star Prince"). What appears as mercy could simply be another attempt to obscure his deceptive motivations and stay unpredictable.

Educators tend to know that when students are not learning, it leads to misbehavior, not like the joking and teasing that occurs between an instructor who has actual rapport with students. By behaving obnoxiously, this leads students to reciprocate and become tricksters themselves. According to scholar Lewis Hyde, "[T]rickster can also get ensnared in his own devices. Trickster is at once culture hero and fool, clever predator, and stupid prey" (19). Due to his eccentric behavior, despite Chang's having taught at Greendale for some time, his students dislike him. They fear him at first and then consider him a joke later, trying to outwit him. For example, in "Communication Studies" (Episode 1.16) he receives a letter from Princeton, indicating interest to hire Chang and offer him a high-paying salary. When Chang figures out that the letter is false, he punishes his suspects — Abed and Troy — by making them wear pantsuits to a school dance. He adds coercion to get his way: if the two were to renege, they would fail the class. According to Savage and Savage, "[P]sychological intimidation interferes with learning and invites power struggles between individuals"

(53). Moreover, "[i]ndividuals ... in an environment of constant criticism and intimidation will develop low self-esteem. This, in turn, will influence their feelings of security and their willingness to learn" (Savage and Savage 54). Later, when Jeff remarks that he has not learned anything in his semesters taking Spanish, the fault, does not only lie with Chang but with the shenanigans of the students as well. Chang has made his students complicit in their own lack of progress by teaching and encouraging them to be tricksters themselves. This serves his ultimate goal — obscuring his lack of qualifications.

Any lack of student academic progress is not Chang's fault alone, however. Chang is also a part of a fictional academic culture that deceives. By browsing the official Greendale Community College web site, viewers may think it is like any other community college (besides the fact that it ends in .com and not .edu). At first glance, things seem quite normal. In the 5 A's webisodes with Professor Patrick Isakson (played by creator Dan Harmon) the list of the available courses are sung by the college's acapella group, the Tune-ition Payments: "forensics, linguistics, business logistics," physics 1, 2, 3, and advanced physics, "history, mystery, humanities, film studies," as well as different types of "engines and motors, and front end rotors," "transportation, education, cake decoration," and so on. These all seem like regular courses at any community college.

Chang's faculty profile actually makes him seem very inviting. Chang has been teaching all three levels of Spanish for the past six years. He appreciates Latin culture, particularly salsa dancing and salsa eating. He even sprinkles in some Spanish in his self-introduction, having met some *Gente Interesante* and his *favoritos*, which are Columbian Timba and spicy mango. He even ends the self-introduction with "¡Muchas gracias!" showing knowledge of his grasp of Spanish punctuation (Greendale Community College). Chang has built a persona as a Latin-culture loving instructor. He builds ethos by pointing out the time he has spent at Greendale and even sprinkles in some Spanish in his introduction. He also uses informal language in his rhetoric to possibly draw students to Greendale or to take his class. However, students who see his profile on the web site are deceived — he is nothing like this persona he has built.

Despite the fact that Spanish is a typical college class and that Chang's class appears to be quite normal despite his personality, throughout the seasons, viewers can see for themselves the range of ridiculous classes and outlandish behavior of parodic and substandard professors at Greendale Community College. In "Introduction to Film" (Episode 1.3), Jeff enrolls in an accounting class in which the professor encourages students to "seize the day" as homework assignments. On Day 1, he has them stand on their desks, throw away their expensive books, and take off their shoes. This spontaneous expression is hilarious in an accounting class. In "Messianic Myths and Ancient Peoples" (Episode 2.5), psychology professor and Jeff's client/friend, Ian Duncan, becomes the replacement professor for anthropology and allows them to watch YouTube videos the entire time. In another episode, "Conspiracy Theories and Interior Design" (Episode 2.9), Jeff tries to take a class that does not exist, "Conspiracy Theories in U.S. History," taught by Professor Professorson, whom nobody has ever seen. It turns out that he was another professor who created the whole system of night classes in which there are no classes, professors, or students. In "Curriculum Unavailable" (Episode 3.19), there is mention of classes in Baby Talk, Advanced Breath Holding, "Can I Fry That?" and Ladders. And in "History 101" (Episode 4.1), they all fight to get into a course called "History of Ice Cream," which is naturally filled. While the webisodes with Professor Isakson are recruiting tools that make the school somewhat normal enough to draw students, when the students get to Greendale, the courses are not always relevant to the subject they believed they would be studying and the professors are all a little nutty. All of these absurd courses and lazy, eccentric, and unqualified professors serve the writers' humorous purpose in lampooning the institution of community colleges. The deception lies in the seriousness with which these students themselves engage with their classes. Most of the time, the students seem unaware how ridiculous their classes are. Although the absurdity of Jeff's accounting class is obvious to the home audience, he must still take it seriously in order to reach his goals. The entire college is set up as a trickster's paradise, and Chang is an extension of this.

After the first half season of the show, Chang's tiger façade begins to crack for his students, and his deceptive strategy breaks down. In actuality, Chang is only a paper tiger pretending to be a real tiger. The idiom, "paper tiger," refers to "an apparently dangerous but actually ineffectual person or thing" (Oxford Dictionary of Idioms). Though this has been a long-time idiom of Chinese culture, Mao Zedong revived the term when he was referring to his opponents. He even uses this as an epigram for a chapter entitled "Imperialism and All Reactionaries are Paper Tigers" in *Quotations from Chairman Mao Zedong*, also known as *The Little Red Book*: "All reactionaries are paper tigers. In appearance, the reactionaries are terrifying, but in reality they are not so powerful. From a long-term point of view, it is not the reactionaries but the people who are really powerful" (Mao 72; Strong 100). When Chang loses his tiger façade, he begins to be seen by the school and the viewers as an ineffective reactionary. Rather than being deceived by his confusing persona, they begin to define him for themselves.

In "Environmental Science" (Episode 1.10), Chang is already breaking. According to Kevin Hilke, "Chang has deteriorated to a depressive nadir." He confesses to Jeff tearfully about his loneliness and suicidal thoughts as Jeff allows him to "rest his head on his pecs like a child at its mother's breast" (Hilke). Jeff understands when Chang is in trouble. When Chang asks Jeff how he knew

Chang and his wife had broken up, Jeff replies, "Well, when you pick juries, you learn to read the little stuff. Same shirt twice in one week, teaching us the word *esposa* means 'liar.'" Here, we see one student beginning to glimpse the real Chang. This is Chang's mistake in getting close to someone: much later, he reveals his secret to Jeff.

In "English as a Second Language" (Episode 1.23), Annie accidentally records Chang's confession to Jeff: "So I did what any man would do. I faked my way into a job teaching Spanish at a community college using phrases from *Sesame Street.*" In a weak moment, Chang has let Jeff become close to him, and his secret is disclosed. Having proof that Chang is not who he says he is, Annie reports him to the Dean; this is Chang's first fall. The Dean sheepishly admits on the PA system: "I've received an anonymous tip that Chang had misrepresented certain aspects of his qualifications, for instance, having them. Word of advice: If an Asian man says he's a Spanish teacher, it's not racist to ask for proof." The Dean himself has been deceived by the trickster, and he looks foolish. Since we also understand the Dean's obsession with diversity, his statement leads the audience to wonder about his own qualifications. Chang looks bad because he was lying, yet he actually seems clever for being able to last as an instructor for so long.

Despite the fact things go downhill for Chang, Hyde explains this normal occurrence for the trickster: "[T]rickster simply suffers ... loss; it happens to him. He may benefit from it, but the benefit is accidental, not a fruit of his own cunning or design" (31). For Chang, being caught leads to his dismissal as an instructor. Ian Duncan is ecstatic because he has been trying to get Chang fired for years. He foreshadows Chang's lack of qualifications by referring to him as "Teacher Chang" instead of "Professor Chang" ("Advanced Criminal Law," Episode 1.5), and when it is discovered that he is a fraud, Duncan takes advantage of the situation and insults him. Chang punches him in the face, leading Duncan to obtain a restraining order against Chang. Chang decides to make the best of it and return as a student. In "The Psychology of Letting Go" (Episode 2.3), Duncan, who is temporarily teaching anthropology, uses Jedi-like force to push Chang out of the classroom. Due to the restraining order, Chang is not allowed to be inside the anthropology class and must watch from the windows outside the doors. Chang also has his clothing stolen at the YMCA ("Beginner Pottery," Episode 1.19); his wife leaves him for cheating on her with Shirley, leaving him homeless; and he has lost his job and livelihood. We find out later that he has been living in the air ducts in the school and has been beaten up by a monkey. Despite the fact that he brought it upon himself, the audience begins to feel pity for Chang who used to wield so much power. This pity is the nadir of his resurgence as a trickster, however. He begins to use this pity for his own purposes. First, when he obtains a restraining order against his enemy, Duncan, and culminating with his infiltration of Greendale as the amnesiac, Kevin, in Season 4. Joe Vasicek points out that the trickster, "a dirty, lying cheat, capable of taking any disguise and throwing the victims of his pranks into any moral quandary just for laughs ... may even be more of an ally than an enemy — but he definitely is not to be trusted."

After he loses his authority, Chang realizes that he had mistreated the members of the study group and tries to make amends; he moves from the trickster with ulterior motives to a possible ally, as Vasicek mentions. He has lost his role as an authority figure and must seek somewhere to belong. Because he is so desperate to be a part of the study group, he tries to prove himself. At the Pop-and-Lock-athon in "Accounting for Lawyers" (Episode 2.2), he dances by himself to the point of exhaustion. When the study group does arrive, they decide to lose the competition and not care about him, leaving their decision to accept him or not in the air. This does not deter him. Chang also steps in to save the day in "Celebrity Pharmacology" (Episode 2.13) when the group is assigned to educate children on the dangers of drugs. While Pierce is dazzling the children with the crazy and fun aspect of drugs and ruining their objective, Chang takes over. When a young person in the audience says he is not Drugs, he responds: "Oh, but I am! Disappointed? Did you expect me to stay the same forever? 'Cause that's not what drugs does, baby! I'm gonna deep fry your dog and eat your momma's face! And I'm gonna wear your little brother's skin like pajamas! I control your lives, and there is nothing you can do." As an authority figure, an adult among children, he tries to use rhetoric of fear once again, very much like he did on the first day of Spanish class. While a threat like this would surprise and disgust any normal person, the children in the audience are undeterred and proceed to seriously beat him. This is one of the few times that the study group is grateful for his help. They fuss over his wounds, and he is welcomed as hero of the day. This fleeting acceptance, however, cannot make up for his years of deception. As Hilke states, "Chang's course may be the structural lynchpin of the show, but he belongs absolutely nowhere in its world." Chang had his place as an instructor at Greendale, loses it, and searches for another role he could play while being demoted to a student. Hilke states that "Chang's centrality was always precarious and uncomfortable ... Chang seems perpetually unwelcome, even in his own first-season classroom." That is when we see the study group fear him at first and then fight back later. Despite the group's back-and-forth decisions to let him study with them, sometimes he is in the room only as a device for the audience to see his need and want for acceptance. Hyde says this is because the trickster does not really have any place (in the story):

> In short, trickster is a boundary-crosser. Every group has its edge, its sense of in and out, and trickster is always there, at the gates of the city and the gates of life.... He also attends the internal boundaries by which groups articulate their social life.

> We constantly distinguish — right and wrong, sacred and profane, clean and dirty, male and female, young and old, living and dead — and in every case trickster will cross the line and confuse the distinction [7].

This might support the idea that no matter how hard he tries, Chang is unable to settle anywhere — he is rootless, homeless, friendless. As Hyde states, "Trickster is the mythic embodiment of ambiguity and ambivalence, doubleness and duplicity, contradiction and paradox" (7). By being unpredictable, Chang has successfully alienated himself and precluded any real chance of belonging as an equal in the study group. Personal stability is out of his reach.

On Day 1 of Spanish class, Chang certainly is unusual; in "Anthropology 101" (Episode 2.1), we really find that he is mentally unstable. While the audience sees him talking to someone else in the study room, he is actually by himself, complaining to another personality lurking within. Ultimately, the constant rejection leads his evil inner personality to overcome. In "Anthropology 101" (Episode 2.1), we see that he has another more sinister personality within him that is hell-bent on destroying the study group for exposing him, humiliating him, and ruining his life. Much later, we see that the Dean, who has a soft spot for minorities, has given Chang a job as campus security. After building a band of adolescent minions whom he dubs the "Changlorious Basterds," he takes over Greendale for "The First Chang Dynasty" (Episode 3.21). This is the tiger reasserting itself. This is apparent in the episode as Chang demonstrates dictatorial capacity when he assists with the kidnapping of Dean Pelton and takes over the school. In his victory, Chang subverts expectations by dressing up in a Napoleonic outfit.

When Chang is finally defeated by the study group, he disappears for a while. Chang reappears in "Alternative History of the German Invasion" (Episode 4.4) with a paper sign that says, "My name is Kevin. I have Changnesia." His previous deceptions leave several members of the study group leery. The new Chang is much milder, nicer, and almost has a child-like innocence — the tiger is gone. The group prefers this version of Chang and they open their arms to him, except Jeff, who stops at nothing to expose Chang.

Chang's *Lord of the Rings* Smeagol-Gollum dichotomy may be used to demonstrate a good person inside him battling a darker force. If Chang cannot possess any authority and wield it, he must switch to his other personality, which contains goodness. This shows the trickster's duality. Viewers might even believe that his new persona, "Kevin," is an example of how good has prevailed over evil, or has it? The audience is aware that Chang is manipulating the study group again. Kevin has even melted Shirley's heart; she allows him to work at her sandwich shop on campus. However, he is simply a false amnesiac, trying to let people see that he has changed and through their sympathy is almost accepted as part of the team. This is where the danger lies. At the end of Season

4, viewers find he has been plotting with City College to bring down Greendale; in Season 5, we can expect another kind of uprising from Chang, this time with more backup. This exposes the "Kevin" gambit for what it is — another deception. Chang is a trickster incapable of genuine interaction.

In her discussion of tricksters, Helen Lock argues, "the trickster performs such fundamental cultural work: in understanding the trickster better, we better understand ourselves, and the perhaps subconscious aspects of ourselves that respond to the trickster's unsettling and transformative behavior." Initially, viewers believe *Community* is about a study group and their relationships; I believe the show centers around their interaction with Chang. At the end of Season 4, Chang passes out flyers at the mall where all the study group members, before knowing one another, are at a frozen yogurt shop. The Greendale flyer inspires them to change their lives and go back to school. Although Chang has been depicted as a villain, he is the lynchpin that holds them together, as Kevin Hilke says. He has been the trickster of Greendale, keeping everyone on their toes. As the audience, we delight in being tricked and praise the writers for their cleverness; through the show and in life, we are being deceived by fictional and real tricksters, like O'Bagy and Patterson. With Dan Harmon's return in Season 5, we can only anticipate what befalls the study group and see what kinds of tricks Chang has up his sleeve.

Works Cited

"Accounting for Lawyers." *Community*. NBC. 30 September 2010.
"Advanced Criminal Law." *Community*. NBC. 15 October 2009.
"Advanced Documentary Filmmaking." *Community*. NBC. 14 March 2013.
"Alternative History of the German Invasion." *Community*. NBC. 28 February 2013.
"Anthropology 101." *Community*. NBC. 23 September 2010.
"Beginner Pottery." *Community*. NBC. 18 March 2010.
"Celebrity Pharmacology." *Community*. NBC. 27 January 2011.
"Communication Studies." *Community*. NBC. 11 February 2010.
"Conspiracy Theories and Interior Design." *Community*. NBC. 18 November 2010.
"Curriculum Unavailable." *Community*. NBC. 10 May 2012.
Du Plooy, Heilna. "Interfaces and Liminal Spaces: Survival and Regeneration in Ingrid Winterbach's *Niggie* (Cousin)." *Beyond the Threshold: Explorations of Liminality in Literature*. Eds. Hein Viljoen and Chris N. Van Der Merwe. New York: Peter Lang, 2007. 29–44.
Ellis, Larry (Lawrence). "Trickster: Shaman of the Liminal." *Studies in American Indian Literatures* 5.4 (1993). Richmond University. Web. 24 September 2013.
"English as a Second Language." *Community*. NBC. 13 May 2010.
"Environmental Science." *Community*. NBC. 19 November 2009.
"Epidemiology." *Community*. NBC. 28 October 2010.
"The First Chang Dynasty." *Community*. NBC. 17 May 2012.
Geeser, Michael. "Dr. Fake: Making up Your Resume." *8NewsNow*. WorldNow and Klas, 19 May 2013. Web. 24 September 2013.
Greendale Community College. Greendale Community College. 2009. Web. 24 September 2013.
Hilke, Kevin. "Community: Senor Chang's Changing Insinuations." *Plasma Pool*. Plasma Pool. 14 February 2011.

"History 101." *Community*. NBC. 7 February 2013.
Hyde, Lewis. *Trickster Makes This World: Mischief, Myth, and Art*. New York: Farrar, Straus and Giroux, 2010.
"Introduction to Film." *Community*. NBC. 1 October 2009.
"Introduction to Statistics." *Community*. NBC. 29 October 2009.
Lock, Helen. "Transformations of the Trickster." *Southern Cross Review*. n.d. Web. 24 September 2013.
"Messianic Myths and Ancient Peoples." *Community*. NBC. 21 October 2010.
Newton-Small, Jay. "The Rise and Fall of Elizabeth O'Bagy." Swampland. *TIME*. 17 September 2013. Web. 24 September 2013.
"The Psychology of Letting Go." *Community*. NBC. 7 October 2010.
Ritz, Erica. "'I Didn't Even Graduate': 'PhD' Comes Clean in Hilarious Obituary." *The Blaze*. The Blaze. 18 July 2012. Web. 24 September 2013.
Savage Tom V., and Marsha K. Savage. *Successful Classroom Management and Discipline: Teaching Self-Control and Responsibility*. 3d ed. Thousand Oaks: Sage, 2010.
"Spanish 101." *Community*. NBC. 24 September 2009.
"The Trickster AKA Trickster Archetype." *TV Tropes*. TV Tropes Foundation, n.d. Web. 24 September 2013.
Vasicek, Joe. "Trope Tuesday: The Trickster." One Thousand and One Parsecs. *One Lower Light*. 28 August 2013. Web. 24 September 2013.

PART II: THE POLITICAL PLAYGROUND

Inculcating Victorian Masculinities at "Loser College": Jeff Winger's Male Poses

Lindsy Lawrence

At first glance, Jeff Winger, the central figure in *Community*, is far removed — both in time and action — from the nineteenth-century masculine ethos of work, duty, and self-discipline, a masculine ethos honed and disseminated through university education. A raffish cad with no apparent moral compass beyond fueling his own wants, Jeff enrolls at Greendale Community College to enable his return to being a corporate lawyer, not from any desire to improve himself or obtain a real education. In the pilot, Jeff proclaims, "if I wanted to learn something, I wouldn't have come to community college" (Episode 1.1). However, Greendale does provide Jeff with an education in proper masculinity, punishing his pose of corporate excess and flash.

Throughout the nineteenth-century, as more upper-middle-class families sent their sons to Oxford and Cambridge in England or an Ivy League institution in the United States, a university degree became a requirement for entry into professional life. Attending an "Oxbridge"— the conflation of Oxford and Cambridge — or Ivy League university did more than merely prepare men for a job. The university experience trained men in the proper forms of manliness. According to Gerald Graff in *Professing Literature*, American colleges "scorned vocational concerns in favor of 'liberal' studies, studies designed to form gentlemanly character rather than train directly for a vocation. College presidents spoke of 'gentle breeding' as a primary concern, and saw the study of literature through the classics as a form of acculturation for 'the cultivated gentleman'" (20). While Graff focuses on nineteenth-century American universities, British universities also participated in the enculturation of gentlemanliness, training men in the cardinal Victorian male traits of duty, work, honesty, and self-discipline.

While Oxbridge seems distinctly different from Greendale, campus narratives have long illuminated the complicated ways universities participate in the processes of gender enculturation, particularly of proper masculinity.[1] I am not suggesting *Community* is directly or intentionally influenced by nineteenth-century campus narratives such as Thomas Hughes's Varsity novel *Tom Brown at Oxford* (1861) or Margaret Oliphant's *The Story of Valentine and His Brother* (1875). Like Scott D. Banville in his work on the connection between sitcoms and the Victorian music hall, I see how *Community* draws inspiration from the "historical [resonance] of Victorian cultural practices" (16), particularly in regards to how universities form proper, productive men. James Eli Adams, in *Dandies and Desert Saints: Styles of Victorian Manhood*, posits that masculinity is a constructed category dependent on the "anxious conjunction of discipline and performance" (10). University life with its regulatory apparatus consisting of coursework, interactions with professors, and organized social events disciplines men into fitting the cultural mode; in effect, university life is precisely the kind of framework for inculcating gendered performance. Oxbridge taught men this performance in the nineteenth-century, and the wider range of universities today still do this cultural work. One of the reasons pundits and other commentators spill anxious ink over the gender imbalance in the contemporary university—more women matriculate into universities than men—is because of this assumption that university life is designed to do this gendered cultural work when it comes to shaping manliness.

In representing the university and university life, campus narratives depict both the process of this enculturation and the tensions between this proper form of masculinity and other, less desirable male types. Paul R. Deslandes argues in *Oxbridge Men: British Masculinity and the Undergraduate Experience, 1850–1920* that "the authors of university novels frequently demarcated and reinforced boundaries that separated insiders from outsiders, marked the universities off as special, privileged places, and emphasized an exclusivity that epitomized Britain's rigidly class-bound society" (ix). While Deslandes's cultural history focuses on Oxbridge, his point about university novels or campus narratives using the distinctive features of the university to reinforce boundary lines informs how this narrative form is able to explore the web of cultural tensions that fashion the university into a space where men learn their performance of gender. Even a community college such as the fictional Greendale participates within this system of exclusion, except the narrative structure positions Greendale as "loser college." Responding to the news that Jeff is now enrolled at Greendale, his sometime friend and previous client, Professor Ian Duncan tells him, "Well, that cannot be an inspiring journey" (Episode 1.1), which reveals the series' entire narrative thrust. As a space structured around the concept of failure, Greendale inverts the code of campus narratives, which tend to emphasize the protagonist's success, even if that success involves rejecting university life. In mocking, often derisively, reasons why people attend community college, creator Dan Harmon depicts the performance of proper masculinity as a fabrication of the narrative of self-improvement that structures many campus narratives.

Drawing from Banville's use of the concept of remediation, "specifically the idea that 'media [...] become systematically dependent on each other and on prior media for their cultural significance" (17), this essay explores how *Community* employs nineteenth-century conceptions of masculinity in its depiction of Jeff. Using the connection cultural critics such as Jeremy Kaye have drawn between the late twentieth- and early twenty-first-century metrosexual and the nineteenth-century dandy, I argue that Jeff's performance of this role is key to *Community*'s narrative structure. In the world outside of Greendale, Jeff is a successful lawyer; his pose of metrosexuality is part and parcel with his financial and professional success. At Greendale, however, this pose is repeatedly revealed to be a performance at odds with Greendale's loser aspects. Instead, the narrative coerces Jeff into moralistic self-abnegation, a hyper-realized form of the traditional version of nineteenth-century masculinity. At Greendale, he must relinquish his desires to be a good person, a process that means he must perform proper nineteenth-century masculinity, even when that performance ensures his continued "loser" status.

Styles of Masculinity in the University and the Campus Narrative

In 1890, *Punch, or the London Charivari*, a popular weekly comic magazine, began publishing a multi-part series called "Modern Types."[2] Each installment satirizes a different gendered character type of late nineteenth-century life, including the "The Invalid Lady," "The Giddy Society Lady," and "The Dilettante." The series satirizes two university types: "the Precocious Undergraduate" and "the Average Undergraduate." In the June 14, 1890, issue, the profile on the Precocious Undergraduate describes a profligate young man more interested in the fast society offered by the university. An avid athlete and club man rather than a scholar while at public school, the Precocious Undergraduate finds "the sudden emancipation from the easy servitude of school was too much for him. The rush of his new existence swept him off his feet, and yielding to the current, he was carried day by day more rapidly out to the sea of debt and dissipation, which in the end overwhelmed him" ("Modern Type. The Precocious Undergraduate" 285). The modifier, "precocious," is misleading. *Punch*'s Precocious undergraduate is not more mature or advanced. Without the discipline provided by public school life, the Precocious Undergraduate finds himself adrift on the sea of possible enjoyments offered by the university. Gambling, wine parties, boating, cricket, and other entertainments are more enticing than reading for his degree.

The profile on the Average Undergraduate, published in the November 1, 1890, issue, presents a different picture of university-produced masculinity. The Average Undergraduate may make mistakes of the same variety as the Precocious Undergraduate, but they are different in degree. By hewing to the cardinal virtues of English masculinity, the Average Undergraduate avoids the pitfalls that cause the Precocious Undergraduate to fall from grace. The article explains that the Average Undergraduate

> as he exists, and has for ages existed, is not, perhaps, a very wise young man.[...] He has his follies, but they are not very foolish; he has his affectations, but they are innocent; he has his extravagances, but they pass away, and leave him not very worse for the experience. On the whole, however, he is a fine specimen of the young Englishman — brave, manly, loyal, and upright. He is the salt of his university, and an honour to the country that produces him ["Modern Types. The Average Undergraduate" 205].

Despite the comic tone, the qualities enumerated here — bravery, manliness, loyalty, and uprightness — define proper manliness. This male type is essential to the university and to the functioning of the nation. As the space that trained Church of England clergyman, civil servants at home and for the Empire, teachers, and other professional men, the health of the nation depended on the university producing this idealized man.

These two types were just some of the male styles on offer from nineteenth-century Oxbridge. Deslandes notes, "Athletes, reading men, aesthetes, and sporting or gambling men, to mention but a few of the distinctive brands or styles of masculinity present at Oxford and Cambridge in the late Victorian and Edwardian eras, all coexisted (sometimes harmoniously and sometimes not) within the precincts of these two cities" (9). In *Tom Brown at Oxford*, Thomas Hughes identifies four male types: gentleman-commoners, the boating set, studious or reading men, and a small subset of the reading men whom were nominally Tractarians or followed the High-church party.[3] The proliferation of male types, what James Eli Adams terms "styles of masculinity" (3), belies the normative construction of nineteenth-century manliness as monolithic. Much work has been done in masculinity studies since the publication of Adam's 1995 text, *Dandies and Desert Saints*, to explore the ways manliness and proper masculinity were constructed in the nineteenth-century against a variety of male self-fashioning performances. Drawing from the work of feminist scholars such as Judith Butler, the work of Adams and cultural historian John Tosh, among others, complicates the narrative of Victorian masculinity. Instead of the one model of the upright, virtuous, stiff–upper lip, athletic, and unemotive man, Adams identifies five main categories of male styles in the nineteenth-century: "the gentleman, the prophet, the dandy, the priest, and the soldier" (2). All of these styles offered men a variety of cultural models for performing manliness. As Butler argues, "Gender ought not to be construed as a stable identity or locus of agency from which various acts follow; rather, gender is an identity tenuously constituted in time, instituted in an exterior space through a *stylized repetition of acts*" (179). Manliness is a culturally constructed performance, one that can change over time as the signifying acts that make up the gendered identity change. For instance, the type of manliness inculcated in public schools and Oxbridge shifts during the nineteenth-century from the self-sacrificing, emotive evangelical mode at mid-century to the more emotionally controlled, athletic mode present at the end of the century.

The two types illuminated by Adams and Tosh of the manly man and the dandy are important for understanding the masculine styles of the Average Undergraduate and the Precocious Undergraduate, as these university types are drawn from these cultural forms. The modern variations of the self-sacrificing good guy and the metrosexual are inheritors of these male styles. While Tosh cautions, "historical parallels between the [late nineteenth-century] and the present should not be overstated" (23), it is possible to see how the structure of *Community* positions Jeff into specific gender performances that echo the two types of undergraduate that dominated nineteenth-century literature about Oxbridge. It is between the poles of gentlemanliness and the dandy, between the Average and Precocious, that Jeff's performance of masculinity is staged.

Both the dandy and the gentleman-commoner are defined by their consumptions habits. According to Ellen Moers, the dandy is an attitudinal performance of masculine indifference and control of form. She argues in her work tracing the dandy in English and French culture and literature: "The dandy's achievement is simply to be himself. In his terms, however, this phrase does not mean to relax, to sprawl, or (in an expression quintessentially anti-dandy) to unbutton; it means to tighten, to control, to attain perfection in all the accessories of life, to resist whatever may be suitable for the vulgar but is proper for the dandy" (18).

While Moers's description is of the Regency dandy, an older style of masculinity than the Precocious Undergraduate, similarities abound between the two styles. Both are controlled performances of manliness based on the performance of absolute status. This control is not about following a moral code; the entire purpose of the dandy focuses on perfecting the pose of the dandy. Similar to its more modern counterpart, the metrosexual, the dandy is a pose of exclusivity. For Hughes, the problem with the Oxford that he is detailing lies in the exclusivity of the gentleman-commoners, the equivalent of *Punch*'s Precocious Undergraduate. This male type is drawn from the sons of the wealthy new industrialists, "paid double fees to the college" (Hughes 2), a fact giving the gentleman-commoner a great deal of latitude within the college. Hughes saw this type of man as a drain on the university, tempting other men like Brown away from a path of moral certitude and upright manliness. Hughes describes the fast set of the gentleman-commoner as being devoted to

> the most reckless extravagance of every kind. London wine merchants furnished them liquers at a guinea a bottle, and wine at five guineas a dozen; Oxford and London tailors vied with one another in providing them with unheard of quantities of the most gorgeous clothing.[...] Their cigars cost two guineas a pound; their furniture was the best that could be bought; pineapples, forced fruit, and the most rare preserves figured at their wine parties; they hunted, rode steeple chases by day, played billiards until the gates closed, and then were ready for *vingt-et-une*, unlimited loo, and hot drink in their own rooms, as long as anyone could be got to sit up and play [1].

The gentleman-commoner's position is secured through his display of wealth and taste. Wealthy and extravagant, the gentleman-commoner is a male pose dependent on the performance of this luxury.

When Tom first meets Drysdale and St. Cloud, the representative gentleman-commoners in *Tom Brown at Oxford*, both young men are lounging in Drysdale's room, drinking heavily, and ordering extravagant clothing: "three light silk waistcoats, peach-color, fawn-color, and lavender" and a pair of boots ordered and forgotten the previous term (Hughes 27). Drysdale sees the moral quagmire of these consumption habits but does nothing to amend his behavior. In *Punch*, the Precocious Undergraduate also gambles, orders expensive cigars and clothes, and is generally profligate in his habits. Finally unable to pay his debts, he tries to finish his degree, but fails to pass examinations. Forced to find an occupation, in the *Punch* account, he "creep[s] about London in a hang-dog fashion for a year or two" (285) before immigrating to the United States and perishing in a Wild West brawl. Hughes gives this male type a less melodramatic ending. Drysdale is sent down — forced to leave the university — but he is not so dishonorable that he does not help Tom as a form of moral repayment for Tom's help with a monetary debt.

The Average Undergraduate, however, is defined by his character through his actions not his consumerism. Much of *Tom Brown at Oxford* is devoted to highlighting Brown's moral development through his navigation of temptations presented by gentleman-commoners of his acquaintance and the model of manliness embodied by his friend and mentor, John Hardy. Hardy is at Oxford as a servitor, a student who works for professors in exchange for free tuition. As such, he does not have the financial means of the gentleman-commoner. While his poverty excludes him from this set, Hardy's outsider position also protects him, allowing him to see the dangers of this mode of masculinity. Athletic, intelligent, and morally upright, Hardy embodies proper manliness, a construction dependent on the performer "paying more attention to the promptings of his inner self than to the dictates of social expectation" (Tosh 87). Hardy's society expects excess and moral laxity, yet he refuses such a performance. When Brown compromises himself with a bar maid, beginning down a road leading to a misalliance or losing his moral uprightness by giving into extramarital sexual desires and ruining her future in the bargain, Hardy confronts him: "Can there be any true manliness without purity?" (236). Hardy goes on to indict all of Oxford: "'And where, then, can you point to a place where is so little manliness as here? It makes my blood boil to see what one must see every day. There are a set of men up here, and have been ever since I can remember the place, not one of whom can look at a modest woman without making her shudder" (236). This set of men, the gentleman-commoner or the dandy, is thus set in opposition to the "true manliness" embodied by Hardy and later Brown.

This model is still being upheld by *Punch* in its profile of the Average Undergraduate. At the end of the article, Punch declares that the Average Undergraduate

> is truthful and ingenuous, and although he knows himself to be a man, he never tries to be a very old or a very wicked one. In a word, he is wholesome. In the end he takes his degree creditably enough. His years at the University have been years of pure delight to him, and he will always look back to them as the happiest of his life. He has not become very learned, but he will always be a useful member of the community, and whether as barrister, clergyman, country gentleman, or business man, he will show an example of manly uprightness which is countrymen could ill afford to lose [205].

Thus, the manly man is the winning style of masculinity in the nineteenth-century, a pose that supports the health of the nation. As the *Punch* article suggests, education as in actual knowledge gained is not the purpose of the university experience; rather, the university is the space designated for the enculturation of this masculine style. Nineteenth century campus narratives such as *Tom Brown at Oxford* and the *Punch* profiles reveal the process by which privileged men gained the necessary moral traits to embody this style or pose.

This narrative form still does this cultural work "because higher education has become common culture in American [and British] life" (Williams 578). Jeffery J. Williams argues, "Contrary to the image of its being an elite experience, college has become mass culture, and the proliferation of both campus and academic novels, as well as films and television shows, obviously responds to the greater centrality of higher education in ... [the Anglo-American world]" (577). It is not only that more attend university in the twenty-first century, although the increasing numbers of people obtaining some college education certainly contributes to making the structures and tropes of university life part of common culture. The prominence of college sports, particularly American football and basketball, means a larger group is familiar with some facets of university life, especially its focus on male styles. After all, the representative face of the university is often the male student-athlete performing feats of physical prowess.

David Lodge also argues, "One reason, perhaps, [for the great appeal of the campus narrative] is that the university is a microcosm of society at large, in with the principles, drives, and conflicts that govern collective human life are displayed and may be studied in a clear light and on a manageable scale" (261). The campus narrative's enduring focus on fomenting "true manliness" is a result of accelerating forms of consumer culture that produce so many more styles of masculinity in the twenty-first century than in the nineteenth-century. As the nineteenth-century, twenty-first century campus narratives like *Community* allow for exploration of cultural anxieties produces by the proliferation of these male types within a contained structure. On the other hand, *Community*'s brand of self-destructive comedy inverts the narrative of improvement found in nineteenth-century campus narratives. Hughes structures his narrative so that the true man wins in the end; he cannot entirely eradicate the dominance of this other male type. In other words, universities can produce styles of masculinity at odds with the ideal strictures of manliness. The likelihood of an undesirable style of masculinity being produced is more possible in a space less elite than Oxbridge. *Community* asks its audience to consider what it means for a "loser college" to be the space where men learn a style of masculinity. The rest of this essay explores how Jeff is made to embody both the dandy and the true man.

Jeff's Poses: Victorian Styles of Masculinity in the Twenty-First Century

The pilot episode establishes *Community*'s focus on the loser or losers of twenty-first century culture. It opens with Dean Pelton giving a supposedly uplifting convocation address, the kind of speech designed to motivate students at the beginning of the academic year. The speech falls short of this mark. It takes place outside, with an audience consisting of a handful of passing students. Dean Pelton's earnest attempt to introduce his unwieldy group of community college undergraduates to the life of the mind is hampered by his own ineptitudes — he leaves out half the speech — and his own over-awareness of the student body's "loser" status. He pompously intones: "What is community college? Well you've heard it called all kinds of things. You've heard it's loser college for remedial teens, twenty something drop-outs, middle-age divorcees, and old people keeping their minds active as they circle the drain of eternity. That's what you've heard. However, I wish you luck" (Episode 1.1).

Inspiring the collection of high school drop-outs, middle-age returning students, and older students seems to be beyond Dean Pelton's abilities. His list of students is indicative of the stereotypes about people who attend community colleges, and the concomitant cultural tag that these types are losers of some sort, an impression born of both the community college's plebian status and the socio-economic background of the student population. Community colleges serve a wider population than Oxbridge or Ivy League schools. According to Mike Rose, "the majority of the more than 10 million students in community colleges [...] are from low- to modest-income backgrounds" (*Back to School* 9). In "Second-Chance Collegians: Inside the Remedial Classroom," Rose also notes that "Over the last thirty years, the percentage of people over age forty attending college has more than doubled" (41). In describing a remedial English class at a community college, Rose observes that "The ages of the students in English 55 range from nineteen, right out of high school, to two people in their fifties" ("Second-Chance Collegians" 42). *Community*'s cast of characters mostly reflects this demographic reality. The study group formed by Jeff in the pilot episode is designed to represent the variety of groups that the community college system serves. Of the main characters, Annie Edison, Troy Barnes, and perhaps even Abed Nadir, constitute traditional students though they are attending a community college rather than a bachelor's-granting institution because of academic failures on the high school level. Britta Perry, Shirley Bennett, and Pierce Hawthorne are the "twenty something drop out," divorcee, and old person, respectively. Only Jeff is omitted from Dean Pelton's description of community college denizens.

As a cisgendered, upper middle-class, white male, Jeff is not the typical community college student, making him an oddity at Greendale. Unlike the rest of the study group, Jeff is not attending Greendale to improve himself; Greendale is merely the easiest solution to reinstating himself as a corporate lawyer after his fake degree is uncovered. Nothing taught at Greendale will help Jeff be a lawyer; the series firmly establishes that Jeff is quite good at his career without formal credentials. In the pilot episode, Jeff boasts to Duncan about his argumentative abilities: "I discovered at a very early age that if I talked long enough, I could make anything right or wrong. So, either I'm God or truth is relative, and in any case, booyah" (Episode 1.1). The "booyah" at the end of this speech is designed to provoke and indicate Jeff's verbal, if not moral, superiority. Jeff, who "reeks of moral ambiguity" ("Accounting for Lawyers," Episode 2.2), does not need his university experience to teach him how to navigate masculinity identities. He has found one in the role of metrosexual corporate lawyer.

Like the dandy, the metrosexual is a tightly controlled performance dependent on the right luxury car, fashion choices, condo, and other displays of wealth and privilege. As Mark Simpson explains, "The typical metrosexual is a young man with money to spend, living in or within easy reach of a metropolis — because that's where all the best shops, clubs, gyms and hairdressers are" (qtd. in Kaye 108). The metrosexual is a "man in touch with his feminine side" (Kaye 108), but being "feminine" does not equate to homosexuality. Jeremy Kaye concludes his examination of the connections between the nineteenth-century dandy and the twenty-first century metrosexual: "The reality is that metrosexuality is an exclusively straight phenomenon. Gay men are by definition not allowed to be metrosexuals. Metrosexuality steals 'gay male style' and appropriates it for straight ends" (122). This style of masculinity is just as disciplined a performance as the dandy. Also, a thread of sensitivity runs through the metrosexual. Warren St. John claims, "America has a long tradition of sensitive guys. Alan Alda, John Lennon, even Al Gore all heard the arguments of the feminist movement and empathized. Likewise, there's a history of dashing men like Cary Grant and Humphrey Bogart who managed to affect a personal style with plenty of hair goop but without compromising their virility" ("Metrosexuals Come Out"). Metrosexuality as a pose of sensitive men is not necessarily about sensitivity to others; rather, it is a pose of consumer awareness of what a perfectly styled life could look like. The sensitivity of the metrosexual should not be read as moral uprightness. As a figure in twenty-first century television series, metrosexuals like Schmidt on *New Girl* (2011–) or Jeff are more invested in perfecting the pose of the perfect life than in the process of real moral improvement. When Jeff is locked out of his condo because he cannot pay his mortgage, he laments the loss of his marble countertops and perfect taps and the cultivated life style they represented. In effect, metrosexuality is a style of masculinity that performs coolness.

The complicated ways *Community* parses male coolness can be seen in "Physical Education" (Episode 1.17) when Jeff takes a billiards class to fulfill his P.E. requirement. Jeff changes his typical attire of a dark, tailored T-shirt or button down, fashionable jeans, hoodie, and carefully styled hair for a black leather jacket and wallet chain. The punkification of his wardrobe is part of Jeff's pose as an expert pool player. It is a momentary expression of coolness thwarted, however, by the gym teacher, Coach Bogner, who requires students to wear the a P.E. uniform: short gym shorts and a tight T-shirt, a style of gym wear from the 1980s. Jeff feels strongly that this attire infringes on his coolness, telling Bogner that his rejection of the shorts is not a testament to his playing abilities: "Hey listen man, you're implying I'm some kind of pool poseur because I don't want to wear a bathing suit." As he storms out of Bogner's office, he quips that the billiard's class uniform rule is "the desecration of America's coolest sport." Bogner responds, "This hipster is dropping this class because he cares more about what he looks like than how he's playing." This last insult from Bogner stings since Jeff is not a hipster.

While the hipster is a twenty-first century male style also dependent on fashion and consumer habits, it is a different style of masculinity than the metrosexual. According to Mark Greif, "The hipster is that person, overlapping with the intentional dropout or the unintentionally declassed individual — the neo-bohemian, the vegan or bicyclist or skatepunk, the would-be blue-collar or postracial twentysomething, the starving artist or graduate student — who in fact aligns himself both with rebel subculture and with the dominant class" ("What Was the Hipster?"). None of these identifiers apply to Jeff who desperately wants his position in the dominant class re-established. Bogner's misidentification of Jeff's male style stems from the fact that the most recognizable aspects of the hipster and the metrosexual are based in fashion; Bogner does not differentiate between different forms of male fashionability and coolness. Jeff, however, inhabits a world in which masculine coolness is rigidly defined. The metrosexual and the hipster are not substitutable for Jeff since he needs the metrosexual identity to retain a sense of who he was before Greendale. Needled by the hipster comment, Jeff complains to the study group: "Do you know he called me a hipster? Hipster! I mean, do hipsters walk around wearing $300 jeans from Italy?" His frustration in being associated with the hipster is not directed at Bogner alone. In the same episode, Abed tells Jeff that his impression of him involves "10% Dick Van Dyke, 20% Sam Malone, 40% Zach Braff in *Scrubs*, and 30% Hilary Swank in *Boys Don't Cry*." Jeff glares at him, saying "Zach Braff," an association Abed apologizes for. Braff's character on *Scrubs* is also a hipster type. The multiplication of available male styles — conforming student, hipster, metrosexual — causes Jeff a moment of panic. He seems to be losing his sense of self.

Abed, being coerced in being less himself to get a girl in the B-story line, tells the group he was fine with changing for them since it seemed important. Supremely confident in himself, Abed tells them, "When you really know who you are and what you like about yourself, changing for other people isn't such a big deal." Inspired, Jeff returns to Bogner's class in the gym shorts, challenging Bogner to a pool game: it is a match about masculine honor. Jeff taunts Bogner: "Now, do you want to talk about clothes like a girl? Or use tapered sticks to hit balls around a cushioned table, like a man?" Bogner replies, "Balls, like a man." They both end up stripped down, naked, and posturing for each other as they play the game. The act of stripping re-establishes Jeff's sense of self and coolness, since stripping displays Jeff's hard-bodied physique, negating the embarrassing effects of the gym shorts, nor does he really follow Abed's advice in challenging Bogner. He does not truly change for anyone; he merely perfects his pose.

Jeff is deeply aware of the loser status of Greendale; he struggles to maintain his own sense of self within the college in spite of it. The doubts Bogner raises about his male identity are not the only ones Jeff must confront. As a self-destructive satire, much of the comedy of the show is fueled by Jeff's own self-sabotage, as he repeatedly tries to assert his metrosexuality only to be coerced into a male pose of self-sacrifice. I use the term, "self-destructive," deliberately here. Harmon's series of podcasts, *Harmontown*, describe him as a "self-destructive writer,"[4] and the characters in the show often display nihilistic tendencies. For instance, "The Art of Discourse" (Episode 1.22) juxtaposes Jeff and Britta against a group of high school students taking classes at Greendale. Mark, the ringleader of the group, overhears Jeff celebrating a good grade. He sneers at Jeff: "So we were just wondering, can you tell us what you did in your lives to end up here so that we don't make the same mistakes? [*snickering from the friends*]. Because if I end up 35 and celebrating a 'B' in nutrition in community college, I'll kill myself." The bullying posturing on Mark's part is an attempt to assert some kind of winning male dominance in a space that does not provide such a model of masculinity. Jeff attempts to seduce Mark's mother in revenge, but it is a move that backfires on Jeff. When she finds out his plan, she states, "I raised a winner who will continue to crush junior college losers like you." The whole situation dissolves into an immature battle of juvenile antics between Britta, Jeff, and the teenagers, the absurdity of which reinforces the "loser" status of Greendale and potentially Jeff.

According to Merritt Moseley, "If satire is the act of ridiculing a person, belief, or situation in order to expose its evils, then, by this reasoning, the academic [television series writers] writes out of an urge to reveal, and perhaps punish, the follies and shortcomings of the academic institution in which he or she has been a dweller and participant" (7). Much of *Community*'s comedy comes from the ways it satirizes and "punishes" the shortcoming of those at Greendale, particularly Dean Pelton's constant need for Greendale to be a "real" university. In "Advanced Criminal Law" (Episode 1.5), he proclaims, "Boy, I don't know about you, but this sure feels like a real college to me," despite the fact that Britta's disciplinary hearing for cheating is taking place by the school swimming pool; the Dean wanted to use the fancy new judges' table. Just the fact that a disciplinary hearing is taking place makes Pelton think his college is gaining legitimacy, a fact the bickering between Señor Chang and Professor Duncan and the hearing's location radically undermines. The episode pivots on a semi-inspirational speech by Jeff:

> But, do we really want to make it a crime to be crazy at Greendale? I mean, look at us. I mean, you two [Chang and Duncan] are arguing about status at a college that correspondence schools make fun of. Dean, you want so bad for this place to be Ivy League that you are putting us at risk of electrocution. Everyone on this

campus is nuts.[...] Because if crazy people can't be at Greendale, then where are we supposed to go?"

Jeff's speech, while successful in defending Britta, reemphasizes the core theme of *Community*'s narrative structure: its insistence on community colleges as a space for losers. This space inculcates a male style where the disinterested, moral uprightness of the Average Undergraduate, a performance of masculine strength and fortitude in nineteenth-century campus narratives is both sensitive in the true sense of the word and a losing form of masculine identity.

Jeff's metrosexuality is a commodity at Greendale that imbues him with authority and desirability even as it is undermined by Greendale's social economy. Pierce tries to mimic his style of dress and his quips, blackmailing Annie into letting him wear a leather jacket like Jeff's in "Celebrity Pharmacology" (Episode 2.13). Pelton seems obsessed with Jeff's coolness, although it is an obsession tinged with homoeroticism. One time, Pelton makes off with an advertising poster of Jeff the group is using for their drug prevention play. In numerous other instances, he expresses erotic interest in Jeff or touches him unnecessarily. When Pelton appropriates Jeff's coolness to advertise Greendale in "Feminism, Football, and You" (Episode 1.6), Jeff confronts him: "If someone from the outside were to find out that I'm a student at a community college, that could have a negative impact on my future career." In "Introduction to Statistics" (Episode 1.7), when he first tries and fails to convince Professor Michelle Slater to go on a date, he complains, "It's this campus. It feeds on my coolness. I've got no moves anymore." The cultural milieu of Greendale needs Jeff's status, his metrosexual coolness, even as the campus structurally strips that factor from his masculinity. Jeff desperately and absurdly heeds Chang's advice to beg Slater to sleep with him, a move which surprisingly works. As they leave the school Halloween party together, however, they pass by the library and Pierce's Ecstasy fueled melt down. Unable to abandon Pierce, Jeff pauses, telling Slater,

> JEFF: I can't believe I'm doing this. I uh, I think I have to say goodnight.
> SLATER: Are you like a court-appointed guardian for these people?
> JEFF: Uh, no. Um, they're my classmates.
> SLATER: Goodnight, Jeff [*leans in to kiss him on the cheek*].

As seen through the dialogue, self-humiliation is the only way for Jeff to win the girl; self-denial is the only way to help his classmates. The metrosexual cannot survive in this loser milieu, only the good guy can.

Episode after episode traces Jeff's vacillating moral transformations as the narrative structure of *Community*'s self-destructive comedy pushes and pulls Jeff between the metrosexual and upright masculinity of the good guy. He typically reverts back to form at the beginning of an episode, but by the end, Jeff reluctantly pursues an ethical course of action for the greater good of the study group. In some episodes, Jeff's selfish behavior is recast as self-interest that in fact actually helps others. When Chang is temporarily separated from his wife, Jeff at first befriends Chang in order to get out of writing the extra twenty page-assignment. Eventually, he reunites Chang with his wife to rid himself of Chang as a companion. In "Comparative Religion" (Episode 1.12), Jeff makes a decision to not fight the bully, Mike, to appease Shirley. He, and the study group, winds up fighting Mike and his posse, but only after Shirley tells Jeff to "kick his ass," releasing him from his resolve to do the right thing. In "Investigative Journalism" (Episode 1.13) when Buddy (Jack Black) tries to join the group after the winter break and makes a sexual joke about Annie, Jeff corrects him, saying, "Annie's pretty young, so we try not to sexualize her." The group places him in a position of authority, asking Jeff to intervene with professors like Chang on their behalf as well as appealing to him to resolve arguments and other issues, usually silencing Pierce's inappropriate commentary.

This performance of manly uprightness, of being the good guy, is almost always a false one done to appease a study group member. As early as the seventh episode of the series, Jeff sarcastically claims, "Well, it's funny. I enrolled here as a selfish loner, but you and the group have given me a crash course in friendship" ("Introduction to Statistics"). Jeff does the morally correct thing, but only after someone else in the group persuades him to do so, usually through manipulation. For instance, in "Basic Genealogy" (Episode 1.18), Annie convinces Jeff to spend time with Pierce and his step-daughter Amber during family day, gently flirting with him as she asks him what he would be willing to do for her. While he agrees to help Pierce, Jeff acknowledges that it is for Annie's sake, not from any sense of disinterestedness. He tells her, "You're becoming dangerous, Anne. It's those doe eyes.[...] Disappointing you is like choking the Little Mermaid with a bike chain." After he still sleeps with Amber even though she is extorting $25,000 from Pierce, Jeff confesses to Annie because he wants to feel like a good person, but he also claims that he should be credited for showing a modicum of restraint in not sleeping with Amber twice as he wanted, displaying the smallest amount self-denial possible.

However, there are moments where Jeff's performance of the self-sacrificing good guy appears genuine. "Advanced Dungeons and Dragons" (Episode 2.14) highlights how Jeff can occupy a position of manly uprightness. The episode centers around a student at Greendale nicknamed "Fat Neil." The opening voiceover explains Jeff and Annie noticing that Neil is dangerously depressed because of the taunting of his obesity. Concerned that he may harm himself, the study group asks Neil to play Dungeons and Dragons with them as a way to bond with him. As the voiceover claims, "What Fat Neil needed the most was to feel like a winner for a change." They make the decision to leave Pierce out this group activity under the reasonable impression that Pierce's gross insensitivity would actually hurt Neil. In retaliation, Pierce sabotages the game and reveals that Jeff is the source of the nickname. Jeff's reason for using the modifier fat was to distinguish him from the other Neil standing near him who is bald, thinner, and black, but Jeff "doesn't look at the world through that lens," the lens of race. Traumatized by Pierce's fat-shaming, Neil tells Pierce that he pities him, causing Pierce to make a fatal error in the game. The episode is set up as a moral lesson for Pierce, yet Jeff's immoral behavior and subsequent guilt over the consequences of his words is the impetus for the whole episode. His insensitive blunder, a true awkward mistake of his own making, causes Jeff to do actually do the right thing. Pierce may sabotage his endeavors, but this episode is one of the few in which Jeff's performance of the good guy, the Average Undergraduate, is genuine.

In insisting on the loser nature of Greendale, *Community* shies away from a full exploration of the nexus of class, political, and economic struggles that inflect much work done in higher education today. Larry Abramson, in an *All Things Considered* piece reviewing the show after its first episode, claims, "The characters in 'Community' face the same existential dilemma that community colleges themselves face. They have to rise above their own low self-esteem" (qtd. in Brand). Somewhere along the way, the community college went from being the people's college to loser college. Rose argues in *Back to School*, "people also go to college to feel their minds working and learn new things, to help their kids, to feel competent, to remedy a poor education, to redefine who they are, to start over" (141–142). None of these reasons for returning to school make a student a "loser" or less worthy, yet *Community*'s dark, often self-destructive strain steers the show away from more positive depictions of community colleges.

Community's focus on losers in the twenty-first century complicates our understanding of how campus narratives represent manliness. Jeff's vacillation between two poses of masculinity reveals just how difficult inculcating proper masculinity is in the twenty-first century university. Admittedly, *Community*'s inversion of the narrative structures of the Victorian campus narratives makes locating an ideal pose of masculinity almost impossible. Unlike *Tom Brown at Oxford*, there is no moment in which Jeff must not only relinquish the things he wants most, but also do so with equanimity and self-reflection. Brown must give up his liaison with Peggy; he spends much of the latter half of the novel atoning for this misdeed. He genuinely feels that making things right for Peggy, and by extension, her working-class love interest, Harry, is the right thing, though the more he is involved with both, the less likely it is he will be able to woo and win Mary Procter. *Community* provides no such narrative of self-sacrifice, disinterestedness, or eventual triumph. Brown does win Mary's hand in the end. Jeff has smaller moments of triumph, in which the rest of the study group helps him thread the needle between the metrosexual and the ideal man. In "Modern Warfare" (Episode 1.23), Jeff and Britta discuss being fake:

> JEFF: Oh, please, I invented phony. You care about people. I accused you of faking to convince myself I'm not such a jerk.
>
> BRITTA: Jeff, you help people more than I do, and you don't even want to. You're not — you're not a jerk. You're fine.

It is a short lived moment — Jeff after all cannot remain between these two styles indefinitely — but nevertheless, it reveals that the good, upright guy is not always the loser at Greendale.

Notes

1. In comparing two texts, I am deliberately avoiding the canon of campus novels since the early twentieth century. The term "campus novel" typically refers to novels about faculty life and the publish-or-perish stresses of academia. David Lodge argues that "campus novel" is a genre of fiction examining faculty at a regional, four-year university whereas the varsity narrative is "about the goings-on of young people at Oxbridge" (vii). Sally Dalton-Brown reinforces Lodge's definitions: "One must distinguish between Bildungsroman tales of student life such as Donna Tartt's *A Secret History* (1992), and classic campus tales that focus on the academic, not the student" (n. 1 599). Professors are almost completely absent from *Tom Brown at Oxford* and while faculty feature prominently in *Community*, the narrative remains focused on the study group, particularly Jeff, the reluctant leader. For an examination of the campus novel in the twentieth century see Showalter, *Faculty Towers* and Williams, 56–89. For more information on the campus novel versus the varsity novel see Dalton-Brown 591–600; Lodge v–vxii; Scott 81–87; Showalter 2; and Williams 56–57.

2. "Modern Types" ran in irregular installments from 1890 to 1891.

3. The Tractarian Movement was a religious movement in the early nineteenth century that took issue with the perceived laxness of the Church of England, as well as the Church's inability to acknowledge its Catholic roots. It began in Oxford.

4. Harmon demonstrates self-destructive tendencies in a June 2013 *Harmontown* podcast. Harmon was removed as showrunner and head writer at the end of Season 3 due to differences between him, NBC, and actor Chevy Chase. Since Chase has left the show and the show had an uneven Season 4, Harmon was asked back for Season 5. In the podcast, he lambasted Season 4. His lengthy apology on his Tumblr blog, *Dan Harmon Poops*, further reveals his self-destructive tendencies, while he calls it "apoloblogging." He says, "As usual, it was then that I started to consider how my words might affect other people if viewed as headlines. After five seconds of thinking, I realized, as usual, that other people might be hurt, and that I really need to do this whole 'saying things and thinking about other people' cycle in a different order at some point" ("It Won't Happen Again Again"). This self-destructiveness can be seen throughout *Community*, especially in Jeff and Pierce's behaviors.

Works Cited

"Accounting for Lawyers." *Community*. NBC. 30 September 2010.
Adams, James Eli. *Dandies and Desert Saints: Styles of Victorian Manhood*. Ithaca: Cornell University Press, 1995.
"Advanced Criminal Law." *Community*. NBC. 15 October 2009.

"Advanced Dungeons and Dragons." *Community.* NBC. 3 February 2011.
"The Art of Discourse." *Community.* NBC. 29 April 2010.
Banville, Scott D. "'A Bookkeeper, Not an Accountant': Representing the Lower Middle Class from Victorian Novels and Music-Hall Songs to Television Sitcoms." *The Journal of Popular Culture* 44.1 (2011): 16–36.
"Basic Genealogy." *Community.* NBC. 11 March 2010.
Brand, Madeleine. "Will Colleges Give NBC's 'Community' Good Marks?" All Things Considered. *National Public Radio.* n.d. Web. 23 April 2013.
"Celebrity Pharmacology." *Community.* NBC. 27 January 2011.
"Comparative Religion." *Community.* NBC. 10 December 2009.
Dalton-Brown, Sally. "Is There Life Outside of (the Genre of) the Campus Novel? The Academic Struggles to Find a Place in Today's World." *The Journal of Popular Culture* 41.4 (2008): 591–600.
Deslandes, Paul R. *Oxbridge Men: British Masculinity and the Undergraduate Experience, 1850–1920.* Bloomington: Indiana University Press, 2005. Ebrary Reader. 14 October 2013.
"Football, Feminism and You." *Community.* NBC. 22 October 2009.
Graff, Gerald. *Professing Literature: An Institutional History.* Chicago: University of Chicago Press, 2007.
Greif, Mark. "What Was the Hipster?" *New York Magazine.* New York Media. 24 October 2010. Web. 16 October 2013.
Harmon, Dan. "It Won't Happen Again Again." *Dan Harmon Poops.* 18 June 2013. Web. 24 June 2013.
Hughes, Thomas. *Tom Brown at Oxford.* New York: A.L. Burt, n.d.
"Introduction to Statistics." *Community.* NBC. 29 October 2009.
"Investigative Journalism." *Community.* NBC. 14 January 2010.
Kaye, Jeremy. "Twenty-First-Century Victorian Dandy: What Metrosexuality and the Heterosexual Matrix Reveal about Victorian Men." *The Journal of Popular Culture* 42.1 (2009): 103–25.
Lodge, David. "Introduction." *Lucky Jim.* Kingsley Amis. London: Penguin Classics, 2000.
____. "Robertson Davies and the Campus Novel." *The Academic Novel: New and Classic Essays.* Ed. Merritt Moseley. Chester, UK: Chester Academic, 2007. 261–67.
"Modern Types. No. XIII.—The Precocious Undergraduate." *Punch, or the London Charivari* 14 June 1890: 285.
"Modern Types. No. XXI.—The Average Undergraduate." *Punch, or the London Charivari* 1 November 1890: 205.
"Modern Warfare." *Community.* NBC. 6 May 2010.
Moers, Ellen. *The Dandy: Brummell to Beerbohm.* Lincoln: University of Nebraska Press, 1978.
Moseley, Merritt. "Introductory: Definitions and Justifications." *The Academic Novel: New and Classic Essays.* Ed. Merritt Moseley. Chester, UK: Chester Academic, 2007. 3–19.
"Pilot." *Community.* NBC. 17 September 2009.
"Physical Education." *Community.* NBC. 4 March 2010.
Rose, Mike. *Back to School: Why Everyone Deserves a Second Chance at Education.* New York: New, 2012.
____."Second-Chance Collegians: Inside the Remedial Classroom." *Dissent* (Fall 2012): 41–45. *Project Muse.* Web. 18 April 2013.
St. John, Warren. "Metrosexuals Come Out." *New York Times.* New York Times. 22 June 2003. Web. 16 October 2013.
Scott, Robert F. "It's a Small World, After All: Assessing the Contemporary Campus Novel." *The Journal of the Midwest Modern Language Association* 37.1 (Spring 2004): 81–87.
Showalter, Elaine. *Faculty Towers: The Academic Novel and Its Discontents.* Philadelphia: University of Pennsylvania Press, 2005.
Williams, Jeffery J. "The Rise of the Academic Novel." *American Literary History* 24.3 (July 2013): 56–89. Web. *Project Muse.* 18 April 2013.

Feminist and Postfeminist Discourses: Reading the Britta Problem
Jessica Ford

> Makeovers, they sure have us programmed right. I am a female pleasure unit. I require a new coat of paint. —BRITTA PERRY, "Football, Feminism and You" (Episode 1.6)

Dan Harmon's television series constructs a complex meditation on second-wave, third-wave, and postfeminist notions of gender and femininity, and in doing so, reflects the competing discourses within contemporary feminism and popular culture. With the exception of Britta, all of the other characters work to uphold to the postfeminist framework that is constructed within the series.

Britta is a college dropout in her late 20s who could be seen as an embodiment of activist and gender politics of second and third-wave feminism. Throughout *Community*, Britta is consistently undermined and characterized as redundant or "the worst" and her name is used as a verb, which means to ruin something. The question of feminism is rarely explicitly discussed within the series, except when Britta raises issues of gender and identity politics. The other female characters, such as Christian single-mother Shirley and type-A high-school graduate Annie do not identify as feminists, at least as far as the series makes explicit. Shirley and Annie's traditional heteronormative femininity is emphasized in comparison to the harsh, ball-breaking persona of Britta. I am not arguing that *Community* is a feminist text; however, the friction between these competing portrayals of femininity and womanhood creates discourse that resonates with how contemporary feminisms are represented in popular visual culture.

Community is participating in an expansive discourse emerging within female-centric comedies about the role of feminism in contemporary popular culture. Comedy series such as *30 Rock* (2006–2013) and *Parks and Recreation* (2009–) present strong unapologetic female characters that identify as feminists, while newer series such as *New Girl* (2011–), *Girls* (2012–), and *The Mindy Project* (2012–) reflect a burgeoning diversity of "funny women" and a willingness to discuss explicitly the issues facing women in a postfeminist context. Each of these uses humor to empower female characters and depict a postfeminist context in which they dictate their own stories.

Unlike the series listed above, however, the lead character in *Community* is a white, upper-middle class male; therefore, female empowerment is not innately woven into the premise of the narrative. Unlike Liz Lemon, Leslie Knope, Jessica Day, Hannah Horvath, or Dr. Mindy Lahiri — who are all the narrative centers of their respective series — the female characters of *Community* are participating in a feminist media discourse from the position of the Other. Furthermore, each of the aforementioned series and characters have been created by female creators and showrunners who often also star in the series, with the exception of *Parks and Recreation* (created by Greg Daniels and Michael Shur); however, Amy Poehler is a credited writer and creative force behind the series.

Irrespective of identity-politics, the series' premise is constructed around Jeff, who, although is a white, wealthy male and seemingly the center of the narrative, brings together many disparate races and genders to form the series' core characters. The structure of the series dictates that Jeff's existence is the impetus for the creation of the study group; however, it results in each of the character being defined against him as Other.

The series constructs this in a particularly overt way with the character of Britta. The audience is first introduced to Britta in the pilot episode through Jeff's eyes as he refers to her as "the hot girl from Spanish class"; through his words, she is immediately defined by how aesthetically pleasing she is to the male gaze, but she is also positioned as the foil to Jeff — unlike the other characters, she is not easily won over by his charm and persuasion. From the beginning of the show, Britta is constructed as the "anti–Jeff" in her willingness to engage meaningfully with other members of the group, evidenced in her participation in Annie and Shirley's protest against the repressive regime in Guatemala ("Spanish 101," Episode 1.2). The irony of this episode is that Britta is seemingly unaware of the actual regime in *her* life, the study group, which is consistently used by the writers to undermine the legitimacy of her convictions. This episode represents the limits of Britta's feminist liberalism in its current form because of her inability to adequately engage with others about the women's issues.

This essay's discussion of feminism in *Community* will focus firstly on how Dan Harmon and his writers attempt to construct a post-gender world through narrative and dialogue, with particular attention to how politics of gender are undercut using humor, often satire. Secondly, I will examine how the character of Britta represents the values and rhetoric of second and third-wave feminism within a postfeminist context and how any "serious" meditation of gender politics are undermined in the process. Comedies have proven a fertile ground for discussing the interaction of feminist and postfeminist discourses on television, because as Amanda Lotz points out, "feminist discourse is predominantly found in the comedy genre because of narrative and generic qualities that both introduce and then contain potentially subversive content" (111). In her critique of *30 Rock*, Linda Mizejewski examines how Liz Lemon functions as a liminal figure able to express feminist views while still being contained within the postfeminist discourse of the diegesis (4). The expression of feminist ideas with a postfeminist diegesis in *Community* will be examined through a case-study format which looks closely at two episodes from the first two seasons, followed by a brief discussion of how feminist discourses have changed in Season 3 and the beginning of Season 4. The case studies will focus on two episodes that explicitly concern issues of gender and femininity: "Football, Feminism and You" (Episode 1.6) and "Psychology of Letting Go" (Episode 2.3). Both episodes will be examined, broadly, in terms of the friction between different ways of constructing femininity, feminism, and gender, specifically in terms of how Rosalind Gill's stable identifying features of postfeminism can be seen to be undermining Britta's feminist agency within the narrative.

Understanding and exploring how the character of Britta embodies the politics of second and third-wave feminism is complicated by the lack of stable understanding of the specific ontologies of each of these terms. While second-wave feminism is largely understood to concern the theorizing of women's history and the insistence on equality that came through the groundbreaking works of Simone de Beauvoir's *The Second Sex* (1949) and Betty Friedan's *The Feminine Mystique* (1963), any attempts identify the defining characteristics of the feminist movement of the 1960s to 1980s would be lead to a gregarious oversimplification. For the purposes of this essay, I have identified Britta's activist tendencies or desire to enact change through political action as a manifestation of second-wave ideals. Her desire to affect systematic change is seen in how she tries to help people, whether it is Abed's dream to go to film school ("Introduction to Film," Episode 1.3) or Pierce's being brainwashed by a cult ("The Science of Illusion," Episode 1.20).

Britta can be seen to enact much of the gender and identity politics that characterized the third-wave. Ednie Kaeh Garrison outlines the impossibilities of creating a singular and stable meaning for the feminisms present in understanding the "third-wave."

> The very claim to know what third wave feminism means is riddled with contradictions and problems. Few can agree about what and whom it encapsulates —

advocates and detractors alike. The only general consensus to have emerged is that it has become a name for young women who identify as feminists (but not the feminists of the sixties and seventies) and, especially among its detractors, it is a name assigned to those who have no real clear sense of what feminist ideology/ praxis, feminist movement, or feminist identity have meant across time and place [qtd. in Gillis, Howie, and Munford 24].

Britta fits this description in that she identifies herself as somewhat of a feminist, as well as a contemporary woman who owns her sexuality. She does not apologize for being sexually active; however, her seriousness or hardness often alienates her from the other members of the group.

In "The Science of Illusion" (Episode 1.20), Britta articulates this when responding to the study group's criticism of her:

> Because I'm a buzz kill, that's why. Because that's who I am. That's my role. You guys create fun, and I destroy it. Of course, a silly little joke ends with a dead body on the lawn. I should have known that, but I wanted to do it anyway 'cause I wanted to be like you. I wanted to be funny. Knock, knock.
> Who's there?
> Cancer.
> Oh, good, come on in. I thought it was Britta.

As she continues Britta gets more upset and by the end she is on the verge of tears. This kind of emotional vulnerability is rare for Britta, while the other characters often taunt her she usually reacts defiantly and stands her ground, even when wrong. Both Annie and Shirley respond emotionally and empathize with Britta's desire to be liked and included. Whereas Jeff, Abed, Troy and Pierce are further alienated by their overt displays of emotion. Like in the episode "Football, Feminism and You," which will be discussed in detail later, when Britta cries she becomes weak in the eyes of the male characters, while the Annie and Shirley see her as more feminine in this moment. In this monologue, Britta touches on how Toril Moi and Garrison describe contemporary understandings of feminism as overly serious and unable to appreciate humor (Moi 1737; Garrison 26). Britta's attempt to engage in a harmless practical joke ends with disastrous consequences, which reflects how Britta begins to see herself in the same way that others do.

Moreover, ridiculing Britta is a constant source of humor within the series. When Vaughn, Britta's beau, finds a reason to dump her, he writes a song, "Getting Rid of Britta," with such lyrics: "I'm getting rid of Britta. I'm getting rid of the B," with Pierce in the background singing "She's a no good B ... She's a GDB" ("Home Economics," Episode 1.8). Later, we find out that Pierce's nickname for her is "Sour Face" ("Intermediate Documentary Filmmaking," Episode 2.16), and a few episodes after that, Annie gleefully whispers to Shirley, "Everyone hates Britta" ("Critical Film Studies," Episode 2.19). Throughout the course of the first three seasons, Britta internalizes the study group's assumptions about her, and by the third season, she appears to be a pale imitation of the complex, politically engaged feminist that was introduced in the early episodes.

Through Britta, *Community* engages with the debates around feminism, in particular the gender/sex binary as Judith Butler deconstructs in *Gender Trouble* (1990). Considered one of the founding texts of third wave feminism and queers studies, in it Butler deconstructs many stable ideas, including woman as subject and gender as performance, which underwrote much of the theoretical work of second-wave feminism. Butler considers the implications of linking a discursive category (gender) with a biologically determined category (sex). She explains,

> This very concept of sex-as-matter, sex-as-instrument-of-cultural signification, however, is a discursive formation that acts as a naturalized foundation for the nature/culture distinction and the strategies of domination that that distinction supports. The binary relation between culture and nature promotes a relationship of hierarchy in which culture freely "imposes" meaning on nature, and, hence, renders it into an "Other" to be appropriated on its own limitless uses, safeguarding the ideality of the signifier and the structure of signification on the model of domination [Butler 50].

Butler's assertion about the relationship between sex and gender highlights the implications of allowing sex, and by proxy gender, to be a cultural signifier of meaning. Britta often talks of how the other female characters are "selling out their gender," by which she creates a direct correlation between a person's sex and gender, without allowing for the pluralization of gender beyond its culturally prescribed links to sex. Butler's exploration of the discursive ontology of gender challenges us to think of how the "Other" is created through language. The narrative structure of *Community* renders each of the characters (except Jeff) as "Other"; in addition, Britta's articulation of the function of gender and sex results in her also discursively constructing herself as "Other."

Britta's repeated use of the term, "gender," as opposed to "sex," implies a stable meaning of gender, which is linked to the biological hierarchy Butler warns about. In the one episode, when talking about their upcoming Women's Studies class, Britta says, "We're gonna find our roots in that class and stop defining our gender by theirs" ("Aerodynamics of Gender," Episode 2.7). This may indicate that if gender is inherently culturally linked and determined by sex, as well as being plural and performative as Butler suggests, then Britta's statement negates itself. Insofar as one gender is defined by another or as the "castrated Other," it is complicated by the assumption that there is a concrete definition of femininity outside of its relationship to masculinity — something which the series does its best to disprove. While Butler assert that the determinist gender/sex binary, which underpins definitions of gender as discursively dangerous for feminism, I argue that the postfeminist framework of *Community* deconstructs any illusions of a world without the male dominance.

Due to the complexity of determining exactly what can and cannot be considered third-wave feminist, while, I will be heavily drawing on Butler, I also refer to Garrison who argues that the notion of third-wave feminism cannot be considered outside the framework of postmodernism and its counterpart postfeminism:

> the emergence of third wave feminism cannot be explored without also considering the popular construction of the political object postfeminism as a term that discursively (and recursively) distances multiple cohorts of young women after 1980 from those who participated in the "feminist" decades of the sixties and seventies [qtd. in Gillis, Howard, and Munford 30].

Garrison alludes to the divide within contemporary discourses around women's studies, between those who were active within the second-wave movement and those of younger generations who have benefited from this activism.

Catherine M. Orr suggests, "Postfeminism assumes that the women's movement took care of oppressive institutions ... now it is up to individual women to make personal choices that simply reinforce those fundamental societal changes" (34). Orr's reading of the third-wave/postfeminist divide is centered on the emphasis on communal efforts versus individual. She explains, "'feminist' practices become matters of personal style or individual choice and any emphasis on organized intervention is regarded as naive and even oppressive to women" (34). This is reflected in my analysis of *Community*, examining how postfeminism's emphasis on choice and individuality actively undermines feminist activists who are attempting to enact structural change through communal action, such as Britta. Underscoring this is the irony that it is the study group's communal efforts to undermine the individual political efforts of Britta that consistently reestablish postfeminism as the status quo.

Regarding discourses around what specifically postfeminism encompasses are complex and at times contradictory, some scholars recognize a "backlash" against feminism a defining feature of postfeminism (Faludi), while others identify the popular cultural absorption and universalization of core feminist values such as equality and empowerment as a trademark of the postfeminist era (McRobbie). Susan Faludi's seminal work, *Backlash: The Undeclared War Against Women* (1991), characterizes the rejection of feminism that Faludi believes occurred in the 1980s. Faludi is particularly concerned with the prevailing belief that "the women's movement, as we are told time and again, has proved women's own worst enemy" (2). Building on Faludi's work, almost 20 years later, Angela McRobbie argues in *The Aftermath of Feminism: Gender, Culture and Social Change* (2009) that there is a "new kind of anti-feminist sentiment which is different from simply being a backlash against the seeming gain made by feminist activities and campaigns in an earlier period, i.e. the 1970s and 1980s" (1). McRobbie contends, "Elements of feminism have been taken into account and have been absolutely incorporated into political and institutional life" (1).

Both Faludi and McRobbie infer that one of the stable defining features of postfeminism is the lack of explicit rhetoric within media culture around feminism and an unwillingness to take up the title of feminist. Toril Moi characterizes the popular image of feminists as angry, out of touch women who are full of hate. Moi argues that it is this image that has caused "a whole new generation of women who are careful to preface every gender-related claim that might come across as unconventional with 'I'm not a feminist, but...'" (1736). *Community*'s female characters embody each of these aspects of postfeminism that Faludi, McRobbie, and Moi discuss to varying degrees.

The understanding of postfeminism that I will be primarily working from, however, is from Rosalind Gill's studies of media cultures and postfeminism. Gill articulates a new way of understanding postfeminism:

> Postfeminism is understood best neither as an epistemological perspective nor as a historical shift, nor (simply) as a backlash in which its meanings are pre-specified. Rather, postfeminism should be conceived of as a sensibility. From this perspective postfeminist media culture should be out critical object — a phenomenon into which scholars of culture should inquire — rather than an analytical perspective. This approach does not require a static notion of one single authentic feminism as a comparison point, but instead is informed by postmodernist and constructionist perspectives and seeks to examine what is distinctive about contemporary articulations of gender in the media [148].

Gill's emphasis on understanding postfeminism as a sensibility, emphasizes the plurality of contemporary feminisms. Gill's conception of multiple feminisms informs my approach to *Community,* especially in regards to understanding how each of the female characters — Britta, Annie and Shirley — represent different ways of internalizing contemporary media articulations of postfeminism. In her analysis, Gill identifies several stable defining characteristics of postfeminism, such as "femininity as a bodily property" (149), "the makeover paradigm" (156), and "irony and knowingness" (159).

"Football, Feminism and You" (Episode 1.6)

This episode is the first dealing explicitly with issues of feminism and femininity. Britta's feminist and activist roots have already been established in earlier episodes as the second one in the first season when Britta challenges Annie and Shirley to consider how human rights are being oppressed in the third world

("Spanish 101," Episode 1.2). From early on, the study group has already accepted Britta as the politically engaged one and have internalized the assumptions that come with that. For Pierce, that means calling Britta a "lesbian" ("Advanced Criminal Law," Episode 1.5) as though it is simultaneously an insult and a logical conclusion. Britta is characterized as the "hard" one, both discursively in she interacts with the other characters, as well as through her costuming, which is primarily mono-chromatic and genderless.

In the episode, Britta engages with Gill's "makeover paradigm": This requires people (predominantly women) to believe, first, that they or their life is lacking or flawed in some way; second, that it is amendable to reinvention or transformation by following the advice of relationship, design or lifestyle experts and practicing appropriately modified consumption habits [56].

While this episode does not strictly fit the makeover paradigm, the episode rests on the underlying assumption that something is wrong with Britta and that she can be "fixed" by discovering her inner softness and femininity. Britta accepts this premise: "I'm willing to try some more mainstream feminine stuff." The assumptions inherent in that statement are problematic, yet accept a stable meaning of "feminine" and privilege certain aspects of femaleness.

The episode considers how female bonding supposedly takes place in the bathroom. In doing so, it raises issues of gender segregation and the concept of "women's space." Gill identifies the establishment of personal shame as the first step in the makeover paradigms (156). During Britta's first communal trip to the bathroom with Shirley, she reveals what she "should" be ashamed of:

SHIRLEY: I think my Mom might visit this weekend. I think she and I are gonna get makeovers at that spa—
BRITTA: Makeovers. They sure have us programmed right. I am a female pleasure unit. I require a new coat of paint.
SHIRLEY: Just something I thought might be fun.
BRITTA: Here's something I think might be fun. Let's find out the number of makeup companies that are owned by women. I'll save the trouble; it's zero. Of course, you're saying, "Britta, aren't you a hypocrite? You're plastered with glitter and goo from head to toe like the rest of us." Well, I also pay income tax and pull over for cops, but that doesn't mean that I support a country that oppresses its citizens, restricts voting rights....

As Britta goes on, Shirley is clearly not impressed and appears to be emotional. It is clear that Britta is not interested in engaging Shirley, but she intends to lecture her. Shirley responds with a glare directly toward the camera. Britta is shown to be at fault here because of her inability to communicate effectively with Shirley. Britta speaks with little to no consideration for the Shirley, an older woman of color more likely to understand what it means to live as Other. Britta essentially stops listening to Shirley, and the dialogue descends into a diatribe whereby Britta is lecturing Shirley and the audience. Britta is calling out the makeover paradigm while unknowingly beginning her own reinvention. The episode's editing contradicts Britta's demand to be heard as the hand dryer muffles her dialogue and her rant is eventually severed when the scene cut to a conversation between Pierce and Dean Pelton. Britta is literally silenced in favor of voices of two white men in positions of power. In relation to the scene, Gill articulates how the subject of the makeover is shamed or humiliated into recognizing that women need to change themselves after which "participants are then variously advised, cajoled, bullied or 'educated' into changing their ways and becoming more 'successful' versions of themselves" (156). This can be seen after their first bathroom experience together; therefore, during the rest of the episode, Shirley tasks herself with fixing Britta by making her softer, more feminine. We see this in a later dialogue:

> SHIRLEY: You think you can't talk about your own business, but you insinuate my mama's a robot because she and I want makeovers. That is the ladies room, Britta, a place where ladies go to share, listen, support each other, and discretely eliminate waste. And I like you, too. I even like that you're a little hard, but if you can't learn to be soft in there, you need to pee alone.
> BRITTA: I've peed alone my whole life. Women have always hated me. I don't even know how it started. Maybe it was when I got boobs before everyone—
> SHIRLEY: Not out here. In there *(gesturing to the bathroom)*.

When Shirley ushers Britta into the bathroom, she is on the verge of tears. Shirley sees this emotional response as a sign of weakness that should be expressed in a women's only space. Shirley makes the argument for women-only spaces because she feels that in co-ed spaces, women are not allowed to be vulnerable; therefore, that space is created in the bathroom. Shirley insinuates that for women to be liked by other women, they need to be "soft," feminine, and vulnerable. Britta's acceptance of her need to change begins what Gill calls the "second chapter," in which she comes to understand her own failings through Shirley's mentorship (156). By inextricably linking femininity with softness, Shirley is limiting how it is socially acceptable for Britta to perform her gender. Shirley, as an instrument of postfeminism, is undermining Britta's brand of femininity (decidedly asexual in Season 1) to get her to conform and partake in the makeover paradigm she rejected earlier in the episode.

The secondary storyline of the particular episode concerns Jeff trying to get Troy to play football for Greendale, while Annie is determined to keep him away from football. When Annie is upset about Troy's choice to play, Shirley sends Britta into help her, and she finally "proves" herself "soft" enough to be one of the girls. Britta's advice to Annie is, "Oh Annie, screw him. There are guys out there that would kill to be with you. And if Troy isn't one of them, that's him failing your standards. You got that?" Britta's advice is a message of self-reliance and empowerment, but simultaneously reinforces a heteronormative notion of happiness, and in doing so, any conception of gender plurality she may have previously possessed is absent.

Although she has been the voice of feminism, in the episode Britta succumbs to the notion that she needs to be more feminine or "soft" to be socially accepted by other women. Despite her apparent staunchly feminist beliefs, Britta begins to internalize the postfeminist sensibility of her surroundings and in doing so enacts Butler's assertion that the sex/gender binary perpetually reinforce the existence of one another.

"Psychology of Letting Go" (Episode 2.3)

While the last episode considers how feminisms manifest in contemporary discourse about women, "Psychology of Letting Go," debates whether femininity and sexuality can be considered a feminist's tool. In this particular episode, Britta and Annie build a diorama on the effects of an oil spill and attempt to raise money to help the injured animals. While Shirley is jealous that she is left out of the discussion, Annie and Britta use different approaches to attract donations. Britta is aggressive and assertive in stating the facts to passersby, with a male student responding, "You don't have to yell at us. Nobody is on the only side of this issue." On the other hand, Annie is overtly girly and meek, to the extent that Professor Duncan calls her, "You with the boobs," when calling on Annie in class and she has little to no response.

Each embodies their feminism in contrasting ways, with an emphasis on physical or outward expression. Gill argues that one of the most striking shifts from earlier representations of women is the emphasis on the body and the belief that "femininity is defined as a bodily product rather than a social structural or psychological one" (149). Gill terms this "femininity as a bodily property" and explains,

> [I]n today's media, possession of a "sexy body" is presented as a women's key (if not sole) source of identity. The body is presented simultaneously as women's source of power and as always unruly, requiring constant monitoring, surveillance, discipline and remodeling (and consumer spending) in order to conform to ever narrower judgments of female attractiveness [149].

The idea of the female body as a source of feminine power is enacted in this episode. Both Annie and Britta voice their criticisms of how each other performs their gender, but ultimately it is sex that sells their cause.

In the episode, each of the female characters advocate for a different kind of feminist discourse. Britta represents that of second- and third-wave feminisms' activist intentions and emphasizes communal acts. Annie takes a more individual approach, emphasizing traditional embodiment of femininity and embrace of the male gaze, while Shirley represents the silent minority. After witnessing how Annie is supposedly using her sexuality to attract male students to donate money to their cause, Britta makes the following accusations:

> BRITTA: Come on, Annie, you know guys are giving you money because of the whole sexy schoolgirl routine.
> ANNIE: I have a routine?
> BRITTA: Yeah, y'know the one where you use posture as an excuse to stick out your chest and you laugh at guys' unfunny jokes, pretending not to know that they have a sock at home with your name on it.
> ANNIE: Um, that's me. And if a guy wants to make a puppet of me, that's hardly your concern.
> SHIRLEY: Well, I may just be an outsider here because I was never called to participate, but it seems to me that Britta's upset because she's raising less money than you.
> BRITTA: Yeah, I'm raising less money because I'm not jump-starting date rapists.

Britta explicitly uses the language of gender performance in her assertion that Annie is doing a routine, while also accusing Annie of not being authentic. The most alarming part is Britta using the conservative rhetoric of victim blaming and claims. When Annie attempts to defend herself, she locates the agency outside herself, through the double entendre of "if a guy wants to make a puppet of me." Although seemingly unaware of the masturbatory allusion of Britta's statement, she makes it about external male validation rather than sense of internal self-worth. While Britta is advocating for a gendered response to the inherent misogyny within Annie's embodiment of femininity, which Britta sees as a feminist issue, however, Annie takes the postfeminist approach of individual responsibility.

The next day, Britta comes to Greendale without her trademark leather jacket, instead wearing a full face of makeup, with a tight sweater and a black mini-skirt. She begins to imitate Annie, her posture has changed to accentuate her breast and posterior and the register of her voice has gone up to indicate flirtatiousness. Annie and Britta satirize each other's gender performance, while Shirley is further ostracized and silenced,

BRITTA: Wow, it really is easy to raise money when you sell out your gender.
ANNIE: I'm sure it's even easier when you're not standing next to this: "Hey jerk ... you're stupid. Give me money. I know more than you." *(imitating Britta)*
BRITTA: Oh no, I don't know anything. I need boys. Saving the planet makes my back hurt. *(imitating Annie)*
ANNIE: Oh, I obviously don't need guys for anything. That's why I wear stripper boots during the day and eat only celery and mustard for lunch.
BRITTA: Oh, I never stop smiling.
ANNIE: I never start.
BRITTA: My sweaters keep shrinking.
ANNIE: I get up an hour early to ever so slightly curl my hair.
SHIRLEY: Yeah, you're both so different, skinny bitches.

Britta's use of the term, "gender," is confusing because while it is intended to be all encompassing and representing all women, she is excluding Shirley. Annie and Britta articulate how they view each other's gender performance. In this exchange it is clear that Annie is projecting an understanding of feminism, as a rejection or even hatred of men and femininity onto Britta. While Britta is clearly not as feminized as Annie, she is far from second-wave image of a "strident, domineering, aggressive, and intolerant" man-hater that Annie is projecting onto Britta (Moi 1736). Annie presumes that Britta's "stripper boots" and hair curling is motivated by a need to be desired by men because that is how Annie understands her own performance of femininity. Britta is arguing for a privileged position for her particular performance of femininity, which is based on empowering the male gaze. In order for Britta to effectively argue that Annie is "selling out her gender," she must place significant currency in the ability of the male gaze to disempower Annie, and subsequently her gender. The series constructs Britta as a paradox, who cannot fulfill her own convictions and fails to enact the ideals that she espouses.

The next day, Britta and Annie are wearing oversized men's style T-shirts, deliberately de-feminizing themselves. Although neither appears overtly masculine, it presents the idea that to perform femininity in a way that is non-offensive, one needs to be de-sexualized to the point of neutrality; however, any serious statements about gender politics are immediately undermined when they knock over the display and are covered in fake oil. Annie and Britta attempt to resolve their issues by wrestling on the ground with a variety of men watching. To add to the spectacle, their bodies become commoditized when onlookers (primarily male) begin to throw money at them. While looking on, Professor

Duncan says, "Now, this is why I came to America," reinforcing the power of the male gaze in transforming a discourse about female empowerment into a scopophilic display. Annie and Britta continue to wrestle as a crowd forms, and money is thrown around. Shirley looks on, shaking her head in disgust. In the fallout of the fight, Annie and Britta stand around while their male onlookers mend their display.

What begins as competing discourses on the representations of femininity and feminism eventually disintegrates into a resolution that blames petty jealousies and poor self-esteem. Britta declares jealousy of Annie and reveals that she only has sexual intercourse with Jeff because she hates herself. Annie replies, "No, but you totally called me on what I was doing, and I only kissed Jeff to see if I could do it. I wanna be cool and sexy like you. I can't believe how gross I am." Not only have Annie and Britta have internalized the postmodern sensibility that their power lies within their sexualized bodies, but they have embraced it. The realization continues:

> BRITTA: And you know the reason that we raised more money in five minutes of oil wrestling than in two days of fundraising?
> ANNIE: Because men are even grosser?
> BRITTA: And when we forget that, they win.

Annie and Britta nod in agreement, before hugging each other. Annie and Britta choose to use the heteronormative system to their advantage, but in doing so, they have to surrender their personal gender performances for one informed by the male gaze. Britta's attempt to pursue a third-wave conception of gender as performance is ultimately undermined by the postfeminist framework of the series, which co-opts any sense of empowerment by establishing the male gaze as the ultimate power.

Episodes from Season 3

The third season represents an interesting character turn for Britta as she becomes more integrated in the group and her defiant feminism is muted. While the undermining of Britta's agenda in the first two seasons was mostly subtle and nuanced, in Season 3, it becomes explicit and aggressive. From the first episode of the season, "Biology 101," she is represented as dumb for buying a chemistry textbook instead of the biology one. Britta spends most of the first episode of Season 3, trying to help Abed, who is distraught that his beloved *Cougar Town* has been pushed back to a mid-season schedule. While the other characters go about their business, Britta is intent on finding a new television series for Abed. Troy is consistently criticizing Britta's attempts and he says to her, "Britta, you've done enough. Why don't you go start a ruiners' club? Oh wait, you'd probably ruin it." This kind of representation relies on Gill's "irony and knowingness":

> Irony is used also as a way of establishing a safe distance between oneself and particular sentiments or beliefs, at a time when being passionate about anything or appearing to care too much seems "uncool" ... in postfeminist media culture irony has become a way of "having it both ways," of expressing sexist, homophobic or otherwise unpalatable sentiments in an ironized form, while claiming this was not actually "meant" [159].

The Britta of Season 3, as established throughout the earlier episodes and Troy's characterization of her as a "ruiner" in the first episode, is reliant on the audience's understanding of her function within the study group. By Season 3, Britta has softened considerably, in large part due to her failed attempts to change herself and challenge the group. She has internalized the sensibility of postfeminism, and possibly more significantly, the study group is less willing to entertain her activist tendencies or even listen to her stance on gender politics.

This is evident in the second episode "Geography of Global Conflict" (Episode 3.2) when Britta rediscovers her activist roots and holds a one-woman protest where she puts herself in a cage and yells, "This is what the UN is doing to your freedom!" While the group ignores her, absorbed by their own storylines, this seems to act as the last futile attempt to resist postfeminism's sensibility pervasive influence of the series' context. This would appear to be Britta's final attempt to reclaim the determination she exhibited in the earlier seasons, but it was completely ignored by the other characters. In "Horror Fiction in Seven Spooky Steps" (Episode 3.5), it is clear that Britta's status as the "worst" has fully solidified that the group has begun using her name as verb to meaning to ruin something. In a discussion about Britta's failed attempts to work out who in the study group is a psychopath per Britta's psychological tests, she tries to reclaim her name:

> BRITTA: We learned an important lesson tonight. We should never make the Britta of Britta-ing each other's feelings.
> PIERCE: You're using it wrong!
> JEFF: Wow. You Britta'd Britta.

Like the reclaiming of "queer" and "nigger" by other marginalized, activist groups, Britta attempts to reclaim her name, but in doing so, she fails to correctly understand its meaning. This moment of reflexivity reveals how Britta's power and any sense of agency she previously had has been subsumed into the group. The spectator can only comprehend the irony of this reflexive moment if they understand what that Britta has struggled against the study group's stifling of her activist tendencies in the first 2 seasons.

Another episode, "Urban Matrimony and the Sandwich Arts" (Episode 3.12), acts as an interesting conclusion to how Gill's stable defining features of postfeminism can be seen to undermine third-wave feminist discourses within *Community*. This particular episode acts as Britta's submission. Shirley gets engaged and is going to re-marry her ex-husband, Andre; Britta is seen in the background, making a scowling bitter face. The episode follows Britta and Annie's attempts to plan Shirley's wedding, while Shirley goes into business with Pierce, opening up a sandwich shop on the Greendale campus.

This episode relies on the spectators' awareness of the irony of Britta's decent into wedding planning. Irony is woven throughout the two storylines, which effectively undo the feminism of one another. It is evident from the beginning of the episode when Jeff asks Britta to explain what an analogy is and she replies "It's like a thought with another thought's hat on," making a strong understanding of the feminist discourses at work within the series a requirement to fully comprehend the irony of this episode.

The premise of the episode is that Shirley delays setting up her business with Pierce so that she can plan the wedding. Therefore, Annie and Britta offer to take over the wedding planning. In doing so, Shirley becomes the empowered, self-assured woman that she came to Greendale to be. On the other hand, Britta becomes embittered in a cycle of self-loathing that is embedded in the determinism of the sex/gender binary that Shirley had worked to instill in Season 1 in "Football, Feminism and You" (Episode 1.6). Britta, always an advocate for feminism over frivolity, says, "Shirley, you can lie to yourself, but you can't lie to me. Do not use your second wedding as an excuse to limit yourself" ("Urban Matrimony and Sandwich Arts," Episode 3.12). In this moment, Britta constructs weddings and the notions of marriage, which have been embraced within a postfeminist context, as a prison that traps women. While Britta is resisting urge to conform to traditional heteronormative gender roles, it is actually Shirley who is standing up for herself and rejecting her role as simply a wife and mother. In the process of planning the wedding, Britta begins to believe in the determinism of the gender/sex binary that she had previously tried to escape.

Community's third season represents the culmination of the competing feminist discourses, in that Britta internalizes the study group's assessment of her as "the worst" and the postfeminist sensibilities that Gill identifies. The series' approach to depicting the feminisms of contemporary popular culture is ambitious; however, an analysis of the episodes selected reveals how the male gaze reasserts itself at the end of each episode. Unfortunately, the postfeminist framework of the series ultimately undermines the characterization of Britta as a feminist activist concerned with identity and gender politics. Looking towards the fourth season, we can only speculate on how vying feminist and postfeminist discourses will continue to be explored within the series.

Works Cited

"Aerodynamics of Gender." *Community*. NBC. 4 November 2010.
"Biology 101." *Community*. NBC. 22 September 2011.
Butler, Judith. *Gender Trouble: Feminism and the Subversion of Identity*. New York: Routledge, 1990.
"Critical Film Studies." *Community*. NBC. 24 March 2011.
De Beauvoir, Simone. *The Second Sex*. New York: Random House, 1949.
Faludi, Susan. *Backlash: The Undeclared War Against Women*. London: Chatto and Windus, 1991.
"Football, Feminism and You." *Community*. NBC. 22 October 2009.
Friedan, Betty. *The Feminine Mystique*. London: Penguin, 1963.
Garrison, Ednie Kaeh. "Contests for the Meaning of Third-Wave Feminism: Feminism and Popular Consciousness." *Third-Wave Feminism: A Critical Exploration*. Eds. Stacy Gillis, Gillian Howie, and Rebecca Munford. London: Palgrave Macmillan, 2004. 24–36.
"Geography of Global Conflict." *Community*. NBC. 20 September 2011.
Gill, Rosalind. "Postfeminist Media Culture: Elements of a Sensibility." *European Journal of Cultural Studies* 10.2 (2007): 147–66.
"Home Economics." *Community*. NBC. 5 November 2009.
"Horror Fiction in Seven Spooky Steps." *Community*. NBC. 27 October 2011.
"Intermediate Documentary Filmmaking." *Community*. NBC. 17 February 2011.
"Introduction to Film." *Community*. NBC. 1 October 2009.
Lotz, Amanda D. "Postfeminist Television Criticism: Rehabilitating Critical Terms and Identifying Postfeminist Attributes." *Feminist Media Studies* 1.1 (2001): 105–21.
McRobbie, Angela. *The Aftermath of Feminism: Gender, Culture and Social Change*. Thousand Oaks, CA: Sage, 2008.
Mizejewski, Linda. "Feminism, Postfeminism, Liz Lemonism." *Genders* 55 (2012). Online.
Moi, Toril. "'I Am Not a Feminist, But...': How Feminism Became the F-Word." *PMLA* 121.5 (2006): 1735–41.
Orr, Catherine M. "Charting the Currents of the Third Wave." *Hypatia* 12.3 (1997): 29–45.
"Pilot." *Community*. NBC. 17 September 2009.
"Psychology of Letting Go." *Community*. NBC. 7 October 2010.
"The Science of Illusion." *Community*. NBC. 25 March 2010.
"Spanish 101." *Community*. NBC. 24 September 2009.
"Urban Matrimony and the Sandwich Arts." *Community*. NBC. 15 March 2012.

Creating a Colorblind Community: Dean Pelton and the Greendale Human Beings

Melissa Vosen Callens

"We've solved racism" is a bold and presumptuous statement for any person to make, but when it is uttered by a middle-aged white man in a position of authority to a white, male septuagenarian, the statement seems downright absurd. The Dean of Greendale Community College, Craig Pelton, is an eccentric administrator that makes ludicrous proclamations like the one above. Viewers learn Pelton has worked in higher education for nearly ten years, four at Greendale, in which enrollment has steadily increased. Pelton is fearful of legal trouble, however, and throughout the series, we see him become increasingly vigilant against lawsuits based on race, gender, religion, and so on.

Throughout his tenure at Greendale, Pelton has tirelessly tried to promote his school as an inclusive, progressive institution of higher learning. As the main administrator of this institution, he has concerns and wishes to abolish any discriminatory and oppressive practices on campus; unfortunately, his vigilance and initiatives to do so are at best misguided and usually ill-advised by faculty and students, often leading to disastrous results. In three seasons, viewers watch Dean Pelton sponsor several alcohol-laced campus events ("Pascal's Triangle Revisited," Episode 1.25) distribute faulty condoms at a sexually transmitted disease awareness fair ("Politics of Human Sexuality," Episode 1.11), repeatedly sexually harass a male student whom he has a crush on, and plan epic paintball wars that nearly destroy the campus ("Modern Warfare," Episode 1.23; "A Fistful of Paintballs," Episode 2.23; "For a Few Paintballs More," Episode 2.24). One of his most ill-advised undertakings, an undertaking I will discuss later in this essay, is when he creates a new "ethnically neutral" mascot for the school in the episode, "Football, Feminism and You" (Episode 1.6). After watching a few episodes and seeing these events unfold, the viewer should not be surprised to learn that all the schools where he had previously worked are no longer in existence. Thus, the viewer is left wondering whether his reckless behavior had led to serious consequences at those other institutions.

Dean Pelton's initiatives are extreme and, at times, discriminatory. At one point in the series, Pelton admits to ranking faculty and students by physical appearance because he is worried about fraternization, from which legal trouble could ensue. However, he accidentally calls one professor, "Professor Seven," referring to her rank rather than her last name. He openly admits that attractive people are "a magnet for lawsuits, so we do stay vigilant. In fact, physically attractive students and faculty are ranked by their potential to insight fraternization" ("Interpretive Dance," Episode 1.14). His ranking of faculty and students by physical appearance, for example, could even be argued as harassment. There are clearly more appropriate ways of dealing with fraternization between faculty and students. On one hand, viewers may respect Pelton for taking steps to protect and improve his institution as well as admire his ability to make quick decisions. Some viewers may even find him tragically funny in the process. On the other hand, viewers may see his means of protection as preposterous, ineffective, and oppressive. As a writer for *The Huffington Post* notes, "Dean Pelton is one of the funniest characters outside of the study group, constantly trying to up Greendale's reputation as a great school and always failing miserably" ("Dean Pelton's Office Hours").

Throughout the series, in his attempt to be inclusive, progressive, and protective (due to potential lawsuits), Pelton's behavior becomes more outlandish as he gradually becomes more obsessed with political correctness. Ironically, as his affinity for political correctness grows, Pelton's behavior becomes increasingly more inappropriate. Despite his best intentions and desire to be inclusive on numerous occasions, his eccentric behavior reflects a very common and implicit form of racism: colorblindness. In his attempt to build and lead an inclusive, open-minded institution, he actually manages to stifle the diversity of Greendale Community College's student body, ultimately revealing his own naïveté and close-mindedness.

An Implicit Form of Racism: Colorblind Racial Ideology

According to Neville et al., colorblind racial ideology (CBRI) is a theoretical construct that characterizes contemporary forms of racial beliefs and attitudes (236). Pearl Rosenberg argues that colorblindness allows people to deny that "race, especially skin color has consequences for a person's status and well-being"

(257). Colorblindness refutes evidence that racism exists in the United States and that there is privilege obtained from a person's cultural and racial identity. People may claim not to see color (race) to demonstrate they are not racist; colorblindness, however, is problematic because it denies the lived experience of many. Eduardo Bonilla-Silva argues that colorblindness is actually an implicit form of racism because it denies that privilege and discrimination still exist (Bonilla-Silva 2). Kerri Ullucci and Dan Battey add, "Color blindness undergirds a story Whites can tell themselves to 'prove' the fundamentally fair nature of life in the United States" (1230).

While colorblindness is a more subtle form of racism than the kind that existed in America's Jim Crow era, many have researched the subject and documented the serious consequences of it. Edward Taylor contends, "By insisting on a rhetoric that disallows reference to race, blacks can no longer name their reality or point out racism" (184). This may mean that when people claim to be colorblind, they shut down all discussions on race, yet many in different locations across the country in various professions are proud to be colorblind — just like Dean Pelton. Evan P. Apfelbaum, Michael I. Norton, and Samuel R. Sommers would consider that colorblindness is alluring because of its simplistic view on a very complex issue. It also provides a simple solution to racial problems across the United States. In their review on the subject, Ullucci and Battey noted that many pre-service teachers, for example, are proud and/or aspire to be colorblind (1197). Research suggests, however, that colorblindness is actually detrimental to race relations. Apfelbaum, Norton, and Sommers write, "[C]olor blindness is far from a panacea, sometimes representing more of an obstacle than an asset to facilitating constructive race relations and equitable race-related policies" (207). They suggest a different approach — instead of ignoring the differences between people, differences should be discussed, considered, and highlighted. This approach is often referred to as "multiculturalism" (207). While not a perfect approach (the approach can be said to alienate whites), it is one that is often supported and preferred. To combat any feelings of alienation, the researchers argue that whites should also be included in all multicultural conversations and encouraged to "individuate themselves by drawing on unique aspects of their own identity" (208).

At Greendale Community College, it appears that Pelton is *trying* to create a multicultural environment. For example, he is sure to include students from different backgrounds when drafting new marketing materials for Greendale. Other times, however, he repeatedly denies serious discussions on race — or religion or gender for that matter — particularly after he proudly proclaims he has created an ethnically neutral mascot and thus "solved racism." It is a disturbing statement given the Dean's role on campus; he is one of just a handful of Greendale administrators we see on *Community*, leading the viewer to assume he has a very central role on campus. As a leader of an institution of higher learning, much of his behavior discourages students to go to him with any serious concerns regarding racism or any other problems they may be having or discrimination they may be experiencing. It is this perspective that shows the Dean is more colorblind than color-conscious. Or it could be that he is just looking for quick solutions to complex problems.

Given his role on campus, this can be detrimental to the overall campus environment. In their study, Ullucci and Battey discuss the dangers of teachers, much like Pelton, who aspire to be colorblind. Colorblindness "dangerously alters teachers' understandings of their students, rendering those teachers colormute" (1200). They advocate for teachers who are willing to deconstruct Whiteness in their classrooms, validate the experiences and perspectives of people of color, identify and name racist educational practices, and develop a color-conscious repertoire (1210–13). Creating an ethnically neutral mascot certainly does not solve racism — nor does it create a color-conscious campus. Creating such a mascot denies the fact that color exists and simplifies a complex history of race relations in the United States.

Four Frames

Pelton's ultimate mascot, the human being, is just one of many initiatives that impede any serious conversations on race at Greendale. In four seasons, not only does Pelton create what he considers to be an ethnically neutral mascot in a vain attempt to solve racism, but he also decorates campus buildings with neutral holiday décor under the guise of being inclusive. Moreover, he hired an unqualified Chinese man to teach Spanish because he did not want to ask for his qualifications, fearing if he did, he would be perceived as a racist ("English as a Second Language," Episode 1.24). After watching numerous episodes, it is clear that Dean Pelton is not a malicious man; he does generally care for his students. His intentions are good; his approach in many instances, however, is not. His behavior, i.e. constant fear of lawsuits and naivety in regard to racial discrimination, time and time again reflects colorblind racial ideology, CBRI.

In his 2009 study, Bonilla-Silva documents what he identifies to be four frames of CBRI. Based on his analyses of survey data and interviews of 627 college students attending three predominantly white universities and 400 participants in the 1998 Detroit Area Study (DAS), he discovered the following: abstract liberalism, naturalization, cultural racism, and minimization of racism. These frames, Bonilla-Silva asserts, are used by "an overwhelming majority of the white respondents" (26). These frames also name and characterize all colorblind behavior.

While some have criticized Bonilla-Silva for focusing almost extensively on the relationship between whites and blacks, CBRI and Bonilla-Silva's framework can be used to examine situations involving different races as well as other oppressive practices. Abby Ferber writes, "Although the goals of most research on white privilege are to contribute to antiracist activism, approaches which focus only on race have limited potential" (74). Ferber believes research should shift to a sociocultural perspective, a perspective which "examines the institutionalized culture of privilege and oppression" (74).

Michael Omi and Howard Winant write on Bonilla-Silva's research: "While he is understandably suspicious of white responses, Bonilla-Silva can, at times, be tendentious and abrupt in his interpretations of their views" (122). They then argue, "Bonilla-Silva tries to take some of the edge off by recognizing some practical realities: blacks can practice color blind racism too" (122). In this essay, I will show how these frames can be applied to other situations beyond relations between black and white Americans and show how Dean Pelton's behavior consistently falls within this framework. Despite his best intentions and his vigilance in being an equal opportunity institution, Dean Pelton, because of his colorblindness and role as a top administrator on the Greendale campus, limits color-conscious and gender-conscious discussions and initiatives on campus.

Abstract Liberalism

According to Bonilla-Silvia, abstract liberalism relies upon the language of political liberalism, referring to abstract concepts of equal opportunity, rationality, and free choice (35). It is the belief that anyone can succeed who works hard — and that race is an irrelevant factor in the equation. In his study, Bonilla-Silvia discovered that respondents used individualism as a way to justify opposing policies on racial equality (35). Ullucci and Battey add, "Individualism supports the notion that personal characteristics are the sole determinant in one's success or struggle. Thus, if you are hard working, diligent and savvy, and good outcomes will result. Lazy, motivated, and uninspired people create their own demise" (1201).

Because Dean Pelton is fearful he will be perceived as a racist, he hires Ben Chang to teach Spanish at Greendale — no questions asked. From the first few episodes of the series, it is clear that Chang is not qualified, and his Spanish, at best, is mediocre. Later in Season 1, viewers learn that an unemployed and penniless Chang had approached Dean Pelton for a job at Greendale with the hopes that no one, including Pelton, would question his qualifications. Chang unrepentantly confesses to Jeff Winger, "So I did what anyone would do, fake my way into a job as a Spanish teacher at a community college, relying on phrases from *Sesame Street*" ("English as a Second Language," Episode 1.24). At any other institution, Chang would have likely failed in obtaining the job, but because of Dean Pelton's determination to show his colorblindness and his overwhelming fear of being sued, it worked—Chang was hired on the spot.

In the same episode, Dean Pelton admits that he did not want to question Chang's qualifications, alluding to the fact he did not want to appear racist, which is common belief underlying colorblindness: if one is colorblind, one cannot be a racist. Apfelbaum, Norton, and Sommers write, "The logic underlying the belief that color blindness can prevent prejudice and discrimination is straightforward: If people or institutions do not even notice race, then they cannot act in a racially biased manner" (205). Pelton does not want people, including Chang, to think he was questioning Chang's qualifications because he is Chinese. He wants everyone to know that he believes a Chinese man could speak and hence be qualified to teach Spanish. It is possible, of course, for a Chinese man, or woman for that fact, to speak fluent Spanish, but it is also reasonable for an employer to verify that employees, regardless of their race, can speak the language they are contracted to teach.

In Pelton's attempt to be inclusive, to be colorblind, he fails to do something expected in any basic job search: check the candidate's qualifications and references. After learning Chang is a fraud, Dean Pelton proclaims to several students, "Word of advice: If an Asian man says he's a Spanish teacher, it's not racist to ask for proof" ("English as a Second Language," Episode 1.24). Although Pelton's misguided and colorblind behavior was not directed towards his students, his students still implicitly paid the price. After a substitute instructor, an instructor who was actually qualified, took over for Chang, the students were forced to teach themselves almost a full year's worth of Spanish to be able to pass and obtain credit for the course, a general education requirement at Greendale.

Viewers often witness Pelton's obsession with proving he is not racist. In one episode, after stereotyping an entire faction of the student body, Dean Pelton immediately backtracks—worried his biases may be exposed. He exasperatedly utters, "Jeffrey, I am the least racist person in the world. My best friend, when I was six years old, was a black man" ("Investigative Journalism," Episode 1.13). Time and time again, the Dean looks and sounds ridiculous when any mention of race is brought up. In both cases outlined above, despite his best intentions, his behavior causes more detriment to his campus than good.

Minimization of Racism

The second framework is the minimization of racism, which, according to Bonilla-Silva, assumes that racism is no longer a problem in the United States and that the playing field for everyone is equal to near equal (43). Neville et al.

write, "In an ideal world, it would be desirous if race did not matter and that all were treated equally as human beings. Unfortunately, the reality is that the U.S. is a racially stratified society in which racism exists on many levels, including individual and institutional" (237). Because of the material gain of some black Americans, however, many are under the false impression that race is no longer an issue and that the "racial playing field has been leveled and that the pre–civil rights injustices and inequities no longer interfere with African American progress" (Hooks and Miskovic 194).

Based on his study, Bonilla-Silva discovers that many white respondents, however, "believe discrimination has all but disappeared, whereas blacks believe that discrimination — old and new — is alive and well" (43). Denying the existence of racism makes it difficult for people experiencing discrimination to speak up and get help. When people argue they do not see color and/or race, they ignore or minimize the lived experience of others, which hinders racial equality. This is especially problematic if people in administrative positions, like Dean Pelton, prescribe to this line of thinking. Bonilla-Silva and David Dietrich write, "Since most whites, [...] believe discrimination has all but disappeared, they regard minorities' claims of discrimination as excused or as minorities playing the infamous 'race card'" (194).

In some instances, when a discussion on anti-discrimination policies occurs, some, rather than simply minimizing race, may even argue that the policies in place discriminate against the majority, i.e. reverse discrimination. Marianne Modica states, "When discussing affirmative action policies a common belief expressed by Whites is that people of color have been permitted to progress unfairly at the expense of harder working Whites. Through this discourse, Whites portray themselves as victims to a political process that ignores individual responsibility and caters to people of color" (38).

In *Community*, we see Dean Pelton time and time again revert back to this framework when he creates an ethnically neutral mascot, becomes overcome with giddiness when he sees a multicultural study group in the library, and creates a ridiculous new mascot for the holiday season: the non-denominational Mr. Winter. At one point, he actually chastises students for participating in an event that celebrates their own heritage. When he notices German students attending an Oktoberfest celebration, he states, "But you were the only German students celebrating German culture, and here at Greendale that is a big, fat no-no. We frown at anyone celebrating their own cultural heritage[...]. It's why I keep a detailed list of every student's race and nationality — to prevent racism and nationalism" ("Alternative History of the German Invasion," Episode 4.4). The students, of course, are shocked.

In "Football, Feminism and You" (Episode 1.6) Pelton, with the help of Pierce Hawthorne, played by Chevy Chase, goes to great lengths to create an ethnically neutral mascot for the school, appropriately called the Greendale "Human Being." This is an ironic marriage of minds, considering Hawthorne, not Pelton, is likely to be identified as the racist in the series. He is overtly racist, unlike Pelton, calling his friend a "Jew" and "Jewie" ("Comparative Religion," Episode 1.12). In a different episode, Hawthorne assumes his other friend's ex-husband, who happens to be black, is a janitor in the cafeteria and only there to collect his tray ("Asian Population Studies," Episode 2.12). It has been rumored that this overtly racist behavior bothers Chase and is one reason why he wants to leave the show. In 2013, Chase reportedly used a racial slur on set to protest his character's racist behavior because he was becoming "more and more unsettled with the direction of his character" (Lombardi).

Back to the episode under examination, Pelton and Hawthorne spend the majority of the episode studying different physical attributes, attempting to devise a mascot that has, according to Pelton, "no stereotypical identifiers from any race or gender." At one point in the episode, viewers see a wall of eyes, noses, lips, chins, and skin colors, etc. Under each body part, there is a label: the name of the race each part/skin color represents. Pelton, despite good intensions, proudly shows off his human skin color wheel and states, "That is our human color wheel. It goes from Seal to Seal's teeth." It is the Dean's goal to avoid using any of these attributes or skin colors.

After a few attempts, Pelton finishes the new mascot. When he introduces the mascot to the student body, he happily and naively declares he has "solved racism." The episode ends with him brainstorming with Hawthorne what injustice or inequality they will tackle — and eliminate — next. His ignorance is only reaffirmed when he proudly announces he is ready to move on to his next cause: helping "Albino little people." Suggesting that he has "solved racism," and will solve any discrimination against any others groups, is, of course, ludicrous. By insisting racism is no longer an issue on campus, it unfortunately shuts down any additional conversations on the subject — which is detrimental to student life and employee satisfaction.

Edward Taylor argues, "By insisting on a rhetoric that disallows reference to race, blacks can no longer name their reality or point out racism" (184). It can be argued that the Dean had good intentions. He originally was going to choose an animal as their mascot, a common selection for colleges, but he ultimately decides that a human mascot is what the students and campus deserve. Pelton explains his rationale: "It was the Greendale Grizzlies, but I thought that a lot of these students have been called animals their whole lives." Regardless of what the viewer thinks of this statement, this statement does show his intensions may not have been all that bad. Unfortunately, his intensions still have problematic consequences. By creating an ethnically neutral mascot and solving racism, he eliminates any discussion on race — and fails to recognize that some people are proud of their features, including those associated with their race.

After Pelton introduces the mascot, it is clear many students find the mascot not inclusive or welcoming — but rather creepy. The Greendale Human Being is far from human; the mascot is someone in an ambiguous head-to-toe gray spandex suit. When Greendale student Jeff Winger first views the ethnically neutral mascot, he looks at Dean Pelton and quips, "I think not being racist is the new racism." Winger is right to question Pelton. Ulluci and Battey write, "Teachers cannot see racial inequities if they position race as insignificant in schooling and see racism as a historical artifact" (1196). Because Pelton assumes that racism is no longer an issue because of one mascot, the Greendale Human Being is an example of the minimization of racism. At the end of the episode, Dean Pelton proudly proclaims all problems solved. While racially charged mascots are no doubt offensive and their use should be questioned and scrutinized, eliminating any discussion or evidence of racial differences is not necessarily a good idea either.

Several studies have been done on student perceptions of racially charged mascots. While some students and sports fans argue that American Indian mascots, for example, are honoring the traditions of American Indians, it has been found in several studies that these mascots create a hostile learning environment. These mascots are said to impose racialized stereotypes on American Indian students, stereotypes that, according to Ellen J. Staurowsky "far outnumber them in the higher education landscape" (66). One other study, however, found that students can benefit from a discussion surrounding racial differences, stereotypes, and their school mascot.

Even though Greendale did not have a racially charged mascot, students would have likely benefited from being part of the creation of a new one. Neville et al. write:

> Given that there were limited racial differences in students' perception of the Chief, it seems that all students regardless of racial and ethnical background can benefit from interventions of designed to heighten critical awareness about the existence and consequences of racial discrimination, as these interventions have been show to decrease CBR [248].

Dean Pelton could have asked Greendale students to participate in the creation; he could have held open forums or even asked students to submit their own ideas. By doing so, he would have encouraged a dialogue on race relations on campus and hopefully decreased colorblindness in his students.

In the same episode, the Dean is also creating new marketing materials for the school. When drafting these materials, he makes sure a variety of races are represented. While this suggests a more multicultural approach to running the campus, the Dean, as soon as he spies a group of Greendale students studying at the library, exclaims, "Well, look at this group having some meetings and being so diverse. There is just, boy! There is just one of every kind of you, isn't there?" He is giddy from what he sees — the group's presence is affirmation to him that there are no racial boundaries at Greendale, and at that, race is irrelevant.

Ferber argues that CBRI can also be used to analyze and categorize other areas of discrimination — not just race. She writes, "[T]he belief that legal obstacles to equality have been removed and everyone has equal opportunities to succeed, is used to justify not only race, but gender and religious inequality, which is rearticulated as the product of the poor choices of individuals, rather than a systematic issue" (74). In the case of *Community*, CBRI can be applied to religious inequality as well. In a later episode, viewers see Dean Pelton dressed in what looks like an aqua-colored wizard costume. It is not Halloween, however; it is December. Pelton is dressed up as the character, the non-denominational Mr. Winter, another mascot he created for the holiday season, his own version of Santa Claus ("Comparative Religion," Episode 1.12). He proudly proclaims over the school's intercom, "Is that the tippy-tappy of secular boots on the roof? Oh, well, it must be yet another sign that it 'tis the season because rumor has it that non-denominational Mr. Winter is on his way to the student lounge." This immediately infuriates student Shirley Bennett, who is a devout Catholic. Her dismay, however, does not matter to the Dean who happily skips around campus wishing everyone a "Happy Merry." By suggesting that race, or in the case above, religion, does not exist, Dean Pelton continues to minimize the lived experiences of his students. This is not the first time Pelton has been insensitive to the history of an entire religion or race. In a second season episode, Pelton proclaims, "I didn't even know there was a difference between North and South Korean barbeque. I mean M.A.S.H lasted longer than that war, you know, get over it. Am I right?" ("Applied Anthropology and Culinary Arts," Episode 2.22). For many students, their religion and race, and the history of their religion and race, are substantial parts of who they are. To have both dismissed, to say the least, is disheartening.

Naturalization and Cultural Racism

According to Bonilla-Silva, the third CBRI framework is naturalization, which "is a frame that allows whites to explain racial phenomena by suggesting they are natural occurrences" (28). Naturalization suggests that people prefer segregation because people "gravitate toward likeness" (28). In his study, Bonilla-Silva discovered that nearly 50 percent of respondents use this frame to explain limited contact between races (37). In addition, it is used to explain behavior that might be perceived as racist (preference of whites as friends or partners) or racially motivated (residential or school segregation) (37). While the main study group composed of six Greendale students is a very diverse group, Pelton, on many instances, believes that many students prefer to associate with people of their own race. For example, in one episode, Pelton assumes that all African-American students would be interested in seeing an African-American artist perform on campus. In many instances, such as this one, Pelton assumes that the African-American students on his campus group together naturally — because they all must have the same interests.

In addition to naturalization, Bonilla-Silva introduces one final framework that overlaps with the naturalization framework: cultural racism. Cultural racism uses culture to frame arguments that explain the standing of minorities in society (28). Bonilla-Silva provides several common arguments used in this frame. For example, people might state, "Mexicans do not put much emphasis on education" or that "blacks have too many babies" (28). In one episode, "Investigative Journalism" (Episode 1.13) Annie Edison, investigates a text message that was sent to all black students and one French exchange student named LeBron. The text message contained information regarding the start time of an on-campus concert. The headliner for the concert was Toni Braxton, a popular black R&B artist of the 1990s. Edison wondered why all students were not notified and why only black students were. After researching, Edison realizes the text message was sent from Pelton. When she questions him, he nervously states, "I'm not racist. I had twenty minutes to let people know that Toni Braxton was starting early and 273 text messages left before my rates tripled. Racial profiling may not be right, but it can be economical."

In the case of the concert, Dean Pelton assumed that the group of people most interested in attending the concert consisted of African American students because Braxton is black and sings in a genre known for black artists and fans. Even though early in the season he noted the diversity in the show's main characters, the study group, he still assumed that all the black students on campus would have the same interests and want to go to see Toni Braxton. He also assumed they would all want to hang out together. That is what is natural to him. Again, much like other instances, his behavior is detrimental to the students and the overall campus environment. He failed to inform everyone of a free campus event — an event that may have been attended and enjoyed by many — because of his behavior that can best be described as naturalization.

Conclusion

As I have demonstrated with various examples, Pelton is a unique administrator. In some episodes, we see a kind, caring man who simply wants what is best for his students. When closely examining his behavior, however, we see an administrator often careless and reckless with the power associated with his position. We see an administrator who is quick to make decisions although many times those decisions are inappropriate. Dean Pelton is known for making quick decisions, and although he thinks he is doing the right thing, his decisions are often discriminatory. In addition to not carefully examining his options when dealing with campus concerns, Pelton repeatedly ignores the lived experiences of a huge number of his students by denying any discussions on race, religion, or gender. At one point in the series, Shirley, a black Baptist student, proclaims, "I am so sick of the Dean jamming his P.C.-ness down my throat" ("Comparative Religion"). While Pelton may *think* he is being inclusive by arguing that race, religion, or gender does not exist on campus, or rather that it is irrelevant, he is actually causing more frustration because he is denying students their reality. If his behavior continues, a viewer must wonder if Greendale will be left to the same fate as the other institutions where Pelton has worked. Despite his desire to be progressive and inclusive, his racist behavior, as shown in this essay, is often detrimental to his institution. In his attempt to build and lead an open-minded community college, he actually manages to stifle diversity by subscribing to Bonilla-Silva's four frameworks of colorblindness: abstract liberalism, naturalization, cultural racism, and minimization of racism. The Dean's behavior is a reminder for all — especially for people working in higher education — that it is important to remain vigilant against racism as it still exists today.

Works Cited

"Alternative History of the German Invasion." *Community.* NBC. 28 February 2013.
Apfelbaum, Evan P., Michael I. Norton, and Samuel R. Sommers. "Racial Color Blindness: Emergence, Practice, and Implications." *Psychological Science* 21.3 (2012): 205–209.
"Applied Anthropology and Culinary Arts." *Community.* NBC. 28 April 2011.
"Asian Population Studies." *Community.* NBC. 20 January 2011.
Bonilla-Silva, Eduardo. *Racism without Racists: Color-Blind Racism & Racial Inequality in Contemporary America.* 3d ed. Lanham, MD: Rowman and Littlefield, 2010.
____, and David Dietrich. "The Sweet Enhancement of Color-Blind Racism in Obamaerica." *The ANNALS of the American Academy of Political and Social Science* 63.4 (2011): 190–206.
"Comparative Religion." *Community.* NBC. 10 December 2009.
"Dean Pelton's 'Office Hours': 'Community' Favorite Gets His Own Web Series!" *Huffington Post.* TheHuffingtonPost.com, 25 April 2011. Web. 5 February 2013.
"Digital Exploration of Interior Design." *Community.* NBC. 29 March 2012.
"English as a Second Language. *Community.* NBC. 18 May 2010.
Ferber, Abby. "The Culture of Privilege: Color-Blindness, Postfeminism, and Christonormativity." *Journal of Social Issues* 68.1 (2012): 63–77.
"A Fistful of Paintballs." *Community.* NBC. 5 May 2011.
"Football, Feminism and You." *Community.* NBC. 22 October 2009.
"For a Few Paintballs More." *Community.* NBC. 12 May 2011.
Hooks, Debra S., and Maja Miskovic. Race and Racial Ideology in Classroom Through Teachers' and Students' Voices." *Race Ethnicity and Education* 14.2 (2011): 191–207.
"Interpretive Dance." *Community.* NBC. 21 January 2010.
"Investigative Journalism." *Community.* NBC. 14 January 2010.

Lombardi, Ken. "Chevy Chase Used Racial Slur on 'Community' Set, Says Joel McHale." *Cbsnews.com.* CBS News, 7 February 2013. Web. 26 March 2013.
"Modern Warfare." *Community.* NBC. 6 May 2010.
Modica, Marianne. "Constructions of Race Among Religiously Conservative College Students." *Multicultural Perspectives* 14.1 (2012): 38.43.
Neville, Helen A., Jeffrey G. Yeung, Nathan R. Todd, Lisa B. Spanierman, and Tamilia D. Reed. "Color-Blind Racial Ideology and Beliefs about a Racialized University Mascot." *Journal of Diversity in Education* 4.4 (2011): 236–249.
Omi, Michael, and Howard Winant. "Thinking through Race and Racism." *Contemporary Sociology* 38.2 (2009): 121–125.
"Politics of Human Sexuality." *Community.* NBC. 3 December 2009.
Rosenberg, Pearl M. "Colorblindness in Teacher Education: An Optical Delusion." *Off White: Readings on Power, Privilege, and Resistance.* Eds. Michelle Fine, Louis Weis, Linda Powell Pruitt, and April Burns. New York: Routledge, 2004. 257–272.
Staurowsky, Ellen J. "'You Know, We Are All Indian': Exploring White Power and Privilege in Reactions to the NCAA Native American Mascot Policy." *Journal of Sports & Social Issues* 31.1 (2007): 61–76.
Taylor, Edward. "Critical Race Theory and Interest Convergence in the Desegregation of Higher Education." *Race is ... Race Isn't: Critical Race Theory and Qualitative Studies in Education.* Eds. Laurence Parker, Donna Deyhle, and Sofia Villenas. Boulder, CO: Westview, 1999. 181–204.
Ullucci, Kerri, and Dan Battey. "Exposing Color Blindness/Grounding in Color Consciousness: Challenges for Teacher Education." *Urban Education* 46.9 (2011): 1195–1225.

Parody as Civic Discourse in "Basic Lupine Urology": The *Law and Order* Episode

Jeremy W. Cook and *Robin M. Murphy*

> In the criminal justice system, the people are represented by two separate, yet equally important groups: the police, who investigate crime, and the district attorneys, who prosecute the offenders. These are their stories. — Voiceover from the opening segment of *Law and Order* (1990–2010)

"*Law & Order* (is) the longest running crime series and the second longest-running drama series in the history of American broadcast television.... The series has also turned into one of entertainment's preeminent brands using a distinct ripped from the headlines format" ("Law and Order Show Summary"). Its 20 consecutive seasons spawned four spinoffs — *Law & Order: Special Victims Unit* (1999–), *Law & Order: Criminal Intent* (2001–2011), *Crime & Punishment* (2002–2004), and *Law & Order: Trial by Jury* (2005–2006), which all follow the *Law and Order* formula — as well as video games, television movies, and foreign language versions. It is likely the crimes that were "ripped from the headlines" kept the show going for 20 years. The viewing audience wants to relate to the detectives investigation of the crimes and the way the criminal is prosecuted in court because the television crimes are similar to what is happening in real life. The audience can use the show to imagine that is what was happening in the real investigations and real courtrooms, and in a way, making them more engaged, critical citizens through their participation as viewers. Now, with even more access to up to moment media, many viewers and therefore citizens desire this participation even more.

The *Law and Order* formula is an easy-to-follow pattern of behaviors that makes the viewing audience comfortable because while they might not know the outcome of the episode, they know the pattern of events that will lead to the unveiling of the outcome. The *Law and Order* formula is so ingrained into the series that occasional episodes that went away from the formula were noticed much more by than the majority of episodes that followed the formula. The main characters of *Law and Order* continually changed over the course of the 20-year run, yet due to the nature of the formula, and the fact that the show continued to stick to the formula, the show maintained its success. Chuck Barney refers to the *Law and Order* formula as "the greatest programming concept we've seen." Regardless of the stars or the crime, the fans of the show could always rest comfortably in the knowledge that the show would continue to deliver the same satisfying entertainment week after week.

That being said, *Community* is almost the complete opposite. Whereas *Law and Order* lasted 20 seasons with multiple cast and star changes and high ratings throughout that run, *Community* is currently in its fourth season, has essentially maintained the same cast, and has struggled for its existence due to lackluster ratings. While *Law and Order* maintained success throughout its run due to the formula and the similar pattern of events, *Community* is a character driven show that does not follow any pattern of events from episode to episode. In fact, in an article on the AV Club entertainment website, Steven Hyden states that the creator of the show, Dan Harmon stressed "the creative process behind the writing, [saying] that he had to write the show as if it were a movie, not a sitcom" thus emphasizing uniqueness of the show and how it cannot be viewed in the same manner as other, more traditional, sitcoms.

According to *Entertainment Weekly*, *Community* ranks as the number 16 show in the list of 26 best cult shows ever, describing it as follows:

> Technically it's about a group of oddball community-college students who form a study group. But it's actually about seven unlikely friends — helmed by cocky ex-lawyer Jeff Winger (Joel McHale) — who spend their time paintballing, pillow-fighting, parodying movies (and basically anything else you can imagine), and occasionally exchanging longing romantic glances [Naoreen].

Despite its cult status, and the enthusiastic following of the show, *Community*'s ratings have remained low. It is easy to attribute the low ratings to the meta-humor (in jokes) and lack of a pattern (formula) to which people who follow closely can become attached, but the casual fan does not. In fact, "[t]he series' affinity for ambitious, high-concept story lines (how many shows do you watch that are willing to turn over an entire episode to stop-motion animation?), meta humor, and constant pop culture allusions has helped it earn the kind of fervent fan following some of its higher-rated comedic competitors must envy" (Naoreen).

Community strays from conventional sitcom formulas and drifts into various forms of parody and meta-humor that, for those not indoctrinated into the long running themes, can possibly become disenfranchised. While the show as a whole does not stick to any particular formula, its writers have used the stringent *Law and Order* structure as the basis of its parody in the episode "Basic Lupine Urology." However, to be able to understand the critical nature of the parody in the episode, one must first understand the *Law and Order* formula.

The *Law and Order* series has a real-life feel that makes it relatable. The audience feels like they are getting an inside view into the workings of "Law" and "Order" week by week with the same formula. Because it examines crime and justice from a dualistic perspective, the show is essentially divided into two separate halves. It is described on the Internet Movie Database as follows: "The show follows a crime, usually adapted from current headlines, from two separate vantage points. The first half of the show concentrates on the investigation of the crime by the police, the second half follows the prosecution of the crime in court" (Law and Order (1990–2010). If one looks at the opening voiceover, they will see that it clearly describes the premise of the show which is the basic formula of each episode being divided into two halves — "Law" and "Order."

The early section and segments of the show comprise the "Law" segment for which the episode shows the crime or the event that could be a crime; they establish the possible motive and begin the investigation of the suspects. The crime, or what could appear to be a crime, happens in one of the early scenes, if not the very first scene of the episode. Once the audience sees the crime or the event that could be a crime, they observe an investigation by two New York City detectives, and their boss, whom they bring in occasionally to decide the direction of their investigations. The investigation usually contains the typical television crime drama fare of gathering clues, talking to witnesses, establishing whether a crime had occurred or whether the occurrence was accidental or natural. The episodes usually progress in short segments and clips with one piece of the investigation leading to more pieces, as more witnesses are interviewed and more information is made known to the television police and the audience. Once the case is established, after all of these pieces lead to enough evidence to prosecute the potential crime, the episode moves from the "Law" section to the "Order" section. This usually occurs about midway through the episode when the District Attorneys appear and handle the prosecution segments of the episode. It is more or less a part of the episode that segues between the "Law" and "Order" segments.

In the "Order" section of the episode, the case is given over to the District Attorneys for prosecution. They continue the legal process of gathering information and following up on information that the detectives have given to them. Important information for the case can continue to be revealed in the "Law" segment. Much, but not all, of this section of the episode occurs in the courtroom, where the prosecution plays out. The episode continues to progress in short segments and clips, dispensing portions of information to fill in information gaps that the officers or attorneys, and also obviously the audience, might have. The "Order" section is told from the prosecutions point of view. This is when the courtroom drama occurs and, as it occurs in real life, sometimes characters who appear to be clearly guilty are acquitted and released. After reading the verdict, the episode usually ends in the District Attorney's office where the characters discuss and summarize the events of the courtroom and thereby discuss and summarize the episode. The vast majority of episodes fit this pattern and formula of events for both the "Law" section and the "Order" section.

As the cliché goes, "Parody is the sincerest form of flattery," which is what *Community* does best. Arguably, one of *Community*'s finest 22 minutes is "Basic Lupine Urology," a perfect parody of pastiche and burlesque, which follows the *Law and Order* formula so closely that it bests the original series and results in bricolage or gives *Community* a new, more critical identity than the meta-humor it is known for by its cult following.

Though satirical, the "Lupine" episode targets the audience as participatory and asks them to engage critically in the procedures of the law enforcement community via the "Law and Order" formula. In that way, John Locke's theory of civic (rhetorical) discourse, which centers on the idea that communication should be for the benefit of the audience and for the public good, is applicable here as a lens to reveal the episode's critical inner workings.

In Locke's theory of civic discourse in "An Essay Concerning Human Understanding," he claims that communication is for civil and philosophical means. He states, "First, by their civil use, I mean such a communication of thoughts and ideas by words, as may serve for the upholding common conversation and commerce, about the ordinary affairs and conveniences of civil life, in the societies of men, one amongst another" (Book II, Chapter IX). This idea applies to the episode's critical shift in identity through its ability to communicate to a different audience than its cult following — the drama's audience — through the *Law and Order* formula as a commonplace. However, by using the burlesque here, the episode is able to keep its own audience, too, while appealing to the sensibilities of the fans of the drama. This complicates the role of *Community* as a sitcom and more firmly places it in the rhetorical situation of cult classic. According to Locke's theory of communication by philosophical means, words "serve to convey the precise notions of things, and to express in general propositions certain and undoubted truths, which the mind may rest upon and be satisfied with in its search after true knowledge" (Book II, Chapter IX). The episode uses the *Law and Order* formula as the "undoubted truth" as its basis to build its discourse community and include the drama fans. By doing so, it asks its cult fans to critically engage in the sitcom in a different way than its usual parodic content; it asks them to participate with law procedure, like the drama fans, pursuant to the *Law and Order* formula.

Whereas Locke's theory of communication serves as a lens to point out how the episode uses parody to place itself in the larger echelon of cult classic, one must also examine the smaller details within the episode to be able to confirm this. This is where symbolic interaction, a micro-sociological theory that examines the words and actions of the individual instead of the larger groups in society as its foundation, is helpful. According to sociologist Jon M. Shepard, Symbolic Interactionism is "the theoretical perspective that focuses on interaction among people based on mutually understood symbols" (24). One of the founding fathers of symbolic interaction theory, George Herbert Mead, developed the idea that the concept of self, one's personal identity, comes out of the social interactions that that person takes, is the cornerstone of the symbolic interactionist philosophy (Cronk). Mead called this idea, "social behaviorism," which was later coined as "symbolic interactionism" by his former students and colleagues. It was Mead's thought that the self, or what can be called the development of the person's own individuality, of a person develops out of the social interaction that the person has with other people. The self is an emerging process. It is constantly changing and evolving to suit the needs of the person (Cronk). The use of language is one of the easiest and most common mutually understood symbols that people use to interact and develop their concept of their "self" (Cronk). Therefore, combining Mead with Locke through theories of communication makes sense in this case.

The use of language is a key element in the structure of societies. Mead says, "Human society, then, is dependent upon the development of language for its own distinctive form of organization" (235). A society is "a group of human beings broadly distinguished from other groups by mutual interests, participation in characteristic relationships, shared institutions, and a common culture" (The Free Dictionary). Using this definition, one can see that community colleges and the students who attend like them are societies unto themselves. Because community colleges can be defined as societies unto themselves, Mead's concept that the behavior of individuals can only be examined when examining the behavior of the society in which that individual is a member is easily adapted to the study of community colleges. They shape the communication, learning, thinking, and behaviors of the students who attend the community college. The uniqueness of this particular society and how it affects the behaviors and development of the self of the students is on display throughout the entire series but none so more than in "Basic Lupine Urology." So, though the episode is in itself a parody of *Law and Order* since the sitcom's success is based on a particular subgroup of community college students, the characters never truly stop communicating who they are in this episode.

The importance of the use of language, considered a mutually understood symbol, is the foundation of symbolic interactionism. Therefore, to ensure that the language used within this analysis is mutually understood and for the purposes of the following analysis of the "Lupine" episode, we define these terms in the following way:

> *pastiche*—a stylistic imitation (Merriam Webster) and in this case, "Basic Lupine Urology" follows the *Law and Order* formula;
> *burlesque*—a literary, dramatic or musical work intended to cause laughter by caricaturing the manner or spirit of serious works (Oxford English Dictionary);
> *mimic*—to ridicule by imitation (Oxford English Dictionary);
> *bricolage*—though usually used to mean the processes by which people acquire objects from across social divisions to create new cultural identities (Wikipedia), in this case, the episode acquires the *Law and Order* formula to create a more complicated TV identity;
> *meme*—a unit for carrying cultural ideas, symbols, or practices (Wikipedia) and in this case, the *Law and Order* formula is so engrained in the show's success and audience, *Community* is able to use it in the form of a meme.

"Basic Lupine Urology" begins as burlesque from the title itself. A scoff of mimicry at both the producer of *Law and Order* Dick Wolf's name and product, this title promises to follow Wolf's (lupine) "piss" (urology) of a formula. And, as Mead stated, "It is important to recognize that that to which the word refers is something that can lie in the experience of the individual without the use of language itself. Language does pick out and organize this content in experience. It is an implement for that purpose" (13). Therefore, the title of this episode itself clearly demonstrates the goal of mocking the *Law and Order* formula established by Dick Wolf.

The episode opens with its own mantra, just like all *Law and Order* episodes: "Greendale Community College is represented by two separate yet equally important groups of people: the goofballs that run around stirring up trouble and the eggheads that make a big deal out of it. These are their stories." And so begins the caricature of the *Law and Order* series.

Next, the opening sequence shows the characters of *Community* of actors as shown as in the formula. The opening for *Law and Order* features a black background with the outlines of the letters for "Law & Order" fading in. With "Law &" on top, the letters are highlighted with blue; "Order" on the bottom is highlighted in red. The *Community* version is quite similar: the same black background with the word, "Community" outlined in white letters while "Comm" is highlighted in blue and "unity" is highlighted in red. Along with the gaze of the camera, these are all true to the formula. The looks on the actors' faces, trying to mimic the formula, however, adds to the burlesque. The opening scene is spot on; we see two janitors enter a classroom, talking about an innocuous subject, and then one of them notices the crime scene: a yam in a biology experiment has been "murdered." Cut to the next scene, and Ben Chang, the community college's ex–Spanish-teacher-turned-security-guard is putting up yellow crime scene tape and says, "Move along, nothing to see here." Jeff Winger remarks: "First time those words have actually been true." All of this fits the formula with the classic pastiche style of *Community*, interwoven to also stay true to its firm place in the sitcom genre.

Our favorite study group has been growing a yam for biology class. Naturally, the group's overachiever, Annie Edison, is concerned about her grade. It is midnight and she has called in to the crime scene the biology professor Marshall Kane and Jeff, who is also in her group and acts as the group's leader and spokesperson in numerous cases. The scene is strictly *Law and Order* formula; the banter, typical *Community*:

> JEFF: She got me here on a very misleading text message.
> ANNIE: Jeff, technically you *are* about be screwed in the biology room, because our final project has been destroyed.

Jeff responds to the whole scene by texting. And, after telling Annie she needs to prove her hypothesis that the yam was purposely destroyed, the professor says, "Now, if you'll excuse me, I was watching *Mama's Family*." At this point, the *Community* characters are playing themselves: Annie and Jeff's innuendo, Annie's anxiety for her grade, Jeff texting on his phone, seemingly unattached from the others, and the professor's annoyance at being bothered.

In this short scene, we are not only shown the *Community* characters, but we begin to see which *Law and Order* characters they will become. The voiceover mimics the original; the opening sequence of characters is a perfect parody; the crime scene is discovered; the "Law" section of the formula is set. Therefore, a strong pastiche style is evident from the first scene. As indicated in the following analysis, the civic engagement portion of Locke's communication theory becomes important to understanding our argument of language acting as a venue to search for the "true knowledge" of what happened at the crime scene.

Shirley Bennett, Troy Barnes and Abed Nadir enter the scene and the *Community* characters take on even more of the *Law and Order* characteristics. Annie asks Shirley to head the investigation and because of her experience from watching crime shows when she is bored, she assumes the *Law and Order* role of Chief of Police immediately: "You boys canvass for witnesses, establish a time frame and motive, and bring me a suspect. You've got 48 hours before the trail runs cold, so start with the last person to see that yam alive." Then, to herself, she mutters, "It was a long 15 years."

By viewing Shirley's dialogue through the lens of Locke's civic means of communication theory, the *Community* audience is shown the thoughts and ideas of the *Law and Order* formula by words, not just scenes and actions. The audience recognizes the crime drama tenets in Shirley's familiar dialogue, which she has acquired by watching crime drama herself: "canvass for witnesses, establish a time frame and motive, suspect, 48 hours, trail runs cold"—all of this vernacular is specific to the crime drama and concretely places the "Lupine" episode as meme based on language use alone. At the same time in symbolic interactionism, "language, as we have seen, is communication via 'significant symbols,' and it is through significant communication that the individual is able to take the attitudes of others toward herself. Language is not only a 'necessary mechanism' of mind, but also the primary social foundation of the self" (Mead 10). Furthermore, Locke's philosophical means, though loosely, easily fits here since Shirley's dialogue "conveys the precise notions of things, and to express in general propositions certain and undoubted truths" of the *Law and Order* formula.

The rest of the "Law" half of the episode masterfully mimics the formula's structure. Troy and Abed, when searching for Pierce Hawthorne, find him leading a betting ring for old-men arm wrestling. When questioned about his competence in watering the yam, he admits he could not even get in the door of the lab to damage the yam. "Okay. Whoa. I had nothing to do with that." When pushed by Abed about where he was when the crime was committed, Pierce admits, "I was asleep in a sunbeam." This scene shows (besides Pierce's typical strange behavior) not just a simple matter of *what* language is used, but *how*, such as the context. The way that the language is used makes it a mutually understood symbol within the context of the "Lupine" episode and the "Law and Order" formula.

With Troy's collaboration, they release Pierce as a suspect and move on through the formula in the same way. They interview witnesses, a "sting," a "chase scene" with Star-Burns, a classmate, through the college halls, and as Bill Wyman writes, "Along the way, no one pretends to be anything but what they are. Says Troy when he captures a suspect: 'You have the right to do whatever you want. Nothing you say or do can be used against you by anyone, but we'd really like it if you'd come with us.'" This is a purposefully obvious allusion to the standard chase scenes used not only in *Law and Order*, but in all classic "cop shows." Additionally, Troy imitates the officers' mantra in *Law and Order* when they capture and arrest a suspect, read the suspect their Miranda Rights, and inform the suspect of their right to remain silent. Because this is not a real criminal investigation, and Troy is not a real police officer, but a character on a TV show playing a parodic role from yet another TV show, in burlesque style, he reads his "polite" rendition of the Miranda Rights.

One scene shows Britta Perry sitting at a computer, apparently the IT cop character of the formula, showing Abed, Shirley, and Troy how she can use an app to change a downloaded photograph. When she starts to talk about her Psychology major as a helpful tool in the investigation, however, all of them walk away and the music indicates a scene change. Wyman adds, "There's a brilliant throwaway scene in the school office, with Fat Neil pointlessly moving file folders around as he carelessly delivers his lines — itself a small masterpiece of mimicry." This mix provides a perfect bricolage of the *Law and Order, Community*-fied, which not only complicates the formula for the *Community* audience, who expects the weekly high-end parody, but also complicates the identity of the sitcom formula itself.

Take, for instance, Star-Burns' interrogation scene which takes place in a storage room: Star-Burns says, "You got nothing on me," which is typical "criminal" dialogue true to the formula; however, that line ends with "and I don't have to stay here because you're not cops." Then, there is a knock on an empty fish tank on a shelf nearby that provides a brilliant burlesque moment by symbolizing the one way window in an interrogation room. Troy and Abed go to the other side of the shelf, where Shirley is waiting for them. She says, "He's right." And as more discussion follows, Star-Burns says, "I can both see and hear you."

This scene is a perfect example of how the formula remains true, yet pastiche, and though the dialogue is burlesque, it too stays on track with the typical content of an interrogation scene. The following autopsy scene also follows the formula: the "dead body" of the yam is on a dissecting tray while Troy and Abed ask the doctor typical questions about cause of death and the heinousness of the crime. The doctor responds like a coroner:

> DOCTOR: For a raw yam, you need more than gravity; you need a boot.

In response to violence of the yam's death, Troy makes a vomiting motion. In this instance, Troy is communicating a mutually understood symbol through body language. When he makes the motion, while it is not dialogue per se, he is still using symbolic communication in the burlesque manner yet progressing the episodic "Lupine" content and also the *Law and Order* formula itself.

The next sequence is when the episode moves from the "Law" section to "Order" of the formula. It begins in similar fashion to the how the original show transitions to the "Order" section. As the episode continues, the *Law and Order* formula is adhered to in a strict fashion, but the dialogue continues to be a bricolage of the formula and *Community*. A series of transition scenes are depicted where the episode transitions from the "Law" to the "Order" section. If an audience member did not understand the "language" or gestures (non-verbal) being communicated by these scenes, they would not know the show was transitioning. However, due to the "language" of the long-running structure of the formula, fans of the show understand the language and are able to comprehend the symbolic nature of the transition because "significant communication, as stated earlier, involves the comprehension of meaning, i.e., the taking of the attitude of others toward one's own gestures" (Mead 8). The first such scene is when we see the "detectives," Troy and Abed, with the "lawyers," Annie and Jeff, outside by a street hotdog vendor. The detectives know Star-Burns is guilty, but they do not have any evidence. Jeff encourages them to do anything necessary. Annie objects on the basis of ethics. This standard *Law and Order* scene of transition ends with typical *Law and Order* dialogue by Jeff: "It's too late to get compassionate. There's only time for justice."

The next transition scene shows a janitor opening Star-Burns' locker, a typical probable cause section of the sequence, but with a twist on the dialogue:

> JANITOR: I shouldn't be doing this. Are you sure you heard a kitten meowing?
> ABED: Not anymore. Hurry up.

This dialogue is, again, using language, a mutually understood symbol, within the "Lupine" episode to continue the burlesque theme of parody and meta-humor that is essential to *Community*, while at the same time expanding the targets being mimicked to the formula, and therefore fans of *Law and Order*.

Meanwhile, Star Burns shows up at his locker just when lab supplies fall out his locker, and he runs, instigating the chase scene, which ends with Troy and Abed "pinkie swearing" that they will not tell about the meth lab in Star-Burns' car trunk if he tells them whom he saw in the Biology lab with the yam.

The next scene is another transition segment when Todd Jamison is "arrested" by Troy and Abed. Todd is in a basket weaving class when Troy and Abed burst into the room, in a similar fashion to how the detectives from *Law and Order* burst into rooms to arrest the suspect. However, in this case, it is just two ordinary college students as opposed to authentic police who have the right to actually arrest anyone. The characters, and writers, acknowledge the satire of this situation when Troy offers this version of the Miranda Rights that have to be read whenever any suspect is arrested in reality:

> TROY: Todd Jamison, you have the right to do whatever you want. Nothing you say or do can be used against you by anyone, but we'd really like it if you came with us. Please and thank you.

At that point, Troy and Abed escort Todd out of the basket weaving class. The simple and understated fact that the suspect is sitting in a basket weaving class is the height of the type of humor that *Community* is demonstrating in this episode. In the colloquial language of college campuses, any time a student is discussing what they would call a "blow off" class, a class in which it is easy to make a good grade, the term usually applied to that class is "basket weaving." This class, a mimicry of the community college course offerings, also acts as a symbol or "something chosen to represent something else. It may be an object, a word, a gesture, a facial expression, or a sound. A symbol is something that is observable, something concrete" (Shepherd 24). Therefore, the class symbolizes the long-running joke that Greendale Community College is filled with easy classes that anyone can pass. Some of these blow-off classes include the following: Pottery Class ("Beginner Pottery," Episode 1.19); Pool Class ("Physical Education," Episode 1.17); Anthropology ("Paradigms of Human Memory," Episode 2.21); Conspiracy Theories in U.S. History ("Conspiracy Theories and Interior Design," Episode 2.9), and many more. While this joke about a "blow off" class is not directly referenced in the episode itself, similar to how the entire parody is not directly referenced, it clearly demonstrates the subtle humor of *Community* itself and the need for the audience to pay attention to the details throughout any episode of *Community*. Troy and Abed clearly represent and mimic the detectives in this scene, in a similar manner in the way that *Law and Order* has a duo of investigative detectives throughout its episodes, but the core humor of *Community* as a sitcom is not diminished as a result.

Once Todd is escorted out of the basket weaving class, the screen goes black as it does in all transitional scenes from *Law and Order*, and we hear what sounds like a gavel pounding. This sound symbolizes a clear-cut transition from the Law section to the Order section, as pounding gavels signify the beginning of trials. In this case, the gavel sound alerts the audience to the importance of the revelations about to be disclosed and demonstrates how the episode is transitioning from the "Law" portion to the "Order" portion of the show. The gavel sound is a mutually understood symbol that allows both the television characters and the viewing audience, as a community, to also transition to the courtroom and the events that will take place in the courtroom. It also helps keep the episode clearly on track with the formula.

When the show has transitioned from "Law" to "Order," a courtroom situation must be established. This occurs when Jeff and Annie, who clearly represent and mimic the prosecuting attorneys of this episode, convince their biology teacher and school dean that they have enough evidence, similar to the detectives gathering up enough evidence for an arrest and trial, to put Todd on "trial" and determine if he did indeed destroy their yam and as Jeff states, "steal" their grade.

During the initial court scene, Todd's uncle, Colonel Archwood, shows up to act as his lawyer who calls the whole process and the school ludicrous. The characters move to the professor's office (the judge's chambers) for a meeting. The scene is formulaic, the dialogue characteristic of *Law and Order*, with a few fallacies thrown in:

> JEFF: We agreed to withhold that information as part of a pinky-swear with the witness.
> COLONEL: Pinky-swear. This is ludicrous. This whole school is ludicrous. Who honors the pinky swear of a degenerate over the word of a decorated soldier?
> DEAN: I'm inclined to agree with the man in uniform.
> JEFF: Shocker.
> DEAN: Jeffrey, tell us what Star-Burns was doing in that classroom, or your group can take an F.
> PROFESSOR: Hold on, hold on, hold on. I grade my students. Now what Star-Burns was doing is irrelevant. What matters is what he saw. I'm upholding the pinky-swear.

It is clear in this scene that the *Community* characters are fully into their *Law and Order* roles. The dialogue resembles *Law and Order* in its structure, but the content is pastiche, and the bricolage of the characters is complete; they have become the *Law and Order* characters for all intents and purposes.

The courtroom scene in the Biology classroom continues, with Todd on the stand. The colonel asks him questions about his service and Annie cross-examines him:

> ANNIE: Is that why you hit your wife? Withdrawn!
> ANNIE: Is that why you smoke pot and pop pills? Withdrawn.
> ANNIE: Are you a virgin? Withdrawn.

Annie's perfect parody of saying something untrue and immaterial followed by a withdraw request indicates her transition into this character is complete. Jeff is not to be outdone when they return from another sidebar in the professor's office. He, in classic *Law and Order* fashion, saunters up to the front of the room and starts dropping the other yam projects on the floor. All of them mush on impact because, as Jeff deducted from Todd's burned hand, they were all subjected to boiling water, except one:

> JEFF: This yam isn't boiled. Vicki?
> VICKI: I didn't do it, I swear!

In an archetypal episode of *Law and Order* the accused on the stand is convicted due to the overwhelming evidence presented by the prosecutors, in a rare case the accused is not convicted, and they walk away, but in even more rare cases, a twist occurs unexpectedly. In the case of the "Basic Lupine Urology" episode of *Community,* a complete and total twist occurs when a "key character" who is not accused or questioned and is not even really a major presence in the episode, shockingly blurts out a confession which ends the court session:

> FAT NEIL: I boiled the yams! Vicki's yam never sprouted, and I didn't want her to fail, so I threw off the grading curve so she wouldn't have to go to summer school, and we can finally have sex in my parents' cabin. God forgive me, I did it for love!

Twist illuminated. Case closed in typical *Community* fashion. This is another example of how *Community* parodied the more unusual line of logic in the *Law and Order* formula by wrapping up the formulaic assault in a completely unexpected way with a character that seemed to be innocuous to the plot. The audience, in this case, is caught unexpected, as in *Law and Order,* but instead of being bothered at the shift, laughs at the ridiculous mimicry.

The closing scene wraps up the formula. Jeff, the dean, the professor, and Annie are all sitting around the Dean's desk, talking about the case outcome just like a regular *Law and Order* episode ending with the phone ringing with bad news about Star-Burns. It is then that the show breaks from the formula of *Law and Order* and concludes with the typical *Community* ending: Abed and Troy, in their bunk beds, at the college. Strange Dean-song later, proverbial curtain.

In the end, this episode is a criticism of a TV formula that "works" for the typical audience. It is clear that it follows the *Law and Order* formula in a burlesque fashion —filled with symbolism, parody, mimicry, and meme features — which in turn indicate Locke's theory of communication and Mead's symbolic interactionism. This engagement with the audience at the communication level firmly places the sitcom and thereby its audience as critical participants in the civic procedures of crime. As the episode progresses, the characters become less *Community* in dialogue structure and language choices and more *Law and Order,* which allows the new character identities through bricolage to occur within the characters. However, without the formula to mimic, the meme of burlesque manner and pastiche style would not have been possible. As a result of the communication and symbolic interactionism, the characters become more civically engaged, and in turn, so does the audience. The *Law and Order* formula provides a perfect place for this to occur, not just because of the formula, but because of the intricacies of law woven within it. When we understand the system of the law better, we are better citizens. In this case, the characters of *Community become* the system, and in their portrayal of the events and the characteristics of it, they and the audience, perhaps inadvertently, become critical of it.

Works Cited

Barney, Chuck. "Simple Formula Drove 'Law and Order' Success." *AZ Central*. Gannett. 23 May 2010. Web. 21 January 2013.

"Basic Lupine Urology." *Community*. NBC. 26 April 2012.

"Community." *TV.com*. CBS Interactive. n.d. Web. 21 January 2013.

"*Community* (TV Series)." *Wikipedia*, Wikimedia Foundation. 14 January 2013. Web. 21 January 2013.

Cronk, George. "George Herbert Mead (1863–1931)." *Internet Encyclopedia of Philosophy*. University of Tennessee Martin. 27 June 2005. Web. 21 January 2013.

Hyden, Steven. "How Dan Harmon Went from Doing ComedySportz in Milwaukee to Creating NBC's *Community*." *AV Club*. Onion. 19 September 2009. Web. 21 January 2013.

"Law & Order (1990–2010)." *IMDB.com*. IMDB.com. 2013. Web. 21 January 2013.

"Law & Order Show Summary." *TV.com*. CBS Interactive. n.d. Web. 21 January 2013.

Locke, John. "An Essay Concerning Human Understanding." Columbia Digital Text. Book 3. Chapter 9. *Columbia University*. n.d. Web. 8 September 2012.

Mead, George Herbert. *Mind, Self, and Society: From the Standpoint of a Social Behaviorist*. Chicago: University of Chicago Press, 1934.

Menditto, Mike. "Plot Summary for 'Law & Order.'" *IMDB.com*. IMDB.com. 2013. Web. 21 January 2013.

Naoreen, Nuzhat. "16. *Community*." 26 Best Cult TV Shows Ever. *EW.com*. Entertainment Weekly. 26 August 2012. Web. 21 January 2013.

Shepherd, Jon M. *Cengage Advantage Books: Sociology*. 11th ed. Independence: Wadsworth, 2011.

"Society." *The Free Dictionary*. Farlex. 2013. Web. 21 January 2013.

Wyman, Bill. "*Community* Nails *Law and Order*" Blog. *Slate.com*. 26 April 2012. Web. 21 January 2013.

PART III: POPULAR CULTURE ACROSS THE CURRICULUM

My Dinner with Abed: Postmodernism, Pastiche and Metaxy in "Critical Film Studies"
Elizabeth Fleitz Kuechenmeister

> Everyone else is growing and changing all the time and that's not really my jam. I'm more of a fast-blinking, stoic, removed, uncomfortably self-aware type. Like Data, or Johnny 5, or Mork, or HAL, or KITT, or Woodstock and/or Snoopy, and Spock probably goes without saying....—ABED NADIR, "Critical Film Studies" (Episode 2.19)

This line from the second season of *Community* accurately represents the way the show easily and frequently references popular culture. To a greater extent than any other current sitcom, the NBC comedy relies on popular culture references to develop its characters or advance its plot. The show is famous for having themed episodes structured around movie plots (*The Breakfast Club, Die Hard*), television shows (*The Office, Mad Men*), games (*Dungeons and Dragons*), and even Twitter feeds (@shitmydadsays). These frequent allusions to popular and familiar texts are often what draw fans and have led the show to a small, but loyal, cult following. From their well-known Christmas Claymation episode to their 8-bit video game episode, *Community* builds its fan base (and its storyline) around familiar genres and texts.

Particularly in comedy, it is not rare for contemporary shows to refer to other shows or films to make the viewer laugh. Starting as early as *Rowan and Martin's Laugh-In* (1968–1973) and *Saturday Night Live* (1975–), and ongoing with *The Simpsons* (1989–), broadcast comedy has continued to rely more and more heavily on references to outside works to further the story or (especially in the case of Seth McFarlane's *Family Guy*) just to get a quick laugh. Tina Fey's *30 Rock* has picked up on the referential — and self-referential — humor as well.

From *Scrubs* to *Parks and Recreation*, this type of comedy is becoming more common.

So, what is so unique about *Community*, then? Like the aforementioned comedies, *Community* frequently makes reference to other texts, as well as occasionally shows an awareness of itself as a text. Many viewers tune in each week to see how many references they can "get"—and receive additional entertainment from those in-jokes. While the show is entertaining, and even more so if one can catch the references, *Community* seems to reach a bit further with its use of intertext. Unlike *Family Guy* or *American Dad!*, *Community* uses popular culture references not to merely get a quick laugh, but instead to play with and reinterpret those texts through a new lens. *Community*'s humor goes further than an *SNL* sketch, selecting and adapting culturally familiar references to the story. Indeed, as the show is constructing a new type of culturally based humor, it is itself constructed by popular culture. Even critics, attempting to characterize the series, cannot do so without referencing other shows; these critics ironically describe *Community* in terms of *The Simpsons*, *Seinfeld*, and other classic series. *Community* does not just refer to popular culture; it *is* popular culture.

However, what is the ultimate purpose of these references? Some critics question the show's reliance on pop culture, noting that the show and its characters appear shallow and trivial, accusing *Community* of being too dependent on references and lacking plot content or character development. This criticism may be valid, as this is always a risk with any text that is made to be subject to other texts. Indeed, a better question to ask might be, what kind of effect does this intertextuality have on the series as a whole, and even on the surrounding landscape of network television programming? Perhaps the best place to begin a study of this nature is to explore the concept of postmodernism, as much of the series carries with it a very postmodern sensibility. In fact, it can be argued that *Community*, unlike the majority of other comedies airing on network television, is likely the best example of a quintessentially "postmodern" television show.

Jean-Francois Lyotard famously defines the concept of "postmodernism" as "incredulity towards metanarratives" (*The Postmodern Condition* xxiv). While much as been made of this overly simplified (and frequently misinterpreted) definition, Lyotard is one of the first critics to identify some of the key features of this theory. Neither just a temporal identification nor a particular style, postmodernism is a movement that challenges previous methods of representation and reality, questioning (and disrupting) the previously seamless nature of history and identity. The breaking down of previously held knowledge and hierarchy is characteristic of the theory. As Lyotard describes in later work, he continues his discussion of the collapsing of metanarratives: "there is no longer a horizon of universalization [...] I would say a sort of *bricolage*: the high frequency of elements from previous styles or periods" ("Theorizing the Postmodern"). As Lyotard explains, metanarratives cease to have meaning within a postmodernist framework, as it is characterized by a collage (or more accurately, a pastiche) of previously familiar elements. In general, postmodernism is suspicious of any universally held knowledge. As critic Terry Eagleton notes, concepts like truth, objectivity, reason, identity and others are challenged by postmodernism (qtd. in Richter). Thus, postmodernism works to overturn or erase master narratives (Lyotard, *The Postmodern Condition* xxiv).

Instead of being merely a response or rethinking of modernism, the "post-" in postmodernity (according to Lyotard) "does not mean a process of coming back or flashing back, feeding back, but of *ana*-lysing, *ana*-mnesing, of reflecting" (qtd. in Richter). To Lyotard, post-modernism is not a reaction to a prior time period, but instead a reflecting and rethinking of our current time. In fact, another feature of postmodernism is its self-referential nature. Postmodern texts frequently acknowledge their own status as a work of art. Linda Hutcheon characterizes postmodernism as being self-conscious and self-referential as a way to challenge and undermine: "The postmodern's initial concern is to de-naturalize some of the dominant feature of our way of life; to point out that those entities that we unthinkingly experience as 'natural' [...] are in fact 'cultural'" (Wolfreys 194).

This undermining of master narratives and challenging of "natural" features of society work in a large part through the way postmodernism views culture as a whole. Instead of defining rigid boundaries between elite "high" culture (fine art, classical music, opera) and popular "low" culture (television, advertising, comics), postmodernism collapses those distinctions, erasing boundaries as a way of rethinking the high-low culture dichotomy (Jameson, "Reification and Utopia" 133). This deletion of boundaries allows postmodernism to resist a clear definition.

In a 1982 lecture, Frederic Jameson develops his concept of postmodernism as a way to describe the current state of the capitalist society, begins without a clear definition of the term, but instead a detailed list of examples: John Ashbery's poetry, Robert Venturi's architectural analysis, Andy Warhol's pop art, the music of John Cage, Philip Glass, Terry Riley, The Clash, Talking Heads, Jean-Luc Godard's films, William Burroughs' fiction, and the list goes on ("Postmodernism and Consumer Society"). This extensive list of disparate texts serves to prove that postmodernism cannot be described in a coherent way and resists unification. What all the texts do share, however, is a willingness to challenge and erase the boundaries that separate high and low cultural forms. Jameson recommends that we rethink this high-low dichotomy by using an "historical and dialectical approach," an "approach which demands that we read high and mass culture as objectively related and dialectically interdependent phenomena" ("Reification and Utopia" 133).

If we consider elite and popular culture not in opposition to each other, but as "twin and inseparable forms," which are interdependent with each other, this will allow us a new way of thinking about culture ("Reification and Utopia" 133–134). In fact, by virtue of high culture's refusal to become popular culture, high culture is relating to popular culture, as it defines itself through its dialectical twin. This collapsing of boundaries is also accomplished through the aforementioned referencing of other previously familiar texts: "[postmodernist works] no longer 'quote' such 'texts' as a Joyce might have done, or a Mahler; they incorporate them, to the point where the line between high art and commercial forms seems increasingly difficult to draw" ("Postmodernism, or the Cultural Logic" 56).

Out of this collapsing of boundaries and destruction of metanarratives, Jameson identifies major features of the postmodern, which he names not as a style but as a "cultural dominant," allowing for a wide range and flexibility of features ("Postmodernism, or the Cultural Logic" 56). He identifies several key features, the most relevant to our interests here being depthlessness. He names this as superficiality, claiming that postmodernism has less focus on content and more on surface, thus challenging the concept of identity and of a unified subject ("Postmodernism, or the Cultural Logic" 58–61). Citing the example of Edvard Munch's painting, *The Scream*, Jameson explains that the work is "a virtual deconstruction of the very aesthetic of expression itself" ("Postmodernism, or the Cultural Logic" 61). This artwork exhibits a decentering of the subject, as postmodernism also dissolves the boundaries that define a subject ("Postmodernism, or the Cultural Logic" 63), pointing towards related features of postmodernism such as the weakening of historicity and the increasing shallowness of feeling and expression ("Postmodernism, or the Cultural Logic" 58).

For all the talk of boundary breaking and challenging unified meaning, postmodernism does not reject meaning or claim there to be no (or no more) meaning. As nihilist as it may appear on the surface, postmodernism uses careful and strategic means to challenge and uncover the weaknesses of unified ideology and hierarchy. However, there has understandably been a fair amount of criticism levied at this term, much of which deals with the misunderstanding surrounding the term itself. Even Lyotard admits responsibility for the term's vague meaning ("Theorizing the Postmodern"). The use of "modernism" within the term implies, logically, that the theory will be some kind of response to the previous chronological time period. However, as Lyotard, Jameson, and others argue, it is not a simple reaction or revisiting of the past. Also, the use of the prefix "post" indicates only that the concept comes temporally after modernism; however, the concept is much more complex than temporal limitations (and in fact works to challenge and break down said temporality). So, the term is not an accurate description of the theory, which is problematic.

Critics also note the futility of defining the term itself. Even as postmodernism serves to undermine definitions and collapse boundaries, these goals ironically end up working against communicating its own meaning. Furthermore, the more recent overuse of the "post" affix with any concept (post-feminism, post-structuralism, post-formalism, post-colonialism), plus the multiple iterations (post-post-modernism and the like) only function to elude meaning — and not in the way postmodernism intends. Its overuse can easily become meaningless. As Hutcheon explains, "few words are more used and abused in discussions of contemporary culture than the word 'postmodernism'" (qtd. in Wolfreys 194). Dick Hebdige criticizes the term, saying, "It's clear we are in the presence of a buzzword" (182). Clearly, the concept of postmodernism is problematic. However, all criticisms aside, the features that Jameson and others describe as vital to this movement can be useful to a deeper analysis of popular culture. It is this assumption, that postmodernism can be used as a vehicle to challenge and disrupt our reified notions of culture, that drives the following analysis.

So, what does *Community* have to do with all of this? How is an example of popular culture relevant to a discussion of the postmodern? In fact, the show illustrates many key features of postmodernism. The show's incessant quoting of pop culture texts, collapsing of high-low culture boundaries, and questioning of clear-cut definitions and identities all point towards an essentially postmodern sensibility. Indeed, it is especially fitting that this work of popular culture frequently critiques other works of popular culture — and itself as well.

Analyzing the postmodern nature of *Community* has the potential to explore the concept of postmodernism in more detail, leading to an understanding of how the theory may be relevant — or irrelevant — today. Undeniably, a critical look at this show can not only provide greater insight on the series itself, but also give a better look at how the postmodern is being interpreted (or reinterpreted). Hutcheon, along with other critics, have claimed that postmodernism is long past, and that the concept is outdated (165). However, can *Community* provide some indication about where we are now? Has it developed into some kind of post-postmodernism (as nebulous as that term might be)? Has it regressed into modernist thought? Or does the show illustrate something else entirely? This analysis seeks to answer these questions.

Perhaps this analysis will be clearer through a case study exploration of a single episode of the series. While it is rather challenging to characterize the entire series as a whole, this study will be more effective by focusing on one particularly well-received episode. Billed as "the *Pulp Fiction* episode of *Community*" by NBC promos leading up to its March 24, 2011, airdate, the episode "Critical Film Studies" uses intertextual references in an interesting way between two classic films: *Pulp Fiction* (1994) and *My Dinner with Andre* (1981). The episode focuses on Abed's birthday celebration, taking place over the course of one evening. Shifting between two plots (a pre-party dinner between Jeff and Abed, and the impatiently waiting guests at Abed's surprise party), the storyline allows the viewer to gain more insight into the always-enigmatic character of Abed.

In order to understand *Community*, one must first understand Abed. Considered the de facto pop culture center of the group, Abed Nadir is a film student at Greendale and is highly knowledgeable about all things popular culture. In fact, Abed frequently makes it known that popular culture is more than just a hobby for him — it is definitive in shaping his identity.

He identifies with movies and television shows more deeply than people and often inadvertently neglects others because of his intense focus on the subject. He admits that he can only relate to people through the lens of pop culture, such as in this quote from the pilot: "I thought you were like Bill Murray in any of his films, but you're more like Michael Douglas in any of his films" (Episode 1.1). In this quote, Abed describes his insight on the character of his new friend Jeff Winger, explaining his understanding through a reference to two popular film actors. Abed does not follow up on this statement with additional explanation regarding his reference, and thus the viewer (as well as the other characters in the scene) are left questioning Abed's intentions. Such strange reactions to other people cause his friends to think he might have Asperger's.

The quote at the beginning of this essay best characterizes Abed, as he can only explain his own identity through references to other texts. He speaks in a very emotionless and detached way, though he does prove several times in the series that he truly loves and appreciates his friends, despite his actions. Abed's childhood and current relationship with his family is considered to be difficult. It is only hinted at, but never explored. In "Abed's Uncontrollable Christmas" (Episode 2.11), Abed develops a coping mechanism to deal with the stress of the holiday season and other unstated familial or identity crises by seeing everyone as stop-motion animated characters. However, the series never lingers long on any negative emotions from Abed, keeping him a rather curious and two-dimensional character, satisfied with developing him only to the extent which pop culture allows him. Even so, Abed's character is developed the furthest in the show than any other member of the study group, which is an occasional criticism levied against the series. As it is, Polish-Palestinian-American Abed is the single best character to encapsulate *Community* and its use of referential humor.

In the episode "Critical Film Studies," Jeff and Abed meet for dinner at an upscale restaurant. Jeff is dressed as Vince from *Pulp Fiction*, Abed's favorite movie, and has plans to take him to a surprise *Pulp Fiction*–themed birthday party at a nearby 50s-style retro diner. When Jeff meets Abed at the restaurant's bar, he knows something is immediately wrong. Jeff asks Abed, "Why are you dressed like Mr. Rogers and talking like Frasier?" Abed's entire demeanor has changed, and instead of being his usual introverted nerdy self, he is dressed in a cowl-neck knit sweater and is extremely welcoming and warm. Jeff notes that Abed does not make one single reference to popular culture and is concerned. Meanwhile, the rest of the study group sits, waiting for Abed and Jeff to arrive at the party. They are each dressed as a character from *Pulp Fiction*: Britta as Mia; Troy and Annie as Pumpkin and Honey Bunny; Chang as the boxer, Butch; a cross-dressing Shirley as Jules; and Pierce as the Gimp. Impatient, the group members start to complain and gripe at one another.

Abed, still with Jeff at the restaurant, is unusually talkative and sociable — even charming. Jeff humors him, if only to hurry him up and finish dinner so they could get on to the party. This is very like the relationship between Jeff and Abed, which has always been rather tense. At the ends of certain episodes (such as "Contemporary American Poultry," Episode 1.21), the two men occasionally have a scene to reestablish their friendship, letting the viewer know that despite all appearances, they do care about each other.

For the most part, though, Jeff regards Abed as a freak, however lovable he may be, noting of Abed that "it was as if he didn't want people to like him" ("Critical Film Studies") because of his obsession with popular culture. Abed seems to enjoy Jeff's company, but Jeff (as usual) only tolerates Abed, using thinly veiled sarcasm to express his mild irritation. Jeff observes aloud that Abed has changed, and Abed explains his transformation. A few days earlier, Abed had been invited to visit the set of his favorite show, *Cougar Town*, a running joke in the series. Unexpectedly, he was invited to be an extra. Abed explains his dilemma about this proposition, saying, "if I'm a person who watches *Cougar Town*, how can I be in *Cougar Town*?" ("Critical Film Studies"). Confused about dually playing a part in a show for which he is also its audience, Abed copes by creating a character for himself to play named Chad. Unlike other situations, when Abed normally copes by likening his identity to familiar pop culture characters, Chad is completely original. He describes his experience playing Chad, saying:

> I start remembering things from Chad's life, like his first kiss under the big tree at Cougar Town field. Playing soccer at Cougar Town Junior High. Finding my first chest hair in the shower. My first apartment. My first true love: falling for my best friend. Birthdays, weddings, car crashes, taxes. Playing charades at Thanksgiving. Chad had lived, Jeff. Chad had lived more than Abed ["Critical Film Studies"].

This revelation caused Abed to rethink his life (but not after a hilarious description of him collapsing on set and defecating himself in front of the cast). After playing Chad, Abed wants to live a more "real" life. Commenting on Jeff's gift to him, a replica "Bad MotherFucker" wallet from *Pulp Fiction*, he says, "I was that wallet. On the surface, a reference to some cinematic drivel. But on the inside, empty" ("Critical Film Studies"). Abed vows to give up his obsession with all things pop culture, much to Jeff's dismay. Jeff tries to argue against Abed's decision, even offering some personal childhood memories as a way to engage him in the subject. Abed claims to have achieved real conversation, while Jeff counters by claiming there is no such thing.

Eventually, Jeff catches on that their dinner talk has been a sham — that the "real" conversation Abed has requested was completely false. The waiter lets it drop that Abed has been engaging an unknowing Jeff in his extended reference to the classic film *My Dinner with Andre*. Angry, Jeff accuses Abed of lying to him, and Abed explains his motivation coming from the fact that he and Jeff had not been socializing with each other for a long time. Jeff relents, and the rest of the group (still dressed in full *Pulp Fiction* attire) crashes the dinner, having given up waiting for the pair at the diner. Abed is back to his "normal" self, and appreciates the surprise effort for his birthday. They continue the party by celebrating at the restaurant instead. Jeff, narrating the last sequence over images of the group's festivities, notes, "As parties go, it was quiet, dark, and a little lame. We'd had better parties, and we'd had worse parties. But I doubt I'll ever forget my dinner with Andre/dinner with Abed" ("Critical Film Studies").

It is precisely the dual nature of this episode, the combination of the "A" plot (Jeff and Abed at the restaurant) and the "B" plot (the rest of the group at the diner) that makes it so rich for analysis. The episode upsets the viewer's expectations and disrupts our assumptions for how a sitcom plot "should" transpire. This disruption was further perpetuated by NBC itself, as they advertised the episode more than usual, giving the impression that this would be the *Pulp Fiction* episode of *Community*. Even upon viewing the episode, the most memorable visuals come from the "B" plot and the shock of seeing Shirley dressed as Samuel L. Jackson's character, a bald Chang, and most notably Pierce as the Gimp (which was only made funnier by the fact that Pierce had no idea who the Gimp was, and did not understand the other diners' fear and revulsion at his costume when he appeared at the restaurant). This visual humor was notable, but thoroughly underplayed.

A blogger, in his review of the episode, noted that this *Pulp Fiction*–focused side plot "feels wasteful," since it provides the only laugh-out-loud humor of the episode, but takes up so little of the twenty-two-minute story (The Critical Fan). *Community* took a risk with its storytelling, devoting the majority of its narrative to referencing a relatively obscure film, while a much more popular and familiar film was sidelined. In this episode, *Community* uses a layering of references-within-references to create an interesting tale. As always, the series refuses to adopt one particular visual or narrative style, and this is true most especially of this episode. As this study explores, this episode of *Community* best represents the unique style the series is developing, a style that has roots within postmodern thought but (particularly in this episode) explores ideas beyond that of the postmodern.

The episode illustrates key elements of a postmodern text, one of which is the concept of pastiche. Not to be confused with parody, which often has an element of comedy involved, pastiche is a wholly neutral imitation of another text's style or medley of texts from a number of works ("Pastiche" 369). Parody, a device used in modernism, is usually a comical (and sometimes a respectful) imitation of a familiar text, with the goal of criticism or analysis. Pastiche, on the other hand, is characterized as neutral imitation. It copies without purpose, intent on surfaces instead of content. Jameson describes it as "blank parody," noting that

> pastiche is, like parody, the imitation of a peculiar mask, speech in a dead language: but it is a neutral practice of such mimicry, without any of parody's ulterior motives, amputated of the satiric impulse, devoid of laughter and of any conviction that alongside the abnormal tongue you have momentarily borrowed, some healthy linguistic normality still exists ["Postmodernism, or the Cultural Logic" 65].

In this characterization, Jameson seems to make a judgment call against pastiche. Even as it may be considered "blank" or "dead," it doesn't mean pastiche is by choice: it is an element of the late capitalist era. As Jameson goes on to explain, "the producers of culture have nowhere to turn but to the past: the imitation of dead styles, speech through all the masks and voices stored up in the imaginary museum of a now global culture" ("Postmodernism, or the Cultural Logic" 65).

Community's frequent references to other texts characterize its postmodernist impulse. In this episode, the show's combination of the art house, intellectual *My Dinner with Andre* with the nihilistic, gritty action drama *Pulp Fiction* (the latter of which is a pastiche in its own right) carries the narrative, even if the show makes no explicit comment or statement about either text. The episode uses these two texts neutrally, merely setting these wildly different texts next to each other without a clear interpretation or reinvention of either. This is an ambitious move, as the show has been criticized for overusing pop culture references, or doing so in a way that is empty or shallow — considered by one blogger to be "flat and lifeless" (The Critical Fan). In fact, show creator Dan Harmon along with the rest of the cast tweeted their concerns in the hours leading up to the episode's premiere, worried that fans wouldn't "get it," that viewers would again find their pastiche meaningless and uninspired (Sepinwall).

What drives pastiche is something Jameson names as "schizophrenia," which refers to the breaking down of metanarratives and the erasure of the individual subject. Postmodern texts are frequently cynical in nature (like Jeff), and often detached from emotions (like Abed). As Jameson explains, the postmodern era no longer has a subject that is good at feeling. Unlike the modern era, in which texts carried a distinct personal style or trademark, postmodern texts efface any personal traces and "decenters" itself from a defined subject (Jameson, "Postmodernism, or the Cultural Logic" 63). Indeed, this episode of *Community* plays with the viewer, making her think she can "get" Abed — but then he reveals that it is all a sham, only a text upon another text, and the rug is pulled out from under her yet again. This too is another criticism of the show, as the characters so often appear to lack depth or portray any emotion other than cynicism or sarcasm. However, according to Jameson, this kind of detachment is the most accurate way to represent life in the late age of capitalism. As he reminds us, "This is not to say that the cultural products of the postmodern era are utterly devoid of feeling, but rather that such feelings — which it may be better and more accurate to call 'intensities' — are now free-floating and impersonal" ("Postmodernism, or the Cultural Logic" 64). While it may appear that Abed is detached and without emotion, his feelings are instead expressed through a collection of references to other texts — hence, pastiche. As the opening quote of this essay described, Abed does not just obsess over pop culture; he exists fully (and exclusively) within pop culture.

The Abed/Chad monologue in this episode describes this decentering of identity effectively, as Abed fully acknowledges his existence within pop culture; thus, in order to escape his identity pastiche, he needs to construct an alter ego. This time, it is not Batman (as his occasional alter ego has appeared in the series), it is an original character. However, even this character, Chad, exists within another reference, the world of *Cougar Town*. As Abed realizes, he can never escape. So, he chooses to play within these references, and construct an homage to one of his lesser-known favorite movies at the restaurant, acting out the part of Andre Gregory, the talkative theater playwright, who meets his friend, Wally (played by Jeff) and tells him fantastic stories of his travel. Abed fully inhabits this role, enjoying the character and his ability to play with his identity.

The show's choice of film is quite striking, as the themes inherent in Louis Malle's film are echoed in this episode. As Wally Shawn explains in his opening narration to the movie, his friend, Andre, had recently had an emotional breakdown in response to a particular quote from an Ingmar Bergman movie: "I could always live in my art, but not in my life." This quotation exemplifies Abed's dilemma, as he realizes that he lives more fully through cultural references than through any kind of unified identity. His realization that "Chad had lived more than Abed" allows him to reach the conclusion that reality, or having "lived" at all, is up for question. Of course, all of this may be a moot point, as Abed reveals that his story is false, and it is left unclear whether he ever visited the set of *Cougar Town* at all, much less "lived" as "Chad." Again, the rug is pulled out from under us.

Furthermore, the depthlessness of form and shallowness of content is another hallmark feature of the show, as well as of postmodernism. While culturally these terms often carry a negative connotation, Jameson again explains that they are most accurate to describe our society in the late age of capitalism. In postmodernism, there is a larger emphasis on form and surface, and less of a focus on content and depth. Jameson describes the period as demonstrating "a new kind of superficiality in the most literal sense" ("Postmodernism, or the Cultural Logic" 60). He notes, "depth is replaced by surface, or by multiple surfaces (what is often called intertextuality is in that sense no longer a matter of depth)" ("Postmodernism, or the Cultural Logic" 62).

Again, in this episode of *Community*, there is more focus on the form (the use of these two film references) and less on developing innovative or original content. Even Abed observes that "[they are] like robots exchanging catchphrases and references" ("Critical Film Studies"). Again, this does not intend to imply a negative evaluation of the episode, but to indicate the episode's focus on form as opposed to content.

This is best illustrated by the "B" plot, the obvious underuse of the costumed study group as *Pulp Fiction* characters. Their plot is clearly meaningless; even the characters themselves are impatient and spend most of the episode simply sitting in a diner and waiting for something to happen. What might have been implied by NBC in their promos as a focused homage to the Tarantino film may appear to be no more than a quick laugh or an easy reference to a popular movie. Certainly, Chevy Chase dressed as the Gimp is hilarious and memorable enough to entertain viewers throughout the episode. However, it is precisely this intentional superficiality and focus on the form of the texts (the recognizability of the references) that allows the episode to explore the breaking down of identity and metanarrative.

In "Critical Film Studies," there is no one master narrative or main plot; instead, the episode is an amalgam of themes and referential images. When the viewer tries to grasp onto a plot or onto an identity (like when we initially trust Abed's "Chad" narrative as true), we are immediately disrupted from that and again the narrative is fractured. This episode, like Abed's identity (and indeed like the series itself), disrupts our expectations about what a television show should do and forces us to question itself as a text.

However, it would be doing the show a disservice to characterize it as completely postmodern. Even through all of its lifeless, dead, shallow references, the series still manages to attract viewers and gain a strong fan base. Clearly, the show is more than simply a postmodern conceit. There is, really, a depth to all of this depthlessness. But what is it? As Matt Zoller Seitz explains in his review of the episode, it was not merely a neutral imitation of various texts, but that it "was *Community* at its most stubbornly original. It dove down deep into its own navel and found authenticity." Seitz continues, saying, "Even as it folded and refolded itself, morphing from analytical to sincere and back again, it focused on characters we've grown to know and love, and scrutinized two of them with such compassion that it made them seem more real than ever. [...] The makers of *Community* went beyond homage, into understanding." Originality, sincerity, reality: none of these terms describe postmodernism. Clearly, *Community* is more complex than the definition of postmodernism allows.

A key may be found in the recently coined term "metamodernism." Proposed by Timotheus Vermeulen and Robin van den Akker, metamodernism is a way to describe the state of present society. Instead of using the rather amorphous term post-postmodernism, Vermeulen and van den Akker present an argument in favor of a term to describe the space in between modernism and postmodernism. Metamodernism, they claim, is not a regression back to modernism, nor is it temporally stuck after postmodernism. Metamodernism is an oscillation between modern commitment and postmodern detachment. The term takes its "meta" prefix from Plato's *metaxy*, which refers to a concept "with," "between," and "beyond." In the same way, metamodernism is situated with, between, and beyond postmodernism. Vermeulen and van den Akker argue that metamodernism helps to characterize the "emerging structure of feeling," as these sort of texts express some kind of hopefulness and sincerity even through the surface-level detachment.

Similarly, "Critical Film Studies" demonstrates not a *post*modernist, but instead a *meta*modernist, tendency. Even as it exhibits many familiar key devices of postmodernist work, the show never completely detaches itself from feeling. As blogger and critic Myles McNutt observes, the creators of *Community* "always seem to experiment in different ways, but there's also a consistent drive behind that experimentation, a dialogue with the audience which makes us feel less like guinea pigs and more like willing (and active) participants in the making of the show's meaning." Thus, the show is more than a detached series of shallow references; it is a way to interact with the fans and reach them on an emotional (instead of just a pop-cultural) level.

Even the final scenes, in one of which Jeff and Abed bond at the restaurant bar over the fact that they have not been spending time together recently, and their realization about how much they have missed each other's company, demonstrates earnestness and sincerity of emotion. For as over-the-top and sarcastic as the study group members may act, in the end they always reinforce their friendship. Jeff's final narration remembering the birthday party and his dinner with Abed, a voiceover on top of silent, slow-motion footage of the party, does not reach the level of cheesiness or cynicism. Jeff says, "I doubt I'll ever forget my dinner with Andre/dinner with Abed," and means it.

This emotion and sincerity is infrequent and does not linger, but it is just enough to allow the series to show its viewers how to feel, through a set of references and images, in our contemporary culture. It is this use of metaxy that best describes this episode, and the show as a whole. The show's ability to work with, between, and beyond the nostalgia and emotion espoused by modernism and the blank nihilism of postmodernism demonstrates the series' capacity to engage viewers through a mixture of familiar references and sincerity. This balance between the two philosophies makes for a successful, lasting viewership and helps to explain the loyalty of *Community*'s fans. We, just like Jeff, Abed, and the rest of the study group, value pop culture; however, we equally value friendship — and *Community* understands. After all, how can a show be titled *Community* without a sincere appreciation of friendship?

Works Cited

"Abed's Uncontrollable Christmas." *Community*. NBC. 9 December 2010.
"Contemporary American Poultry." *Community*. NBC. 22 April 2010.
"Critical Film Studies." *Community*. NBC. 24 March 2011.
Hebdige, Dick. *Hiding in the Light: On Images and Things*. London: Routledge, 1988.
Hutcheon, Linda. *The Politics of Postmodernism*. London: Routledge, 1989.
Jameson, Frederic. "Postmodernism and Consumer Society." *The Critical Tradition: Classic Texts and Contemporary Trends*. 3d ed. Ed. David H. Richter. New York: Bedford/St. Martin's, 2007.
____. "Postmodernism, or the Cultural Logic of Late Capitalism." *New Left Review* 1. 146 (July-August 1984): 53–92.
____. "Reification and Utopia in Mass Culture." *Social Text* 1 (Winter 1979): 130–148.
Lyotard, Jean-François. *The Postmodern Condition: A Report on Knowledge*. 1979. Trans. Geoff Bennington and Brian Massumi. Manchester: Manchester University Press, 1984.
____. "Theorizing the Postmodern." *The Critical Tradition: Classic Texts and Contemporary Trends*. 3d ed. Ed. David H. Richter. New York: Bedford/St. Martin's, 2007.
McNutt, Myles. "Community —'Critical Film Studies.'" *Cultural Learnings*. 26 March 2011. Web. 7 February 2013.
Murfin, Ross, and Supriya M. Ray. "Pastiche." *The Bedford Glossary of Critical and Literary Terms*. 3d ed. New York: Bedford/St. Martin's, 2009: 369.
My Dinner with Andre. Dir. Louis Malle. Saga Productions, 1981.
"Pilot." *Community*. NBC. 17 September 2009.
Richter, David H. "Theorizing Postmodernism." *The Critical Tradition: Classic Texts and Contemporary Trends*. 3d ed. Ed. David H. Richter. New York: Bedford/St. Martin's, 2007.
Seitz, Matt Zoller. "My Community Pulp Fictional Dinner with Andre." *Salon.com*. 25 March 2011. Web. 7 February 2013.
Sepinwall, Alan. "Review —'Community'—'Critical Film Studies': My Dinner With Abed." *Hitfix.com*. 24 March 2011. Web. 7 February 2013.
"TV Episode Review: Community "Critical Film Studies." *The Critical Fan*. 25 March 2011. Web. 7 February 2013.
Vermeulen, Timotheus, and Robin van den Akker. "Notes on Metamodernism." *Journal of Aesthetics and Culture* 2 (2010). PDF.
Wolfreys, Julian. "Postmodernity/Postmodernism." *Critical Keywords in Literary and Cultural Theory*. New York: Palgrave Macmillan, 2004: 190–197.

"That's So Meta!"
Allusions for the Media-Literate Audience in *Community* (and Beyond)

Bridget Julie Hanna

Over the years, film and television programs have gradually become saturated in intertextual references and allusions. As a result, they are reliant on a media-literate audience that is able to transfer knowledge across media platforms to understand the significance of an allusion. The television program *Community* (2009–) is highly influenced by codes born from existing media and acts as a particularly fascinating example of how television texts traverse narratives, genres and mediums.

It is the contention of this essay that *Community*'s playful intertextual references reveal two varying degrees of audience understanding. Noël Carroll's two-tiered system of communication is therefore prominent in this exploration of *Community*'s references to other texts. In "The Future of Allusion: Hollywood in the Seventies (And Beyond)" Carroll outlines how 1970s filmmakers used allusions to pay homage to, rework, and reshape the meaning of 1960s films for a two-tiered audience: the film-literate or film-conscious viewers who recognized the reference, and those who could not. Reflecting this film-literate heritage, *Community* is dense in both explicit and subtly encoded references: using parody to produce laughter, reworking genres, paying homage to auteurs, and being self-conscious of its own use of allusionism for the knowledgeable viewer. However, like many intertextually rich television programs, *Community* requires not only a single medium consciousness but rather an all-encompassing media-literacy.

Allusionism and the Two-Tiered System of Communication

Through allusionism, a film or television text has the potential to produce additional levels of meaning. Carroll, discussing the references used by 1970s filmmakers, identifies certain strategies used in allusionism: "quotations, the memorialization of past genres, the reworking of past genres, *homages*, and the recreation of 'classic' scenes, shots, plot motifs, lines of dialogue, themes, gestures, and so forth" (Caroll 52, original emphasis). These allusions do not disperse or defer meaning but rather point beyond themselves to intensify meaningfulness (Orr 139). For instance, *Community* exceeds its own textual narrative by referencing other texts, yet uses the meaning associated with these past texts to enhance the meaningfulness within the context of the show. Mikhail Bakhtin's dialogism outlines how by itself a text only has one meaning, but through the addition of intertexts, that being the referenced text, other interpretations are added, exposing multiple points of view (*Dialogic Imagination* 76; Kristeva 66). Bakhtin calls this auxiliary meaning a text's "heteroglossia" (Dialogic Imagination 76). Through dialogism, "[t]he text lives only by coming into contact with another text (with context). Only at the point of contact does a light flash, illuminating both the posterior and anterior, joining a given text to a dialogue" (Bakhtin, *Speech Genres* 162).

Influenced by Bakhtin, Julia Kristeva coined the term intertextuality to describe "a mosaic of quotations; any text is the absorption and transformation of another. The notion of *intertextuality* replaces that of intersubjectivity, and poetic language is read as at least double" (66). Kristeva, through her discussion on the transposition of sign systems, offers any text the chance to mean multiple things at once through a constitutive state of motion (66). However, these added levels of meaning are not possible without the audience's recollection of the allusion. The viewers who were aware of the dialogue between texts and could recognize the intertext are the audience members Carroll calls the "film-conscious" or "film-literate" (Carroll 56).

The rise of allusionism was a result of sixties cinephiles infiltrating Hollywood. This generation of filmmakers were film school-educated and introduced a system of referencing that, by the early 1970s, became a common aesthetic of Hollywood film and signaled the beginning of postmodern cinema (Carroll 75). These sixties cinephiles, turned Hollywood directors, required serious film-goers that could decipher their allusions. As Carroll states, the serious film-goers were a prerequisite for the directors so that the audience members were "well enough versed in film history to note references and delicate variations" which were required to decode such self-conscious gestures (56). Allusions were structured in a way so that "informed viewers [were] able to recall past films (filmmakers, genres, shots, and so on) while watching the new films" (Carroll 52). It was a new creative system that granted the well-versed and knowledgeable viewer additional interpretations of a text through allusions that could methodically enrich narrative, genre, and stylistic attractions.

Carroll's two-tiered system of communication is reflective of Charles Jencks' postmodern architecture double-coding theory. Carroll's argument, similar to Jencks,' illustrates the postmodern nature of allusionism as a cultural strategy of "mixing high and low codes, subverting the dominant from within" (77). This system of communication allowed films to be interpreted by two types of audiences: for the film-conscious, there were special grace notes that referenced, reworked, and questioned past films; for those unable to decipher the allusions, there was a soaring, action-charged melody (Jencks 77). As Jonathan Gray argues, "[t]exts make sense because of our past textual experiences, literacy, and knowledge" (*Show* 31). The two-tiered system of communication positions the film-conscious as elite, knowledgeable, and informed, leaving the not-so-film-conscious a step behind yet no less entertained, as they are still able to interact with the text through narrative action.

As film and television content converge through allusions, the film-literate audience must also apply their cinematic knowledge when watching a television program. Media-literacy or media-consciousness became a required characteristic of audiences around the late eighties and early nineties when the increased use of media and technology in everyday life was amplified through representation in popular culture (Collins, *Architectures* 92). Today, this has developed into richer media saturation for which every aspect of popular culture seems to be intricately linked and attainable. The accessibility of media and its representation within screen texts demands an audience that is familiar with and can acknowledge the concept of converging media formats. In order to understand or work with television's increasing intertextuality, we need to expand Carroll's film-conscious audience to an audience that is becoming increasingly literate across media platforms.

Parody and Paintballs: Laughter and the Media-Literate Audience

At the beginning of *Community*'s first paintball episode, "Modern Warfare" (Episode 1.23), the screen cuts to black, displaying the words "1 Hour Later," an homage to the apocalyptic off-screen time of Danny Boyle's *28 Days Later…* (2002). Mirroring the camera movement from the same film, we are shown a bird's eye view as Jeff awakes from a nap to find Greendale Community College deserted and covered in paint. He enters the college building and finds Garrett

Lambert, a casualty of the game of paintball, slouched against the wall. A trembling Garrett outlines that the stakes were raised when the Dean announced "The Prize," explaining the campus war zone, yet he is cut off when a rogue paintball hits him in the chest. Jeff turns to see where the paintball originated and discovers Leonard Rodriguez, the most immature of Greendale's mature aged students, standing at the end of the hall, paintball gun in hand.

Leonard begins to chase a confused Jeff down the hall, and, thankfully, Abed comes to the rescue, parodying *Terminator 2: Judgment Day* (1991). In a slow-motion shot, Jeff turns the corner dodging Leonard's paintballs, dropping to the floor and sliding towards Abed. Abed jumps over Jeff, using the wall as leverage and shoots Leonard, removing him from the game. While Jeff is still on the ground, Abed mirrors the powerful stance of Arnold Schwarzenegger, stating, "Come with me if you don't want paint on your clothes," a reference to the famous line from the *Terminator* franchise, "Come with me if you want to live." In this instance, *Community* sets up two types of jokes to produce laughter from two different audiences: slapstick and situation comedy for the not-so-media-conscious and parody with an added level of meaning for the media-literate.

Parody, as a form of intertextuality, playfully exposes and flaunts the dialogue between texts for the media-literate spectator. It is one of the most ancient, widespread, and potentially most powerful art forms for strictly targeting and critiquing another work of art (Bakhtin, *Dialogic Imagination* 51; Gray, *Watching* 4; Gray, *Keeping* 118; Harries 32; Hutcheon, *Theory* 16). Parody provides a heightened level of intertextuality (Harries 23) which is dependent on its power and potential to "write back to and even write over other texts and genres, to contextualize and recontextualize other media offerings, and thus to teach and engender a media literacy of sorts" (Gray, *Watching* 2). As Bakhtin outlines, "[I]n parody, two languages are crossed with each other, as well as two styles, two linguistic points of view, and in the final analysis two speaking subjects" (*Dialogic Imagination* 76). Although *Community* is dense in parodic references, Fredric Jameson pronounced the death of parody in the postmodern era, arguing that it has now dissolved into the "uncritical pastiche" (116). However, through an analysis of contemporary media, it is clear that parody is still alive and relevant. If anything, parody is being utilized in more creative and critical ways, providing another system of communication, as Margaret Rose outlines, between texts, audience, and social context (44).

What differentiates parody from other forms of intertextuality is that the conversation between texts generates an added level of laughter. Bakhtin's discussion of carnival laughter is crucial when outlining laughter derived from parody. He contends that the layers of language within the carnivalesque are "dialogized, permeated with laughter, irony, humor, [and] elements of self-parody," all which emphasize how intertextuality and parody are processes which analyze, question, and create a comic appropriation of the old within the new (*Dialogic Imagination* 7). Two influential writers on the subject of parody, Linda Hutcheon and Rose, overlook the important role of laughter which furthers parody's intent, as laughter has the power to expose and criticize a text from within. As Bakhtin states, "[e]verything that makes us laugh is close at hand, all comical creativity works in a zone of maximal proximity" (*Dialogic Imagination* 23). Although parody must expose and "bring up close" the text being parodied to provoke laughter, it is not always the parodied text that we are laughing at. Parody's intertextual dialogue is capable of bringing elements of the text using parody to the forefront, criticizing itself through the parody of another text.

This is evident in one particular episode of *Community* that parodies the situation comedy clip show through an array of flashback montages: "Paradigms of Human Memory" (Episode 2.21). In the most meta-montage of the episode, the group members fight over past events until Troy suggests the fighting is a good thing; they can air out all their dirty laundry. However, Abed reminds Troy of their camping trip, where in a flashback, Britta states the same point as Troy, to which Abed recalls the same fighting while painting Shirley's nursery. This leads to an *Inception* (2010) style jump into deeper memories and flashbacks. Here, each flashback is commenting on the previous flashback, which is simultaneously commenting on the events that are taking place in the current episode. This use of parody is quite obvious for the media-literate audience; however, to fill in the gaps for the not-so-media-literate and to be even more self-referential, Jeff openly references the shows use of meta-textuality and gives a short definition, yelling, "Abed! Stop being meta! Why do you always have to take whatever happens to us and shove it up its own ass?" While *Community* is mocking the situation comedy clip show, it is ultimately hyperconsciously mocking itself, its genre, storyline, character traits, relationships, and its subtly encoded references to other texts. Hence, when we are laughing at the parody within *Community*, we are also laughing at *Community* (Gray, *Watching* 2) as parody is a form of imitation, though "not always at the expense of the parodied text" (Hutcheon, *Theory* 6). Here, *Community* flaunts the discussion between texts in various creative forms to produce the fundamental element that differentiates parody from another form of intertextuality: laughter.

The use of parody in *Community* is structured for a dual audience. Although many audience members understand that a parody is taking place, they may struggle to recognize the past text and the dialogue between texts, making them unaware of the allusion. In this way, the additional meaning can be lost yet laughter and entertainment can still ensue. Following Carroll's double structure, *Community* provokes laughter through parody by setting up two types of jokes for two different audiences: slapstick comedy for those who do not recognize the intertext and parody for the media-literate.

The segmentation of media-literate and not-so-media-literate spectators arranges an inside and outside position for its audience. Gray states that the knowing inside position is for those that are "in" on the joke and are rewarded for recalling the parodic insertion of intertexts (*Watching* 106). On the other hand, the outside audience cannot identify an allusion and will "merely naturalize it, adapting it into the context of the work as a whole" (Hutcheon, "Parody Without Ridicule" 203). Although television parody "thrives upon recognition" (Ellis 118) recognition is not always essential if the desired effect is merely laughter and not understanding. As Bakhtin states, carnival laughter, the freedom to laugh at all participates in dialogue, "is the laughter of all the people" (*Rabelais* 11).

The difference between slapstick comedy and parody is usually most clear within minor parodic allusions, for which the cues to the parodied text are minimal but effective. The first paintball episode, "Modern Warfare" (Episode 1.23) incorporates multiple humorous parodies of various scenes within two films: *The Warriors* (1979) and *Die Hard* (1988). The allusions to these films can be recognized as parody by the media-literate audience, yet if spectators "miss a parodic allusion, they will merely read the text like any other" (Hutcheon, *Theory* 94). That is, as slapstick comedy associated with narrative action and thus in their reading, the text is no longer using parody.

Community references *The Warriors* in two scenes. Firstly, Britta, Annie and Shirley hide in the men's bathroom stalls and ambush Jeff, Troy and Abed, mirroring *The Warriors*' bathroom invasion scene. Secondly, when the study group is surrounded by a team of roller skaters, "Disco Stu" (an allusion to *The Simpsons*) echoes Luther's famous line, eerily taunting, "Study group, come out and play-ee-ay," a near direct quote from *The Warriors*. *Die Hard* is also parodied multiple times in this episode. After Britta and Jeff have sexual intercourse, Britta attempts to corner Jeff; however, Jeff "one ups" her in a parody of *Die Hard* in which Jeff (as protagonist, John McClane) gives Britta (as antagonist, Hans Gruber) a gun with an empty clip. When Britta discovers she has no bullets, Jeff directly references *Die Hard* when he holds up the paintballs, mocking, "No paintballs, Hans?" At the end of the episode, Jeff, as last man standing, confronts the Dean with a gun strapped to his back, mimicking NYPD officer John McClane's final confrontation with German terrorist Hans Gruber. Although there is no direct allusion to dialogue in this scene, the parody of action along with the previous allusion counts as a cue for the media-literate. These allusions are still inherently entertaining for those who do not recognize the parody as they are humorous in their own right and are commonly followed by witty comments that draw attention away from the parody. For example, Jeff's direct reference to Hans when stealing Britta's paintballs is a clever allusion to *Die Hard* for the media-literate but merely the continued bickering between Jeff and Britta for the not-so-media-literate. These allusions illustrate how *Community*'s use of carnival laughter is directed at both the audience members who recognized the parodied text and those who do not.

Parody provides intertextual cues that are recognizable to the savvy spectator. Hutcheon argues, "[i]f the desired response is a reaction to the recognition and interpretation of parody, then the producer of the text must guide and control the understanding of the reader" (*Theory* 89). For a parody to be understood and encourage laughter, the audience needs to recognize both the similarities and differences from the parodied text. Hutcheon contends that a parody can only be recognized through the dramatization of the differences between two texts, stating that parody "marks difference rather than similarity" (*Theory* 6). On the other hand, Carroll outlines how for seventies film it was a basic rule, "that a similarity between a new film and an old film generally can count as a reference to the old film" (52) yet in order for parody to work effectively, that is to induce laughter through recognition, both similarities *and* differences need to be present in the dialogue between texts (Harries 24). This allows the audience a greater chance to acknowledge the intertext, and the comic nature of the reference.

Parodic cues can also be described as what Jerry Palmer calls "the logic of the absurd" for which the ridicule of a text is indicated through the opposition it creates from the text which we are familiar with (199). Therefore, one dimension of a parody is similar to the target text to ensure logic and recognition of the text being parodied, and another to produce difference and create absurdity, allowing for humor to occur through parody (Harries 9). As Gray outlines, "[c]omedy works most often by wedding sense and the expected to the unexpected, by colliding discourses and moving one into the realm of the other" (*Watching* 105).

Most references in *Community* display both similarity and difference and the logic of the absurd to signal the parody. Towards the end of "Modern Warfare," Señor Chang, the Spanish teacher, enters the game of paintball assassin and in an absurd and humorous scene parodies multiple texts. Firstly, Chang walks into the library study room holding a paintball machine gun in a stance that is reminiscent of Tony Montana in the final shootout of Brian De Palma's *Scarface* (1983). After his paintballs run out, he reveals two golden guns which is an allusion to the film, *Face/Off* (1997), in which Nicholas Cage's character's trademark is his two golden guns. Chang and Britta then have a slow-motion shoot out where their paintballs curve and collide in mid-air, a reference to the film *Wanted* (2008). To add to the absurdity of this scene, Chang, in a high-pitched manic laugh, reveals a paint bomb strapped to his chest ready to self-destruct, parodying the end of the film, *Predator* (1987). All of these cues aim to activate the media-conscious audience's knowledge of the reference. Specifically, the similarity created to the original texts by the episode's plot and the gun-centered allusions, and the difference and absurdity produced through the various situations in which the weapons do not cause injury or death (although the character's dramatic reactions make it appear this way) but merely ends a student's game of paintball assassin.

The division between the media-literate and not-so-media-literate spectator is dependent on the recognition of the parodic text through parodic cues and the added level of meaning or heteroglossia associated with it. It is as Hutcheon accurately contends: "When we speak of parody, we do not just mean two texts that interrelate in a certain way. We also imply an intention to parody another work (or set of conventions) and both a recognition of that intent and an ability to find and interpret the backgrounded text in its relation to the parody" (*Theory* 22).

Through the recognition of allusions, *Community* rewards its knowledgeable audience members by providing additional meanings and insider jokes. Hutcheon discusses the position of the "sophisticated subject" who, like the media-literate, is able to recognize background texts (*Theory* 94). She states that the act of recognition "would parallel the parodists' own synthesis and would complete the circuit of meaning" (*Theory* 94). The position of the media-literate is one of the insider or knowing audience, a sought-after position whose competency allows for a more in-depth entertainment experience of most media consumption (Gray, *Watching* 31).

Community seems to take intertextuality to the next level by continuously crossing mediums within its references, at times *expecting* media-literacy from its audience. The second paintball episode, "A Fistful of Paintballs" (Episode 2.23), not only parodies Sergio Leone's spaghetti western, *A Fistful of Dollars* (1964), but also the work of Quentin Tarantino who is renowned for his use of intertextuality and reworking of genre. As we are introduced to each member of the study group, the camera quickly tracks and zooms into a close-up of their face, framed with a cartoonish paint splattered background and identified by a playing card. This image is accompanied by a sudden dramatic change in non-diegetic music emphasizing the absurd alteration in visual aesthetic. The exploitation of the dramatic close-up is used multiple times in Tarantino's *Kill Bill: Vol. 1* (2003) and *Kill Bill: Vol. 2* (2004). However, Tarantino borrowed this aesthetic from Leone whose trademark was dramatic camera movements and extreme close-ups that played with the western genre's conventions through exaggeration. The media-literate audience would recognize this as an allusion to Tarantino, rather than Leone, through the use of parodic cues that reference Tarantino, such as the use of color filtering and Annie's role as the attractive lone female lead that mimics *Kill Bill*'s protagonist, The Bride. In this way, *Community* is taking its use of intertextuality a step further and exposing the discussion between texts for the media-literate audience in a parody of a parody.

Through such extreme means of allusionism, we see how intertextual meaning is reliant on a media-literate audience that is able to transverse multiple texts and make sense of a work that is riddled with parodic references (Ndalianis 26). Gray outlines how texts can talk back and revise other texts, and in the process connect meaning between previous texts (*Show* 44). Within this parody, *Community* is using stylistic techniques to talk back to Tarantino's *Kill Bill*, which was talking back to Leone's *A Fistful of Dollars*, which influences the heteroglossia the audience associates with the current text, *Community*. Most importantly, the heteroglossia associated with *Community*'s self-conscious recognition of its use of intertextuality through its parody and reference to a film that is rich in allusions.

Genre Parody: Text, Audience, and Creator

In "Contemporary American Poultry" (Episode 1.21), *Community* reconstructs the gangster genre as Jeff schemes to take over the cafeteria's distribution of chicken fingers. This quickly evolves into a homage to Martin Scorsese's *Goodfellas* (1990). Here, Abed, mirroring the protagonist, Henry Hill, begins as the fry cook and ends up with the decision-making power, corrupting both himself and the study group. One particular scene that portrays many gangster genre traits is the montage and voiceover narration that explains the process of chicken finger distribution. This montage is accompanied by the blues song "Shake Your Money Maker" by Elmore James and, in voiceover narration, Abed describes the role of each member of the study group: "T-Bone was the bag man. He'd move the fingers to a store room where two of the girls did the packaging. We could trust them not to eat the supply because Britta was a vegetarian, and Shirley figured that if she stole, she'd go to hell. They handed the stuff out the window to Annie. She was the leg man, the distributor."

The language used in this narration, with the accompanying music and montage, is a genre trait the media-literate audience would associate with the gangster genre. This episode reassembles the genre by basing the production and distribution on the supply of chicken fingers rather than illegal drugs or weapons. It is through such allusions that *Community* reworks genres using parody, creating a dialogue between texts, and also the show's creator, Dan Harmon. *Community*'s media-conscious viewers position Harmon as maker of heteroglossic meaning, who initiates the conversation between texts and audience.

The use of genre parody within *Community* exemplifies how the show's intertextual density has the power to engage with past texts. Much genre theory is "less interested in how genres are *actually* defined in cultural practices than in identifying the abstract theoretical 'essence' of a genre in idealized form" (Mittell 4, original emphasis). However, as Gray outlines, Rick Altman, Stephen Neale, and Jason Mittell have attempted to modify the cultural definition of genre with the reader as the focal point (*Watching* 29). In this case, genre describes the way films are stylistically classified based on generic criteria, yet "the interpretation of generic films depends directly on the audience's generic expectations" (Altman 14). Genres are "contingent and transitory, shifting over time and taking on new definitions, meanings, and values within differing contexts" (Mittell 17). Translating this logic, genres alter the intertextual relationship with earlier texts by reworking and appropriating what constitutes the structure of a particular genre. Hence, they do not have norms but continually remake norms that can be equally influenced through parody (Collins, *Uncommon* 46).

Gray discusses the conversation between texts which involves a process of dialogue where, "not only will earlier-viewed texts be able to talk to a current text — the current text will also be able to talk *back* to earlier texts" (*Show* 44, original emphasis). By using intertextual references a text has the power to rewrite an understanding of a past text. As Gray states, "[e]ach proliferation, after all, holds the potential to change the meaning of the text, even if only slightly" (*Show* 2). Just as genre parody instills new meaning into *Community*, it can also revise the meaning and genre of the text being alluded to.

For the audience to understand a genre parody, they need to first detect the discussion between texts and then extract the intended meaning of the genre allusion. Each genre has its own "common sense" rules and conventions that the audience internalizes to make sense of future texts (Gray, *Watching* 28). Although Bakhtin contends that "parodied genres do not belong to the genres that they parody; that is, a parodic poem is not a poem at all" (*Dialogic Imagination* 59) genre parody as an intertextual form can revise a genre through its reflective engagement with past texts. Genre parody tends to lean more accurately to Altman's definition of genre where "[l]ike a train, genre is free to move, but only along already laid tracks" (22). Following this analogy, genre parody is then able to revise genres only through the lens of previously set precedents so that the genre parody is able to be recalled.

In "Advanced Dungeons and Dragons" (Episode 2.14), the study group plays a game of Dungeons and Dragons with another classmate who is not a part of the study group, Fat Neil. However, Pierce's jealous nature causes their plan to backfire in a creative parody of the fantasy genre. The opening scene of this episode uses classic fantasy genre shots accompanied by a mythic voiceover to outline the saga of Fat Neil: "As a man he traveled far to a new school," which is accompanied by a traveling shot over a map to the castle of "Greendale." This line is followed by, "A council was called," complemented by the image of each study group member, fading in and out of a black background. Lastly, with the narration, "A game which not only might save a life, but which would forever change the balance between good and Pierce" shows a slow-motion heroic walk of the study group, shortly followed by the overdramatic introduction of the evil villain, Pierce.

This episode demonstrates the way genre produces meaning for the media-literate audience who is well-versed in the way genre works: as a fluid and constantly changing process of intertextuality that must be read through other texts and genres. However, this generic allusion is only activated for those who recognize the parody (Collins, *Batman* 79). Here, *Community* employs the use of genre parody to help entrust meaning into its narrative, producing laughter for those that notice the allusion. Furthermore, the parody "makes the genre quite explicit and culturally active" (Mittell 152) flaunting the constantly changing intertextual process of genre.

While intertextuality presents a discussion between texts, it also promotes a dialogue between creator and audience. When Kristeva coined the term, "intertextuality," she noted that there are three elements, other than the text, under consideration: the author, the reader, and the other exterior texts (Hutcheon, *Theory* 87). Within film studies, auteur theory ("auteur," the French word for author) identifies the dialogue between the director and the potential audience. Just as "[c]inema celebrated the director as the creative source of meaning" (Bordwell 44) television programs saturated in intertextuality, such as *Community*, champion the show's creator as maker of heteroglossia. As Petra Kuppers states of the cult show, *Babylon 5* (1994–1998), television positions the creator as an authorial figure, especially for the knowledgeable fan (46). Generally, television does not allow space for an auteur; however, some programs, particularly in more recent times, have invited this kind of reading. *Community* situates Dan Harmon, creator and executive producer of Seasons 1 and 2, as the auteur who opens up a discussion with the media-literate audience through allusions. Television shows, especially those shows rich in allusionism, give the authorial role to the creator despite the writers, directors, producers, and actors who all contribute to the show's heteroglossia. As Kuppers states of *Babylon 5*, fans identify a television show "not with a network or an industrial work process, but with the ingenuity, creativity, and stubbornness of one man" (46).

The dialogue between Harmon and the media-conscious audience, like auteurism, requires "an operation of decipherment" on behalf of the audience (Wallen 77). Hutcheon discusses this dialogic relationship identifying the auteur as the encoder and the media-literate audience as decoder "in order for parody to be recognized and interpreted, there must be certain codes shared between encoder and decoder, the most basic of these is that of parody itself, for, if the receiver does not recognize that the text is a parody, he or she will neutralize both its pragmatic ethos and its double structure" (*Theory* 26–27).

Within parody, the media-literate audience often associates the telling of the joke with the auteur, and in their decoding and understanding of the joke, they open a dialogic relationship (Bakhtin, *Dialogic Imagination* 47). Collins also looks at the relationship between auteur and audience, arguing that intertextual references reflect "a different dynamic in the exchange between producer and audience, one based on the sophistication of both parties" (*Batman* 170). Hence, the relationship between the creator, Harmon, and the media-literate audience recognizes a shared and sophisticated knowledge between encoder and decoder. As Harries argues, "[t]he fact that most parody films have targets that are popular genres should be of no surprise since both operate by way of 'contracts' between film-makers and viewers in terms of the control of possible meanings" (36). Thus, genre parody as an intertextual form brings together the auteur and the spectator through the recognition of textual and generic references.

Community also acts as an outlet for Harmon to pay homage to the creative authority of other auteurs. In the chicken finger episode, "Contemporary American Poultry" (Episode 1.21), Abed attempts to restore the group's order by destroying the items that reflect their individual corruption. This montage is a nod to Martin Scorsese's *Goodfellas* (1990) and the famous moment when Carmine is found dead in the meat freezer which is mimicked when Annie's new backpack is found torn up and hanging in the hallway. This parody is also reiterated later in the episode when Annie states, "Abed killed my backpack."

Although the episode is based mostly on *Goodfellas*, it also pays homage to Francis Ford Coppola and parodies the famous scene at the end of *The Godfather* (1972). Supported with non-diegetic traditional Italian music, Abed, mimicking the role of the Godfather, asks Jeff to leave the study group. As Jeff exits the room he turns to look back and sees Pierce kissing Abed's hand in the doorway as Troy slowly closes the door shutting Jeff out. Through the allusion to genre, the episode respectfully highlights Scorsese's and Coppola's influence on the gangster genre, just as the 1970s filmmakers paid tribute to their predecessors through recognizable allusions. Here, the media-conscious audience is involved in the dialogue between Harmon as well as the directors *Community* pays homage to. It is because of *Community*'s intertextual density that its use of genre parody can open a dialogue between texts and auteur for the media-literate audience.

Community's conversation between the creator and audience is represented and exposed through Abed's character, whose media-structured mind confirms allusions for the media-literate audience and identifies the genre parody for the somewhat less media savvy. Within the chicken fingers episode, Abed's voiceover narration begins the gangster genre parody when we are shown a freeze frame of Abed's face accompanied by his narration: "As far back as I can remember I've always wanted to be in a mafia movie." This quote is a direct reference to Henry Hill's opening narration in *Goodfellas*, "As far back as I can remember I always wanted to be a gangster." This line acts as a cue for the media-literate audience, preparing them for the dialogue which is about to take place between the two texts, *Community* and *Goodfellas*. Whereas, for the uninformed genre audience, this narration identifies the gangster parody, allowing them a greater understanding of the meaning intended from the allusion.

Abed also exposes the nature of the genre allusion through direct dialogue. For example, when Jeff tells the study group that Abed gets the job of fry cook, Abed replies, "We might be watching different Mafia movies," drawing attention to how the episode is referencing and reworking the genre through the chicken finger parody. Abed's self-conscious comments on the reassembling of a genre initiates Harmon's intended discussion between texts, confirming the depth of the genre parody for the media-literate audience and enlightening the not-so-media-conscious on gangster genre conventions. As Mittell states of *The Simpsons*, the show "does not work to *destroy* generic codes but to *highlight* their cultural circulation and common currency among the show's media-saturated audience" (25, original emphasis). This is true for *Community* as Abed highlights the reworking of genre, opening the discussion between audience, texts and creator through his role as parodic mediator.

Community is dense in intertextual references, using parody to provoke laughter, appropriating genres, paying homage to auteurs, and acknowledging its own clever use of allusionism. Although the series relies heavily on references to popular culture texts, the arc storyline of the show, its lightweight slapstick comedy, and at times, sentimental sitcom genre provides high levels of entertainment for those who do not recognize the allusions. However, the media-literate or media-conscious audience who appreciate the cleverly concealed and obscure references are rewarded through additional levels of narrative understanding. *Community*, being saturated in intertextual references, encapsulates Carroll's allusionism, portraying the relationship between television, other media texts, auteurs, and most importantly the audience's ability to recognize this relationship.

Works Cited

"Advanced Dungeons and Dragons." *Community*. NBC. 3 February 2011.
Altman, Rick. *Film/Genre*. London: British Film Institute, 1999.
Bakhtin, Mikhail. *The Dialogic Imagination*. Trans. Caryl Emerson and Michael Holquist. Ed. Michael Holquist. Austin: University of Texas Press, 1981.

_____. *Rabelais and His World*. Trans. Helene Iswolsky. Cambridge: MIT Press, 1984.
_____. *Speech Genres and Other Late Essays*. Trans. Vern W. McGee. Eds. Caryl Emerson and Michael Holquist. Austin: University of Texas Press, 1986.
Bordwell, David. *Making Meaning: Inference and Rhetoric in the Interpretation of Cinema*. Cambridge: Harvard University Press, 1989.
Carroll, Noël. "The Future of Allusion: Hollywood in the Seventies (And Beyond)." *October* 2 (1982): 51–81.
Collins, Jim. *Architectures of Excess: Cultural Life in the Information Age*. New York: Routledge, 1995.
_____. "Batman: The Movie, the Narrative, the Hyperconscious." *The Many Lives of the Batman: Critical Approaches to a Superhero and His Media*. Eds. Roberta E. Pearson and William Uricchio. London: Routledge, 1991. 164–181.
_____. *Uncommon Cultures: Popular Culture and Post-Modernism*. New York: Routledge, 1989.
"Contemporary American Poultry." *Community*. NBC. 22 April 2010.
Ellis, John. *Seeing Things: Television in the Age of Uncertainty*. London: I.B. Tauris, 2000.
"A Fistful of Paintballs." *Community*. NBC. 5 May 2011.
Gray, Jonathan. "Keeping It Real: Reality and Representation." *Television Entertainment*. New York: Routledge, 2008. 102–130.
_____. *Show Sold Separately: Promos, Spoilers, and Other Media Paratexts*. New York: New York University Press, 2010.
_____. *Watching with The Simpsons: Television, Parody, and Intertextuality*. New York: Routledge, 2006.
Harries, Dan. *Film Parody*. London: British Film Institute, 2000.
Hutcheon, Linda. *A Theory of Parody: The Teachings of Twentieth-Century Art Forms*. New York: Methuen, 1985.
_____. "Parody Without Ridicule: Observations on Modern Literary Parody." *Canadian Review of Comparative Literature* 5 (1978): 201–211.
Jameson, Fredric. "Postmodernism, or the Cultural Logic of Late Capitalism." *New Left Review* 146 (1985): 53–92.
Jencks, Charles. *What is Post-Modernism?* London: Academy Group, 1996.
Kristeva, Julia. *Desire in Language: A Semiotic Approach to Literature and Art*. Trans. Thomas Gora, Alice Jardine, and Leon S. Roudiez. Ed. Leon S. Roudiez. Oxford: Basil Blackwell, 1980.
Kuppers, Petra. "Quality Science Fiction: Babylon 5's Metatextual Universe." *Cult Television*. Eds. Sara Gwenllian-Jones and Roberta E. Pearson. Minneapolis: University of Minnesota Press, 2004. 27–44.
Mittell, Jason. *Genre and Television: From Cop Shows to Cartoons in American Culture*. London: Routledge, 2004.
"Modern Warfare." *Community*. NBC. 6 May 2010.
Ndalianis, Angela. *Neo-Baroque Aesthetics and Contemporary Entertainment*. Cambridge: MIT Press, 2004.
Neale, Stephen. *Genre and Hollywood*. London: Routledge, 2000.
Orr, Mary. *Intertextuality: Debates and Contexts*. Cambridge: Polity, 2003.
Palmer, Jerry. *The Logic of the Absurd: On Film and Television Comedy*. London: British Film Institute, 1987.
"Paradigms of Human Memory." *Community*. NBC. 21 April 2011.
Rose, Margaret. *Parody/Metafiction: An Analysis of Parody as a Critical Mirror to the Writing and Reception of Fiction*. London: Croom Helm, 1979.
Wallen, Peter. *Signs and Meaning in the Cinema*. 2d ed. Bloomington: Indiana University Press, 1972.

My Dinner with Andre/Our Dinner with Abed: Genre and the Audience

Sallie Maree Pritchard

> Abed was being weird. And by that I mean he *wasn't* being weird. He was hugging, smiling, making eye contact. And in 30 seconds, he hadn't made a reference to anything. —JEFF WINGER, "Critical Film Studies" (Episode 2.19)

This is a quote from "Critical Film Studies," which originally aired in the United States on March 24, 2011, on the NBC network. Written by Sona Panos and directed by English actor and filmmaker Richard Ayoade, the episode concerns Abed's birthday. Having helped plan a *Pulp Fiction* (1994) themed party at The Greasy Fork, a 1950s nostalgia diner where Britta works, Jeff is puzzled when Abed requests a quiet dinner with him alone. Unbeknownst to him, Abed's decision threatens to ruin the evening. Thinking Abed has finally become "normal," Jeff opens up to him only to find out the whole evening is Abed's re-creation of a film, *My Dinner with Andre* (1981). While Jeff is having dinner with Abed while also trying to get Abed to come to the surprise birthday party, Troy destroys Jeff's gift for Abed, believing Abed has chosen Jeff over him as his best friend. Consequently, when Abed and Jeff fail to show up at the diner, Britta is fired. Once the fighting has stopped, Jeff and Abed go back to the restaurant and celebrate Abed's birthday.

Phillip McIntyre asserts that, "in order to be comprehensible, culture must be organized in such a way as to enable communication" (122). While *Community* employs the character of Abed to represent the series' investment in popular culture, it is this episode in particular that brings into focus the ways in which *Community* addresses its audience. What do we mean when we talk about the audience? Dennis Kennedy identifies some of the difficulties in understanding the spectator within our culture:

> The reasons for this difficulty are apparent enough: audiences are not (and probably never have been) homogeneous social and psychological groups, their experiences are not uniform and impossible to standardize, their reactions are chiefly private and internal, and recording their encounters with events, regardless of the mechanism used to survey or register them, is usually belated and inevitably partial. Almost anything one can say about a spectator is false on some level [3].

According to Kennedy, the central flaw in theoretical discussions of the spectator is the "psycho-semiotic assumption that the film text governs spectator" (10). This assumption is problematic because it assumes the audience has no authority in the interpretation of texts.

For Kennedy, the central question seems to be, "What is an audience? When spectators congregate in public for a performance, live or recorded, does anything unite them? Among those disparate selves can anything 'universal' occur?" (13). One answer may be that the "universal" thing that occurs among audiences is the way in which they recognize particular structures associated with film and television, namely format and genre.

David Bordwell and Kristin Thompson argue that, "the constant interplay between similarity and difference, repetition and variation, leads the viewer to an active, developing awareness" (49). In order to appeal to an audience, the balance between similarity and difference is tenuous: too many differences and an audience may not be able to engage with the text, but too many similarities means an audience may not want to engage with the text. From the perspective of both producers and audiences, there is a perception that structures are seen as constraints and limit originality and creativity. Conversely, they can increase, rather than reduce, engagement with a text because, as McIntyre emphasizes, "by seeing similar elements in a television programme we can engage in comparisons of characters, events and ideas. Recognizing these increases an audiences' understanding of the dramatic narrative" (123).

This suggests that audiences engage with a text by recognizing familiar content presented in a new or modified way and often form expectations of material presented in a similar way, such as television comedy. As McIntyre observes, "from one perspective narratives are ways of organizing an experience into a coherent set of events that chart the movement, as Tzvetan Todorov explains, from order to disorder and back to order again" (125). This means that a format such as the television comedy relies on a recognizable structure and even a set of recognizable stories that chart this movement from disorder to order, according to Todorov. Television comedy is one example in which this movement is repeated not only across an entire series, but also within each episode.

Jane Feuer identifies the television format as "familiar status quo, ritual error made, ritual lesson learned, familiar status quo" (qtd. in Creeber 69) but argues that this format can provide a space in which the series can transcend these boundaries, if only for the duration of the episode. For example, the British comedy, *The Mighty Boosh* (2004–2007), which aired on BBC3, follows this format of Feuer's "familiar status quo, ritual error made, ritual lesson learned, familiar status quo" (qtd. in Creeber 69) but often provides a space in which the narrative can go beyond the confines of a traditional television comedy. The two main characters, Vince Noir and Howard Moon, often try to improve their situation in life but always end up exactly where they started and usually back at their workplace. These narratives in which they try to improve their situation in life are often surreal in nature, such as a journey to Monkey Hell ("Bollo," Episode 1.3), being kidnapped by a love-starved sea monster with a fondness for Bailey's Irish Liqueur ("The Legend of Old Gregg," Episode 2.5), and a battle with a crack-addicted urban fox ("The Strange Tale of the Crack Fox," Episode 3.4). For the duration of the episode, Vince Noir and Howard Moon stray beyond the confines of their position both in life and within the television comedy.

Brett Mills discusses the television sitcom as a format that uses a strict set of codes and conventions to make clear the sitcom's purpose to the audience:

> while most fiction in any medium attempts to hide the fact that it is a fiction formed around codes of construction, sitcom relies on its artificiality not only as part of its metacommunication, but also for its very effectiveness. Thus "sitcom naturalism" is based on audiences "suspending disbelief in return for pleasure," in which the laughter track, the theatrical shooting style and the displayed performance clearly demonstrate sitcom's artificial status and its clear, precise, single-minded aim: to make you laugh [67].

This argument from Mills suggests that this breaking away from the traditional television format as described by Feuer is merely another element of the television comedy structure. Outlandish characters and incredible situations then become a device for audiences to engage in the text through their understanding of the television comedy.

In *Community*, as Abed tells Jeff, "TV makes sense. It has logic, structure, rules" ("Anthropology 101," Episode 2.1). Even with more surreal or unconventional elements, TV comedies still follow a particular structure for its particular purpose: to make the audience laugh. While *Community* is not a studio-based sitcom and has no laughter track, it follows the sitcom format in the way it uses its artificial nature to alert audiences that it is a comedy. If one of the features of the sitcom format is to be clear and obvious in its purpose, the series also uses this artificiality to provide comment on film and television itself. In "Critical Film Studies" (Episode 2.19), Jeff sees engagement with popular culture as little more than "fake people talking about how fake the world is." On the other hand, Abed sees it as a vital tool for connecting with other people. McIntyre asserts that, "one can see different forms within a culture depending on the way experience is organized and engaged with" (124). The way this experience is organized and engaged with, according to McIntyre, are the structures, such as that belonging to the television series: "All television programmes, for example, have some things in common. They are all audio/visual experiences organized around the particular senses that deal with sound and vision. Not all television programmes, however, share the same organizing principle in terms of their construction or the way they are put together. Dramas, nonetheless, do. It is the way dramas are structured that makes them dramas" (124).

What we can draw from his words is that all television programs are organized primarily by the television format. Not all television programs, however, share the same content and so further formats are required in order to engage a specific audience. The format becomes the structure, but how does a producer then organize the content for an audience? If structures are the ways in which cultural forms are organized so as to be recognizable to an audience, "we can make the declaration that structures are the blueprint of a form, but genre is the subsystem of classification we use when we recognize the organization of the cultural form" (124).

So, perhaps we can conceive of an audience by their ability to recognize structures and formats belonging to the film and television text. According to Daniel Chandler, this is where genre plays a vital role: "From the point of view of the producers of texts within a genre, an advantage of genres is that they can rely on readers already having knowledge and expectations about works within a genre." This means that television series and films of a particular genre will engage spectators already familiar with the genre, and because these structures of the television format and genre are repeated within each episode, spectators new to a television series can, in theory, watch a television series, particular a television comedy, at any point within a given series. A viewer who watches from the beginning, however, will begin to recognize the individual series' particular structures.

In the case of "Critical Film Studies," the producers of *Community* engage a spectator who recognizes particular films and film genres within the series, but also one who has seen at least one other episode, relying on the audience, as Chandler suggests, to recognize not only other works in the same genre as *Community*, but other genres in general. Rather than asserting authority over the audience, *Community* allows the audience to actively engage with and participate in the interpretation of the television series, primarily via genre.

Genre is regarded as an important tool in the creation of codes and conventions that determine the way a narrative is presented or a means of setting up the twin processes of similarity and difference, as theorized by Bordwell and Thompson. As previously discussed, genre is not only important in the way in which it is used to determine format and structure, but in the way it is used to construct and address the spectator. The ways that genre is linked to audiences can be "traced in the different functions of subjectivity each produces, and in their different modes of addressing the spectator" (Gledhill 64). Daniel Chandler adds on to this idea with the thought that genre is often "seen as constituting a kind of tacit contract between authors and readers." This suggests that filmmakers and audiences work together to create meaning in a text, and that the filmmaker relies on the audience's engagement not only with their text but also with other texts. The way the filmmaker addresses the audience depends upon audiences' recognition of particular codes and conventions. This contract between the filmmaker and the audience takes the shape of forms designed to create expectations within the audience. McIntyre argues that "it is the audiences' expectation of following this system that draws them into actively participating in the ongoing process of the creative work" (125). We can argue that audiences choose particular films and television series based on genre, and if they have viewed other examples of a given genre they will begin to make assumptions on how the narrative will develop, based on those previous examples. Chandler argues that audiences do much more than "passively accept the preferred readings which may be built into texts for readers: most would stress that reading a text may also involve 'negotiation,' opposition or even outright rejection." One of the ways in which audiences can negotiate, oppose or reject the text is via genre, through the format and structures of previous examples. Abed himself opposes and rejects texts within *Community*, particularly when he is tired of the way Britta and Jeff's relationship is playing out and attempts to direct it himself ("Anthropology 101," Episode 2.1). In "Critical Film Studies," he rejects the conventions of *Pulp Fiction* and negotiates with Jeff by using the conventions he feels comfortable with, those from *My Dinner with Andre*. In this way, Abed is acting almost as the audience's representative within the series.

In addition, "genre consciously works with these formal expectations. For example, television comedy is often the result of the formal expectations being presented not being met" (McIntyre 125–6). In "Critical Film Studies," the audience's formal expectations are ultimately met precisely because the characters' expectations are not being met. The audience uses *Community*'s format and genre to actively engage and participate in Abed's deception.

Daniel Chandler sets out some of textual features of film and television genres. These include narrative, characterization, themes, settings, iconography, and filmic techniques, such as camerawork, lighting, sound, and editing. Of these elements, Chandler observes that "viewers are often less conscious of such conventions than of those relating to content." In "Critical Film Studies," three different genres are used to engage with the audience in different ways. On one level, the episode employs the textual features of the television sitcom that the series as a whole uses. *Community* makes use of all of textual features as outlined by Chandler, but in the case of *My Dinner with Andre* and *Pulp Fiction*, there is a focus on different features.

With references to *My Dinner with Andre*, close attention is paid to the narrative. The episode begins with Jeff, walking through the city and ending up at a sophisticated restaurant. We learn via Jeff's voice-over that he has been invited to the restaurant by Abed. He describes the ways in which the choice of restaurant does not seem at all in keeping with Abed's character and how he is not looking forward to the dinner.

This is almost exactly the beginning of *My Dinner with Andre*: Wallace Shawn makes his way to a sophisticated restaurant to meet his friend, Andre, describing Andre's character, why they fell out of contact, Wallace's surprise at the invitation, and why he is not looking forward to the dinner with Andre. Furthermore, just like *My Dinner with Andre*, in "Critical Film Studies," Jeff and Abed discuss the reasons for Abed's change of character. While Andre orders the quail, Abed chooses the squab, telling Jeff, "they're out of the quail." Here, Abed is referring to the limits of his homage. He cannot order the quail and so he orders a similar dish. If Jeff were a more discerning viewer (like us), he would recognize Abed's comment for what it may truly be: an apology for not being able to follow *My Dinner with Andre* as precisely as he would have liked.

The filmic techniques, from the long shot of the episode's opening to the heavy use of medium close-ups and close-ups, and a shot reverse-shot structure using over the shoulder shots of each character in conversation, are quite similar to those used in *My Dinner with Andre*. Composition is also similar, with Jeff and Abed sitting in the same positions as Wallace and Andre. Though Abed's characterization and costume is designed specifically for *My Dinner with Andre* (down to his choice of shawl-neck cardigan), and Jeff's for *Pulp Fiction*, Jeff's characterization becomes aligned with that of Wallace from the very beginning of the episode. Jeff's costume matches *My Dinner with Andre* as well as *Pulp Fiction*, as Wallace also wears a suit to dinner.

In the references to *Pulp Fiction*, the choice of costume seems to perfectly match the characterization of everyone in the study group. Britta and Jeff dress as Mia Wallace and Vincent Vega respectively, the star-crossed love interests and dominant presence within *Pulp Fiction*. Annie and Troy dress as Pumpkin and Honeybunch, the young couple whose reckless behavior threatens lives in the diner. Chang dresses as Butch, a man who is self-serving to the point of self-destruction. Shirley dresses as Jules Winnfield, the calming, spiritual presence, and Pierce dresses as The Gimp, a stereotypical symbol of sexual perversion. Aligning the characters within the study group with the characters within

Pulp Fiction illustrates the ways in which characterization becomes the primary generic textual feature, allowing the audience to immediately recognize the source of the film being referred to. The use of the diner too is an important feature, as it is the location of the film's opening scene and it is where they return to at the end of the film.

Not only does this demonstrate the use of settings to denote a particular genre and film, it also reflects the episode's use of iconography to alert viewers to the source of the references. This brings us back to Chandler's explanation of the textual codes employed by a film or television series to alert the audience to its use of a particular genre. Chandler defines iconography as the following: "A familiar stock of images or motifs, the connotations of which have become fixed; primarily but not necessarily visual, including décor, costume and objects, certain "typecast" performers (some of whom may have become "icons"), familiar patterns of dialogue, characteristic music and sounds, and appropriate physical topography."

The diner also serves a double purpose in that it is a nod to both the diner from the opening scene and Jackrabbit Slims, the restaurant at which Mia and Vincent win the twist competition. Annie is even drinking a milkshake identical to Mia's "five-dollar shake."

When the entire study group participates in homage to particular films, television series, or genres, more obvious genres are used: western, war, or horror. Settings, characterization and iconography become the primary generic features *Community* employs. When Abed controls the use of genre and choice of film or television series, there is reference to less obvious genres and less reliability upon iconography, such as in "The Science of Illusion" (Episode 1.20) in which characterization and narrative is used for Abed to manipulate Shirley, Annie and Dean Pelton into taking on traditional "buddy cop" roles. In "Abed's Uncontrollable Christmas" (Episode 2.11), narrative and filmic techniques allow Abed to demonstrate his grief over not spending Christmas with his mother, imagining the college campus and everyone in it has become a stop-motion animated Christmas film. Regarding his response to Britta's story in "Horror Fiction in Seven Spooky Steps" (Episode 3.5), characterization, narrative, and themes are used to make Abed's argument that rational or "realistic" behavior within a constructed universe such as the horror film does not change the outcome. In "Critical Film Studies," Abed's use of genre is different than that of the rest of the group. For the audience who has seen these particular episodes and more, they may begin to recognize the differences in the series' approach to genre, and they may even begin to interpret the reasons for these different approaches.

When Abed tells Jeff he wants a "real conversation," Jeff immediately assumes the role of antagonist, pointing out the artificial nature of the evening's events:

> Okay, you wanna have a real conversation? Here's as real as I get under the circumstances. It's nice that you've learned to dial back your love of TV. But I'd really like you to come have a milkshake with me. But before you do, I'd like you to remember how much you enjoy *Pulp Fiction*. Now that's as far as I can go without defeating the purpose. I'm really tilting the bean can here.

This speech again seems to reveal the episode's approach to genre and the *Community* audience. It is also another red flag for an audience familiar with Abed's particular use of genre and the extent to which the rest of the group understands the way in which Abed engages with them. Here we can also see the way in which *Community* often uses the character of Abed as the perceived representative, within the series, of the audience. Abed often recognizes structures, formats and generic conventions within his immediate world.

For example, in "Cooperative Calligraphy" (Episode 2.8), Abed assesses the tension created within the group when Annie's pen goes missing and draws a connection between the way the group responds and a television format called a "bottle episode." This is an episode in which a few characters (usually the regular cast) are placed in a single location for a particular period of time. Abed dislikes the tension among the group, which makes sense to him because he hates "bottle episodes," declaring that they are "wall-to-wall facial expressions and emotional nuance. I might as well sit in the corner with a bucket on my head."

Community's purpose regarding its audience is perhaps revealed in Alanna Bennett's review of "Critical Film Studies":

> Week to week, *Community* is a show that *plays* on that love of popular culture, lets us *play* around in it for a half-hour without us having to feel guilty about the fact that it takes up so much of our lives; its script — and its characters, for that matter — are so built around what already makes up the pop cultural landscape that it's often hard to tell where the references stop and the show begins.

This difficulty in distinguishing references from the series is a complaint often leveled at one of the filmmakers to whom "Critical Film Studies" pays homage: Quentin Tarantino. Tarantino is regarded critically and commercially as the embodiment of the term "all style and no substance." Chris Trafficante writes that *Pulp Fiction* is "the ultimate 'style over substance' picture. It quickly became known as a film held together by genre fusion and parody." Again, this is a description that could easily be applied to *Community*. The series is often considered to use different genres for comedic purposes. This episode plays on these expectations by presenting one obvious parody (*Pulp Fiction*), and using another to examine and thwart these expectations (*My Dinner with Andre*).

The ways in which *Community* addresses its audience and the series' use of film and television genres is arguably at its most transparent in "Critical Film Studies." The episode draws a connection between those literate in popular culture and the attitudes of others — aligning the study group's attitude toward Abed with attitudes toward Tarantino. For example, Joseph Natoli asks, "Is Tarantino's latest just another pastiche of postmodern cinéphilic references?" This sentiment is echoed by Abed at his dinner with Jeff in "Critical Film Studies" when he says, "You know what I was, Jeff? That wallet. On the surface, a reference to cinematic drivel, but on the inside, empty." The wallet referred to is a brown, leather wallet with the words "Bad Mother Fucker" embroidered on it. It is a replica of the wallet belonging to Jules Winnfield in *Pulp Fiction*, another reference to attitudes toward *Pulp Fiction* and the overall style of Tarantino. However, it is also an attitude the study group has toward Abed, and in particular, Jeff— it is why Abed chooses to single Jeff out and have dinner with him, and why he uses *My Dinner with Andre*, a film in which two men discuss whether it is possible to engage with reality through art, and if truth can ever be found in the adoption of characters or roles outside of oneself.

The episode reflects the attitudes of others toward those fluent in the language of popular film and television culture, but also reflects the debate or tension between structures, formats and genre within critical discussions:

> In the rush to perceive and critique structural constraints, unconventional work is generally valorised over conventional material in the West, leading one to assume that only unconventional material can be considered unique, and thus in the terms used in the discussion, creative. This is to ignore the extent to which the perfection of traditional or conventional material embodies creative work and to also ignore how culturally specific certain assumptions about creativity are [McIntyre 121].

Chandler too notes that this view is often extended toward audiences, particularly in discussions of genre: "As for *reading* within genres, some argue that knowledge of genre conventions leads to passive consumption of generic texts; others argue that making sense of texts within genres is an active process of constructing meaning (Knight 1994). Genre provides an important frame of reference which helps readers to identify, select and interpret texts."

Another characteristic of genre and its unification of audiences is "other pleasures can be derived from sharing our experience of a genre with others within an 'interpretive community' which can be characterized by its familiarity with certain genres" (Chandler). This interpretive community is united, then, by the recognition of other genres within series such as *Community*.

Alanna Bennett argues that "Critical Film Studies" is a prime example of the way *Community* creates a space for audiences invested in popular culture to feel as though they are not alone, their recognition of the television format and particular genres within the series uniting and allowing them to play alongside Abed. The *Community* audience stands to gain from this play in the *Community* space and the audience gains from this play by elevating their status, both among the *Community* audience and the film and television viewers.

The way in which the *Community* audience can elevate their status is via the acquisition of "cultural capital," a concept developed by French sociologist Pierre Bourdieu. According to Bourdieu, "a work of art has meaning and interest only for someone who possesses the cultural competence, that is, the code, into which it is encoded" (qtd. in McIntyre 75). For the audience of a television series such as *Community*, this cultural competence or cultural capital is earned by recognizing familiar cultural works. Chandler too writes that "any text requires what is sometimes called 'cultural capital' on the part of its audience to make sense of it.... Clearly one needs to encounter sufficient examples of a genre in order to recognize shared features as being characteristic of it."

An audience that relates to Abed will necessarily have an increased cultural capital because they will recognize Abed's attempts to converse with Jeff as a meticulous and careful selection of specific genre and film formats. Along this line, then, we should think about some questions: How does a cultural work engage an audience and use that cultural capital effectively? How does that audience discover opportunities to increase their cultural capital? Again, it seems the audience is rewarded for and united by their recognition of particular genres within a particular cultural work. If cultural capital is a reward for those who understand the "code, into which it is encoded," does the recognition of how and why these codes are being used a part of that reward? Is "Critical Film Studies" essentially a game with a prize?

For avid viewers of *Community*, the references to *Pulp Fiction* may appear too obvious, particularly as they are used here to highlight the overuse of popular culture in film and television, with Tarantino as the embodiment of everything that is apparently wrong with continually making reference to film and television. That all the references to *Pulp Fiction* seem so obvious is all but confirmed when it is revealed that even Shirley has seen *Pulp Fiction*. She has seen it on a plane and tells Pierce that it is "a 30 minute film about a group of friends who like cheeseburgers, dancing, and the Bible." Shirley becomes reflective of precisely what Abed is complaining about to Jeff— that references to popular culture have become so obvious that anyone is able to do it.

Abed not only complains that popular culture is now too easy to reference, he also suggests that *Pulp Fiction* is to blame, the film almost all people choose to pay homage to. At dinner, Abed openly criticizes overt references to popular culture, which is very unlike him, and also seems completely uninterested in Jeff's heavy-handed hints about the surprise birthday party. He denigrates *Pulp Fiction* and even ignores the gift of the replica of the wallet belonging to Jules, referring to it only as a metaphor for the problem of investment in popular culture. The study group assumes that a person who makes constant reference to film and television must love the work of Quentin Tarantino and they are punished for it, particularly those who have appeared closest to Abed: Jeff, Troy and Britta.

Jeff is punished by being emotionally manipulated by Abed's homage. Troy is thrown into self-doubt about his and Abed's friendship to the point that he destroys one of Abed's gifts. Britta is punished by being humiliated in front of the group and eventually fired from her job. One can argue the reason for their punishment is their assumption that Abed loves *Pulp Fiction*.

Jeff tells us what he knows about Abed is that Abed likes "chicken fingers, video games, Quentin Tarantino." Then Jeff begins to wonder, does he? The audience can find evidence from previous episodes that Abed prefers stop-motion animated holiday specials, films like *The Breakfast Club* (1985), *Batman Begins* (2005), and *Kickpuncher* (*Community*'s *Robocop* knock-off) and television series such as *Farscape* (1999–2003), *Cougar Town* (2009–), *Who's The Boss?* (1984–1992) and *The Cape* (2011). He has previously mentioned directors like Martin Scorsese in previous conversations with Jeff, but Abed has not mentioned Tarantino until this particular episode. Even with his reference to chicken fingers, Jeff reveals he has missed the point of Abed's extensive knowledge and use of film and television. For a start, it is another reference to Martin Scorsese and the film, *Goodfellas* (1990). But it is not the chicken fingers themselves that held Abed's interest — it was the possibility of being able to directly communicate with others, just as he is trying to do with this dinner with Jeff. Abed explicitly states the reason for his use of *My Dinner with Andre* and why he used it in an attempt to connect with Jeff: "Everyone else is growing and changing all the time and that's not really my jam. I'm more of a fast-blinking, stoic, removed, uncomfortably self-aware type. Like Data, or Johnny 5, or Mork, or Hal, or Kit, or Woodstock and/or Snoopy, and Spock probably goes without saying."

While the references to *My Dinner with Andre* are perhaps as obvious as references to *Pulp Fiction*, they are detailed, meticulous, and sophisticated as Abed is in control of the homage. The reason Abed chooses to refer to the film is the emotional core of the film, while the birthday party waiting for him at the diner echoes Wallace's lament: "That's the only way anything is expressed, through these completely insane jokes!" Abed wishes to connect with Jeff and therefore seeks a film that will allow him to do so. As Abed tells Jeff later at the diner, "I chose *My Dinner with Andre* because it's about a guy who has an unexpectedly enjoyable evening with a weird friend he's been avoiding lately." Feeling as though Abed's inability to interact without the use of film and television is causing Jeff to withdraw from their friendship, he constructs a situation that he thinks will allow him and Jeff to connect. Abed's employment of *My Dinner with Andre* is ultimately more successful than the allusions to *Pulp Fiction*, as Abed eventually achieves his desired outcome for the evening, while the *Pulp Fiction* narrative ends in the destruction of the briefcase (which turns out to be fake) and Britta losing her job at the diner. And though a more iconic *Pulp Fic-*

tion homage occurs at the end of the episode (the group re-enacts the diner sequence that opens and closes the film), it is in service of *My Dinner with Andre*: they return to that film's location, and to the voice-over narration employed at the beginning and end of the film. The music used at the end of the episode is also the same as that of *My Dinner with Andre*: Gymnopédie No. 1, by Erik Satie.

In light of this discussion of audiences, genre, and *Community*, it might make the reader wonder: how has some of the *Community* audience interpreted or engaged with "Critical Film Studies?" Todd VanDerWerff finds the *Pulp Fiction* references a ruse to deflect attention from the episode's even more blatant homage to *My Dinner with Andre*:

> "Critical Film Studies" has been sold as "the *Pulp Fiction* episode" of *Community*. Even NBC, which often doesn't promote the show all that heavily, has run many, many promo slots for the show playing up the crazy costumes and situations involved in the *Pulp Fiction*–styled B-plot. This makes perfect sense. *Pulp Fiction* is one of those cultural touchstone movies that almost everybody is familiar with, like *Star Wars* or *It's A Wonderful Life*.

VanDerWerff seems to suggest that the *Pulp Fiction* homage is almost a private joke that not only the series creators are in on but also NBC. Even promotional commercials for the episode suggest the show is using *Pulp Fiction* to demonstrate its place in popular culture and its use is designed, it would seem, to lure audiences into a reference to a more obscure film, just as Abed lures Jeff away from his goal of getting him to the surprise party. A certain opportunity for smugness is available to those who recognize why *Pulp Fiction* is being used and also to those who identify Abed's true purpose for the homage he has created. VanDerWerff also identifies the homage early:

> I saw *My Dinner with Andre* in high school.... Thus, from the opening minutes of the episode, I was sort of keyed into what the show was doing, had a vague idea that there might be more to Abed's plan than just meeting for a real, human interaction. But that didn't mean that the show didn't find a way to make the *My Dinner with Andre* conceit its own.

Another critic, Joshua Kurp, writes that he "logged onto Twitter right after 'Critical Film Studies' aired last night to see what people thought of the episode." He was mostly unsurprised by the responses, observing that, "half the world loved it and half the world wondered where the jokes were — and half of that half was disappointed that it wasn't a more straightforward parody of *Pulp Fiction*." Kurp sees "Critical Film Studies" as "an homage to the Tarantino classic, using it, along with *Cougar Town* and *My Dinner with Andre*, to discuss how we interact through pop culture." Kurp's review of "Critical Film Studies" seems an exact account of the episode's central themes, and the way in which Abed is used to illustrate these interactions. The way the episode produces these themes is via a strict adherence to generic conventions and an understanding of the *Community* audience.

Along the same line as Kurp, Andrew Daglas suggests that with "Critical Film Studies," *Community* subverts the audience's expectations of the series as a whole. According to him,

> While most of the study group waited in a '50s-themed burger bar, like a joke-stuffed trap waiting to be sprung, Abed was drawing Jeff into a very different, but no less faithful, cinematic recreation. Around the edges, "Critical Film Studies" hints at an overcooked version of the sort of theme episode that in many ways put *Community* on the map ("Modern Warfare," "Epidemiology," etc.). At its core, it's brashly subverting those expectations, the way Abed subverts Jeff's.

Daglas' appraisal of the episode seems in keeping with both the essence of the series and also the episode's larger message; that it is using an obvious reference to popular culture in order to examine how and why genre is used and the expectations audiences have in relation to genre. His reference to the *Pulp Fiction* homage as a trap perfectly demonstrates the series' refusal to take itself seriously, even drawing humor from its own approach to popular culture.

These viewers, along with Alanna Bennett, have concluded many of the same things: that "Critical Film Studies" defies viewers' expectations of an episode dedicated to an easily recognizable cult film within popular culture, thereby providing comment on the ways in which knowledge of popular culture can be perceived; focuses on generic textual features for each film with different levels of subtlety; and analyses Abed's relationship with the rest of the group, drawing on his specific use of film and television to communicate with them. They have all guessed at a central message of the episode and have very similar interpretations of the material. As Matt Zoller Seitz asserts, "'Critical Film Studies' ... was art. And art about art. And entertainment about entertainment. And a free-ranging conversation about the value of stories." The episode focuses on a discussion of film and television's affective powers with a spotlight on genre, thereby providing an illumination of Jeff and Abed's character.

As an avid audience member of *Community* myself, this episode was distinct for me in its particular use of a specific visual style. I was unfamiliar with *My Dinner with Andre* prior to watching the episode, but I recognized the difference in visual style and tone immediately. As someone who identifies very closely with Abed, I found the homage to *Pulp Fiction* an odd choice, given how long the series took to make reference to the film, suggesting the homage itself was being used in a particular way. I would argue that Tarantino is a director who has consistently created spaces for audiences to engage with genre and that this episode is a celebration of that play with the audience, something *Community* does consistently, but not quite the way it does in "Critical Film Studies."

If we see structure and genre as the ways in which *Community* sets up a space that allows the audience to engage and participate with the text, it is possible to view this engagement with the audience as a game, or even a quiz, to see if the audience is paying attention, or figure out whether they can be united, as Dennis Kennedy wonders, by their knowledge of popular culture and its associated cultural works. For the discerning viewer, the game is all but spelled out in the title: "Critical Film Studies." Presented with homages to a cult film within popular culture and a slightly more obscure independent film, those who recognize not only the latter film, but the reasons for the use of both are those who would be more likely to win.

The episode's use of *Pulp Fiction* reveals the ways Abed feels the group perceives him; the use of *My Dinner with Andre* illuminates the group's understanding of Abed's reliance on popular culture. The episode, and the series as a whole, does not try to position the audience in such a way as to understand this reliance, but rather it provides a space in which the audience members can locate themselves in popular culture, using structure and genre. It is a game, one in which the odds are stacked in the audience's favor. This is seen with Jeff's final words: "As parties go, it was quiet, dark and a little lame. We'd had better parties, and we'd had worse parties. But I doubt I'll ever forget *My Dinner with Andre* dinner with Abed."

Jeff briefly relinquishes control of the group to Abed, knowing that despite his best efforts, Abed was directing the events of the evening. He will remember this night as one in which he revealed his superficial understanding of Abed's character and how easy it was to be emotionally manipulated just as he often manipulates the group. Jeff assumes control once more, but it is with a newfound understanding of Abed and his use of popular culture in social situations. He concedes victory to Abed, allowing him to control the *Pulp Fiction* homage, and in doing so he also concedes victory to the *Community* audience.

Works Cited

"Abed's Uncontrollable Christmas." *Community*. NBC. 09 December 2010.
"Anthropology 101." *Community*. NBC. 23 September 2010.
Bennett, Alanna. "Community Recap: 'Critical Film Studies.'" *Give Me My Remote*, 2011. Web. 27 November 2012.
"Bollo." *The Mighty Boosh*. BBC3. 1 June 2004.
Bordwell, David, and Kristin Thompson. *Film Art: An Introduction*. 3d ed. New York: McGraw-Hill, 1990.
Chandler, Daniel. "An Introduction to Genre Theory." *Aberystwyth University*, 1997. Web. 10 December 2012.
"Cooperative Calligraphy." *Community*. NBC. 11 November 2010.
Creeber, Glen. *The Television Genre Book*. London: British Film Institute, 2001.
"Critical Film Studies." *Community*. NBC. 24 March 2011.
Daglas, Andrew. "Community: 'Critical Film Studies.'" *Chicago Now*, 2011. Web. 10 December 2012.
Gledhill, Christine. "Genre." *The Cinema Book*. Ed. Pam Cook. London: British Film Institute, 1985.

"Horror Fiction in Seven Spooky Steps." *Community*. NBC. 27 October 2011.
Kennedy, Dennis. *The Spectator and the Spectacle: Audiences in Modernity and Postmodernity*. New York: Cambridge University Press, 2009.
Kurp, Joshua. "Community Recap: 'Critical Film Studies.'" *Splitsider*, 2011. Web. 10 December 2012.
"The Legend of Old Gregg." *The Mighty Boosh*. BBC3. 23 August 2005.
McIntyre, Phillip. *Creativity and Cultural Production: Issues for Media Practice*. London: Palgrave Macmillan, 2012.
Mills, Brett. "Comedy Verite: Contemporary Sitcom Form." *Screen Spring 2004* 45.1 (2004): 15.
My Dinner with Andre. Dir. Louis Malle. Saga Productions and Andre Company, 1981.
Natoli, Joseph. "The Deep Morals of *Inglourious Basterds*." *Senses of Cinema* 52 (2009). Web. 3 December 2012.
Pulp Fiction. Dir. Quentin Tarantino. Miramax Films, 1994.
"The Science of Illusion." *Community*. NBC. 25 March 2010.
Seitz, Matt Zoller. "My Community Pulp Fictional Dinner with Andre." *Salon*, 2011. Web. 25 April 2013.
"The Strange Tale of the Crack Fox." *The Mighty Boosh*. BBC3. 6 December 2007.
Trafficante, Chris. "Before Django: The Cinema of Quentin Tarantino." *MMGN*, 2012. Web. 7 December 2012.
VanDerWerff, Todd. "Community." *AV Club*, 2011. Web. 10 December 2012.

Advanced Introduction to Liminality: *Community* on the Fringe
Lisa K. Perdigao

Throughout its four seasons, *Community* has experimented with the formula of network television. Like other series, much of its content is informed and shaped by its mode of production and its relationship with its network, NBC; yet the obstacles that *Community* has faced in its run have been made public and, as a result, have become part of the foreground and background of the series, making it a productive site for critical study. Attempting to sustain itself despite problems with program scheduling and marketing, *Community* suggests the possibilities and limitations of televisual narrative in the contemporary age as it demonstrates how a series can survive—and remain relevant—in the space of prime-time programming. *Community* presents these struggles as its diegesis, self-consciously exploring its medium through self-referential plots and commentary, most often directed by its resident television and film expert Abed. However, in season four, a season that was delayed—almost indefinitely—*Community* turns the lens on itself to examine its place within television history. With an inaugural episode that showcases the evolution of television and a final episode that ends with the promise of alternate storylines and seemingly infinite possibilities, the fourth season of *Community* can be read as a study of its own liminality. By evading cancellation and resisting closure in its narrative arcs, *Community*'s almost ending suggests new beginnings—for a new season, for syndication, and for new approaches to television narrative.

While the first three seasons of *Community* are marked by play with "conventions of space and time," the Season 3 episode, "Remedial Chaos Theory" (Episode 3.3), charts a new course for the series. A roll of the dice introduces six alternate timelines into the narrative and the viewers are given glimpses of the possible outcome from each roll, each possible combination. Season 2's episode, "Messianic Myths and Ancient Peoples" (Episode 2.5), presents Abed's pitch for a "Jesus movie" shot from the perspective of a filmmaker; in Abed's representation, "the filmmaker realizes that he is actually Jesus and he's being filmed by God's camera" and "it goes like that forever in both directions like a mirror in a mirror." In a metafictional turn, "Remedial Chaos Theory" returns to Abed's ideas about plot and borrows from the *Star Trek* episode, "Mirror, Mirror" (Episode 2.4), at its center to become a richly intertextual and textualized episode that plays with ideas about its emplottedness. At WonderCon 2012, creator and showrunner Dan Harmon commented on the writers' sources in *Rashomon* (1950), *Run Lola Run* (1998), and *Sliding Doors* (1998) in the episode, but "Remedial Chaos Theory," introducing ideas about recurrence plots as well as divergence, terms that are suggestive for narrative studies as well as physics, is even more expansive, reflecting Jorge Luis Borges' concept of "The Garden of Forking Paths" as the episode regenerates its own storyline.

Rather than playing out alternate storylines simultaneously, offering an either/or scenario like *Run Lola Run* and *Sliding Doors*, Borges' story presents the multiplicity and simultaneity of all versions of the story. As Borges' protagonist, Yu Tsun, an English professor working as a German spy, locates his target, Stephen Albert, a sinologist, he also discovers a family secret. While Tsun's ancestor Ts'úi Pên's idea of a garden of forking paths involves both a book and a labyrinth, Albert reveals to Tsun that they are the same, an infinite novel that presents a world in which "all possible outcomes occur" (2187). Tsun's initial concept of an infinite book is more limited than Pên's, as he notes, "I could think of nothing other than a cyclic volume, a circular one. A book whose last page was identical with the first, a book which had the possibility of continuing indefinitely" (Borges 2186). In contrast, Pên's and Borges' theory is all-encompassing, as Borges writes,

> "The garden of forking paths" was the chaotic novel.... In all fictional works, each time a man is confronted with several alternatives, he chooses one and eliminates the others; in the fiction of Ts'úi Pên, he chooses — simultaneously — all of them. *He creates*, in this way, diverse futures, diverse times which themselves also proliferate and fork [2186].

Community experiments with the space between Tsun's and Pên's descriptions. Rather than functioning as a circular narrative, with a last page (or episode) duplicating the first, the series demonstrates how the narrative is created by proliferating and forking. When Season 4 returns to this concept, offering yet another role of the dice, it does not merely repeat its themes. It generates new material from the combination of its sources.

"The Garden of Forking Paths" concept offers yet another link in the chain, as it is the concept that scientist Walter Bishop repeatedly refers to, and even maps out, to explain the world in/of *Fringe* (2008–2013), a contemporary of *Community*, which, somewhat ironically, ended its run just before *Community*'s fourth season aired. The introduction of "Remedial Chaos Theory" and its multiple timelines in Season 3 evidences the influence of *Fringe* as well as *Fringe*'s sources. Following Borges' and *Fringe*'s paths, *Community* presents the chaotic narrative in televisual form. As a series that experiments with tropes borrowed from other works of science fiction, most notably Mary Shelley's *Frankenstein* as a point of origination, *Fringe* continues the work of *The X-Files* (1993–2002) before it by offering a counter-narrative of what lies out there. *Fringe* does not aim to reveal the "truth" but rather suggests that truth is relative to one's perspective. *Fringe*'s experiment in narrative form provides a productive model for *Community* as the characters in *Fringe* are introduced to an alternate reality and alternate selves (a "Walternate" and "Fauxlivia" most notably). The "Darkest Timeline" bears an uncanny resemblance to *Fringe*'s other world(s), a different world order where antagonist Ben Chang, like the Observers, is omnipotent and omnipresent, even on posters. Posters in the episode feature the lines, "Chang is Leadership" and "Chang is U.S.," even "Chang is Right Behind You." These recall the billboards and signage in *Fringe* stating, "The Future in Order," with the image of an Observer, and, later, "Resist," bearing Peter and Olivia's daughter Etta's face. These alternate worlds show how different choices lead to the creation of alternate histories.

As *Fringe* continues throughout its five seasons, with a truncated fifth season as a prelude and parallel to *Community*'s shortened fourth season, it takes its characters back and forth between worlds, relegating them to a liminal state of in-betweenness. As past, present, and future collide and coexist in the space of *Fringe*, when *Community* borrows from it, it enters the space of experimental contemporary television that pushes the boundaries of its medium, offering new ways of conceiving the construction of episodes, seasons, and series. Following *Fringe*'s lead, *Community* explores its liminal status. Performing in the space between situation comedy, science fiction, fantasy, horror, police procedural, and even cartoon, *Community* becomes a nexus not only for its study group but for the medium of television itself. At the end of Season 4, *Community*'s return to *Fringe* locates the series as part of a larger discussion about how contemporary television continues to generate meaning at the end of its run, the inevitable ending that all series face—whether it be at the network's hand or by the creator's own design.

It is fitting that Abed is our mediator for the ideas presented in "Remedial Chaos Theory," as he continually asserts the presence of science fiction within the story-world of *Community*, along with Troy, introducing seemingly infinite sources of play with his allusions to and borrowings from other plots. Troy and Abed's obsession with *Inspector Spacetime* offers a solid foundation for the series as its source of play, *Doctor Who*, a series sustained over five decades (1963–1989; 2005–), is regenerative like its protagonist. While the borrowings from *Doctor Who* create the "conventions of space and time" that operate within *Community*, "Remedial Chaos Theory" goes even further to offer a metacommentary about how narrative is conceived and reconceived in television to generate new possibilities. In Borges' story, Albert tells Tsun that his ancestor believed in "a growing, dizzying net of divergent, convergent and parallel times," a "network of times which approached one another, forked, broke off, or were unaware of one another for centuries," leading him to embrace "*all* possibilities of time" (2188). Applying Albert's terms to *Community* yields new meanings when contextualized with the story behind the series, the struggles with NBC. In *Community*, the connections between texts — with sources as diverse as Borges and *The Muppet Show* (1976–1981) — create a network of meanings. Where that other network NBC arguably attempts to close off the system, *Community* sustains itself by embracing all possibilities available to and through its medium.

While "Remedial Chaos Theory" demonstrates the creation of these diverse times that result from the roll of the dice, it is the aftermath of the episode that is most suggestive for the series, particularly the trajectory — or seemingly infinite loop — of Season 4. In itself, Season 4 is challenged by time: it was aired out of sync with its regular program schedule, with a start date falling in February rather than October. In the redesigned space of fall and spring programming, *Community*'s Halloween episode, "Paranormal Parentage" (Episode 4.2), appeared on Valentine's Day. In the Season 4 finale, "Advanced Introduction to Finality" (Episode 4.13), Pierce wonders about the timing of graduation as well as the series' end, saying, "I just don't get it. We just had Christmas and now it's warm outside." However, offering an "Intro to Senselessness," the college divides its calendar year into two semesters that are more reflective of television programming: fall/spring and summer/winter.

"Remedial Chaos Theory" and "Advanced Introduction to Finality" can be viewed as subverting — or rejecting — that standard plot and structure prescribed by network programming. Moreover, these episodes provide a blueprint for the design of the series itself. Defining a "poetics of television narrative," Michael Z. Newman identifies how the teleology of television narrative can be measured in beats, episodes, and arcs, constituent elements that are a "product of an advertising-driven industrial context of narrative production" (24) and become "a way of managing story material, of crafting it into a meaningful whole" (24). For Newman, these measures work to compel weekly viewing and maximize ratings yet also "come with the aesthetic functions of generating interest" in characters' "struggles and discoveries," ultimately creating a cohesive narrative by "maximizing formal unity" (24).

As *Community* self-consciously refers to the forces behind its production and calls attention to its own structure, it in many ways complicates what Newman takes to be the more conventional aspects of television narrative. Newman highlights the "direction of influence" that extends from corporate office to the writer's room to the audience, noting that "a kind of feedback loop is initiated between the creative and corporate branches of the industry"; as a part of that loop, "A device like redundancy is seen to serve everyone's interests" (Newman 25). *Community* experiments with this idea of the "feedback loop," subversively playing with its relationship to the corporate branches; the series creates an open circuit, a reconfigured network that generates meaning through critical re-examination, by challenging the viewers' expectations of television's conventions.

The feedback loop that Newman describes is altered in the space of the series and becomes the point of origination — or continuation — for a fourth season that almost did not happen. Part of this is by necessity: its creator and showrunner, Dan Harmon, was unceremoniously fired, breaking that feedback loop in conversations between creative and corporate branches and, losing the showrunner, threatening the continuity of the narrative arc. Performing as an open circuit, Season 4 takes the characters — and the viewers — into various possible futures for the series as the characters face the graduation that looms at the season's (and potentially series') end. However, borrowing from Frank Kermode's text, the "sense of an ending" for the season if not the series was already complicated by the season's beginning.

"History 101" (Episode 4.1), marking the beginning of Season 4, takes the characters through a history of television, from live action studio production to animation to its reality, all mediated by Abed's design and represented as "Abed's Happy Community College Show" and, in another metafictional turn, an animated "Greendale Babies." Borrowing from another *Muppets* show, *Muppet Babies* (1984–1991), "Greendale Babies" offers a world where the characters remain together, static, even infantilized. Where Season 4 ends with Jeff's anxiety about graduation — about closure more generally — it begins with Abed's fear of the group's graduation and separation, the loss of "community" itself. This is not entirely new territory, however; Abed's coping mechanisms lead him to a magical adventure in Season 2, in the episode, "Abed's Uncontrollable Christmas"(Episode 2.11); there, repression, denial, and imagination allow Abed and the other characters an escape from Abed's family dramas (that plot) to the world of Claymation. In "History 101," Abed again retreats to a world of his own making, but in the space of the episode offers a meditation on different modes of production for *Community* itself, exploring what the series could have been — and might still be, even with new casting to fill the vacancy left in Season 4: Pierce is played by Fred Willard.

In *Reading for the Plot*, Peter Brooks states, "If the motor of narrative is desire, totalizing, building ever-larger units of meaning, the ultimate determinants of meaning lie *at the end*, and narrative desire is ultimately, inexorably, desire *for* the end" (52); however, according to Brooks, the "deathlike ending" becomes problematized in many works of fiction, particularly in postmodern literature. He notes that endings "have become difficult to achieve," absent or permanently deferred, leaving one "playing in anticipation of a terminal structuring moment of revelation that never comes, creating the space of an as-if, a fiction of finality" (Brooks 313). At the end of Season 4, *Community* again uses the episode title to highlight the theory it will explore. However, its study of "finality," like many of the episodes before it, suggests the problems with the concept, particularly for its characters, setting, and narrative. While "Advanced Introduction to Finality" ostensibly offers to provide that "sense of an ending," true to form, and true to Brooks' sense of postmodern literature, *Community* leaves its characters and audience "playing in anticipation of terminal structuring moment of revelation that never comes"; "Advanced Introduction to Finality" is the as-if, a "fiction of finality." Brooks' theory about the possibilities generated by the play with endings is suggestive for *Community*'s larger narrative arc, as he writes, "Any final authority claimed by narrative plots, whether of origin or end, is illusory.... It is the role of fictional plots to impose an end which yet suggests a return, a new beginning: a rereading" (109). *Community*'s Season 4 finale challenges any notion of a "final authority" in and on the series, crafting its place as a site for new beginnings rather than closure.

While "Basic Lupine Urology" (Episode 3.17) takes the characters and viewers into the world of forensic science, heavily borrowing from and appropriating markers from *Law & Order*, the season four finale plays with the idea of closure that is a hallmark of the police procedural and instead turns to other narrative forms. *Law & Order* becomes a source of parody and play with the series' narrative; Annie switches majors to forensic science by delaying her graduation, giving her more narrative time. Despite its genre-blurring performances, though, *Community* is still informed by its own formulations, not only the situation comedy but also the bildungsroman. The series documents the growth of its characters throughout their years in school, yet with its setting in a community college that has a poor graduation rate, *Community* already suggests its play with the genre and its own sense of time.

By Season 4, with the imminent end of their college careers marked by the degree timeline, although Jeff's degree is a bit ambiguous in the series and in the episode, *Community* presents itself in the space occupied by the following TV series: *Beverly Hills, 90210* (1990–2000) and a rebooted *90210* (2008–2013), *Buffy the Vampire Slayer* (1997–2003), *Felicity* (1998–2002), *Dawson's Creek* (1998–2003), and, more recently, *Glee* (2009–). The four-year run of *Felicity* documents the character's time in college, with seasons ordered by her school year (freshman, sophomore, junior, and senior); its sense of an ending is achieved with graduation and adulthood. However, even from its very beginnings, *Community* complicates this timeline. Jeff Winger, a successful lawyer, is sent back to college and other characters, most notably Pierce and Leonard, are forever suspended in this stage, representative perhaps of not only *Community*'s design but suggestive of other series within the genre. *Beverly Hills, 90210* had experimented with the space beyond high school, like its contemporary *Saved by the Bell* (1989–1993), which extends its arc into "The College Years" (1993–1994), sending its protagonists to the same university. In the rebooted *90210*, Jennie Garth, Luke Perry, and Shannen Doherty reprise their roles, with Garth's character, Kelly, cast as a guidance counselor.

Fan speculation about Jeff's role after graduation has led to the suggestion that he could teach at the college, performing a role similar to *Glee*'s Finn who returns to McKinley High School after he graduates. However, in another extratextual turn, due to the passing of actor Cory Monteith, it ends that storyline; thus, the third episode of the series' fifth season is to memorialize the actor and character. Ryan Murphy had stated that he would not keep his characters on the series post-graduation, leaving his actors to speculate on their futures in social media as well as in the stories' diegesis; however, Murphy has effectively spun the series into a new location, following graduates Rachel, Kurt, and Santana to New York. And, at home, new characters revisit former storylines, for example, with the introduction of "The New Rachel" and "Britney 2.0." *Community* has played with the tropes in *Glee*, most notably in "Regional Holiday Music" (Episode 3.10), highlighting (and parodying) how *Glee*'s narrative arc always returns to regionals. Borrowing from *Glee*'s masterplot for returning characters is problematic for *Community*, as the transformations of Chang's role attest. With a trajectory that takes him from professor to student to security guard to dictator to amnesiac, Chang's narrative destabilizes the idea of any "authority" much less "final authority" in the series.

As *Community* suggests different possibilities for the sustainment of the relationship between the study group members, that community, it enters a dialogue with other series that cover that ground. After high school and college graduation, *Dawson's Creek* had attempted the metafictional turn, presenting Dawson as a version of creator Kevin Williamson, a filmmaker who fictionalizes the story of his years growing up with his circle of friends. Despite its work to regenerate storylines through these meta-moments, though, closure in *Dawson's Creek* (1998–2003) is finally achieved in Season 6 with the characters' reunion set five years later, when Jen, one of its central characters, dies in its two-part series finale titled "All Good Things..." (Episode 6.23) "...Must Come to an End" (Episode 6.24). That *Fringe*'s Peter Bishop is played by Joshua Jackson,

Dawson's Pacey, is ironic; Peter becomes the key to the masterplot of *Fringe*, regenerating himself and the narrative beyond its finale.

Following this (re)turn to science fiction and fantasy, perhaps the most suggestive comparison for *Community*'s characters' resistance to both graduation and the series' conclusion is *Buffy the Vampire Slayer* (1997–2003) that begins as a high school series, representing threats to adolescents by way of monster metaphors, and graduates to college yet fails to complete that cycle. Buffy's high school graduation almost marks the "End of Days" and she drops out of their local college once her obligations force her to leave adolescence behind. *BtVS* is a series that plays with the idea of endings throughout its run, with a "Big Bad" introduced each season, leading its characters to wonder what the plural form of "apocalypse" is.

David Lavery refers to Kermode's statement that we "make considerable imaginative investments in coherent patterns which, by the provision of an end, make possible a satisfying consonance with the origins and with the middle" (1) as he examines the narrative arc of *Buffy the Vampire Slayer*'s seven seasons, making a case for a "narrative eschatology" that has apocalypses at its foundation. Lavery writes,

> As a television narrative, every episode of *Buffy* offers us a variety of "little deaths," mini-apocalypses as well: the distinctly televisual ends, allowing for commercial breaks, that come within the narrative itself; the ending of each episode…; the endings of narrative arcs; the ending of each season. And finally, we have the final narrative eschatology of *Buffy the Vampire Slayer* itself [3].

Recalling the "last laughs" of comedies *I Love Lucy* (1951–1957), *The Honeymooners* (1955–1956), *M*A*S*H* (1972–1983), *Seinfeld* (1989–1998), and the endings of episodic serials *Dallas* (1978–1991), *Twin Peaks* (1990–1991), and *The X-Files* (1993–2002), Lavery makes a case that "no series ending had ever been so much about ending as the always apocalyptic *Buffy the Vampire Slayer* … by the end of Buffy's story, Buffy herself had already announced, in the story itself, the end of story" (3). For Lavery, *Buffy* is one of "those fictions which continue to interest us, which through their very subject matter and form give to us a 'sense of an ending' and facilitate our imaginative deconstruction and construction of our world" (39).

It is not surprising, given this narrative eschatology, that Joss Whedon's other vehicle *Angel* (1999–2004) is an intriguing case study for a "sense of an ending" in television; in contrast to *Buffy*, *Angel* introduces new complexities which resonate with *Community*'s production. Exhibiting the influence of this unlikely source, *Community*'s fourth season features the episode "Intro to Felt Surrogacy" (Episode 4.9), an episode featuring puppet versions of the characters. *Angel*'s fifth (and final) season presents the episode "Smile Time" (Episode 5.14), in which Angel, investigating a television studio that takes children's lives, is transformed into a puppet. *Community* repeats that televisual magic by turning its characters into puppets as they share their feelings with one another, with Dean Pelton's puppets helping to facilitate the dialogue.

Angel is born as a spin-off from *Buffy*, a necessary extension of *Buffy*'s narrative as the two characters are unable to remain together; the result of their union is the "End of Days," but it is *Angel*'s ending that is most evocative for studying how endings are negotiated in the space of the experimental serial narrative, itself staged in a liminal space between genres — film noir, detective fiction, and the supernatural — and an extension of *Buffy*'s Sunnydale. At the time of *Angel*'s cancellation, occurring a year after the more "natural" ending of *Buffy*, its ratings were up. In an interview with Mike Jozic, co-executive producer of *Angel* David Fury says that, due to the show's success and Whedon's desire to work on narratives that would extend into Season 6, Whedon pushed Jordan Levin, the head of The WB, for an early pick-up for *Angel*'s sixth season; Levin cancelled the show the next day (qtd. in Jozic).

That decision — on both sides — shapes the course of the series and its conclusion that many say occurred too soon. While the end of *Buffy* brings the activation of a generation of slayers (suggesting the viewers' new role as well), it also marks the continuation of its narrative. As the Sunnydale sign falls into the abyss, Giles says, "There is another one in Cleveland. Not to spoil the moment" ("Chosen," Episode 7.22). Roz Kaveney makes a case for how *Angel* sustains its narrative to — and through — the end in its finale, "Not Fade Away" (Episode 5.22). Kaveney compares *Buffy*'s design, where each year "was planned to end in such a way that, were the show not renewed, the finale would act as an apt summation of the series so far" (1), to *Angel*'s, writing, "It has never been the case that endings in *Angel* were so clear-cut and each year culminated in a slingshot ending, an attention-grabber that kept viewers interested by allowing them to speculate on where things were going" (2). Kaveney suggests that the final image, that of Angel continuing the fight despite the overwhelming odds against him, offers the creation of "Schrödinger's Angel, who at this point in the game is neither undead nor dead" (5). Whedon has commented that he left that ending intentionally ambiguous, in case it was renewed or found a new medium, and, for Kaveney, that ending performs a double function: providing a series finale and offering the possibility of continuation, indefinitely.

Season 4 of *Community* presents the writers, cast, and crew with a similar problem. With the loss of Harmon at the helm and an uncertain future, the series returns, as many critics have noted, to the formulas of its early making, including both paintball and the "Darkest Timeline." While the audience is divided in social media over the strengths and weaknesses of the season, Kaveney's comments about the difficulty of performing so many roles extends from the *Angel*verse to *Community* as well. Newman's assessment that "A device like redundancy is seen to serve everyone's interests" (25) is suggestive of at least part of the attempt to sustain season four, particularly in Harmon's absence. Harmon has commented that the season was an "unflattering" impression of his work. Part of the critiques — beyond Harmon's — center on the static nature of the narrative; plotlines introduced in earlier seasons do not seem to go anywhere. In essence, the critiques read like those of the formulaic sitcom, which is in opposition to everything that *Community* has been credited for being. As the criticism attests, *Community* does not serve everyone's interests through redundancy.

The finale creates a playful space in its returns, rewriting its own history. Jeff recalls the plot of "Remedial Chaos Theory" and suggests that they roll to see who will bring soda for the graduation party. Although Abed has not mentioned the "Darkest Timeline" in months, the camera features a close-up of Abed as Jeff rolls the dice. When it fails to land on a number, it re-introduces Borges' theory and seemingly infinite possibilities. The characters agree that it could mean nothing — or everything. As Jeff admits, anticipating the viewers' response, "I was hoping for more" ("Advanced Introduction to Finality"). And it is all about expectations, returning to Brooks' sense of the desire for the end. Jeff, forever the viewer of the series, says that he was expecting a "little more pageantry" for graduation. The episode then turns (or returns) to Brooks' formula, "playing in anticipation of a terminal structuring moment of revelation that never comes, creating the space of an as-if, a fiction of finality" (Brooks 313).

Identifying that something is amiss in the *Community*-verse, again reflecting viewer sentiment as well as the characters' (perhaps noting the disappearance of Harmon and other writers), Jeff traces it back to the earlier source, returning to the episode that Harmon noted would be a standard for greatness for Season 5. Jeff says, "Something happened when I rolled that dice. Something only nerds can understand" ("Advanced Introduction to Finality"). When the evil versions of the characters appear, they bear similarities to the originals, including their self-consciousness. Evil Pierce reappears, a trick of the eye, as Chevy Chase is about to leave the series. "Advanced Introduction to Finality" is Chase's last episode. Both Harmon and Chase left the series in season four. While Harmon returns for season five, Chase will remain absent (although an absent presence) for the remainder of the run. Going back to the episode, Evil Pierce tells them that he faked his death a year ago to teach everyone a lesson, recalling the season two plotline of "Intermediate Documentary Filmmaking" (Episode 2.16). However, when evil Troy asks what the lesson was, Pierce says, "Who can remember? It was more than a year ago" ("Advanced Introduction to Finality"). When Abed and once evil Abed meet, they agree that the episode is *Superman 3* meets that *Star Trek* episode meets season three of *The Cape*. When Abed notes that *The Cape* has been cancelled, the other Abed says, "Not here," and gives him the tape. Alternate histories emerge from these forking paths, including television history. As a "mirror in a mirror," the finale plays with this chain of signification. And it is in the return to its sources that the final episode makes meaning in and for the series. As Abed says to Jeff, "Don't logic this one away from me. We finally found a way to make paintball cool again" ("Advanced Introduction to Finality").

While the episode offers continuous play with its recurring gags and plots (Newman's sense of redundancy that achieves cohesion), it is the return to the "Darkest Timeline" and the final scene that becomes that regenerative source. "Troy and Abed in the Morning" performs as an extension of the diegetic space in the series; the season finale uses this space to counter the other ending of the episode, and, at the time, possibly the series. Jeff's graduation is almost trumped by Pierce's appearance, allowing the character to be at the center of the plot for his final performance, but the graduation and the study group's "final" meeting around the table provide a fitting end to the bildungsroman. In a sense, *Community*'s graduation plays with the more traditional plotline evidenced in series finales like in *Felicity* and *Roswell* (1999–2002) yet it, even in that performance, resists closure. The anchor in reality, albeit a cynical one, Jeff, is taken on an Abed-esque journey to another world. Abed must inform Jeff this time that it is a coping mechanism, reversing the teleology of "Abed's Uncontrollable Christmas" and "History 101." However, "Six Seasons and a Movie" clearly appears on the chalkboard behind Dean Pelton during the "wedding/graduation mash-up" combination borrowed from *Glee*'s musical numbers. When the episode ends, Troy and Abed appear, the doppelgänger versions, at least, to offer a redefinition of *Community*'s reality. The garden of forking paths returns as Troy and Abed present split screens of the different timelines. When evil Jeff appears to tell them that no one is watching, they continue with their show, with Troy winking at the camera as the shot fades out.

The ending of "Advanced Introduction to Finality" is evocative for its parallels to that other extratextual material, the promos that are featured on Comedy Central to advertise the syndicated run of the series on Friday nights. In one of them, Ken Jeong, who plays Chang, throws money into the air and announces, "Guys, we're syndicated!" and Joel McHale, who plays Jeff, replies, "Oh, great, now we cannot be watched by even more people" ("We're Syndicated!"). When Yvette Nicole Brown, who plays Shirley, says that they just need promotion, she and McHale turn to the camera as McHale says, "Holy crap, we're being advertised. What the hell network is this?" ("We're Syndicated!"). In the space beyond the series, in the worlds of alternate timelines and seemingly infinite possibilities, *Community* continues to generate meaning. The finale's "Troy and Abed" conclusion recalls an earlier one, offering yet another return. When *Community* was indefinitely postponed in the fall of 2012, Troy and Abed returned to the camera to present the news and the reasons behind the executive decision to postpone the series. Recalling *Angel* and those "Powers that Be," the Oracles that determine the character's future and possible redemption, Troy and Abed refer to the powers that be that made the decision about their future: the network. Abed says, "Even though the powers that be agreed to put the premiere on October 19th, they couldn't decide *where* to put October 19th.... They explained to us that October 19th isn't just a date. It's a state of mind" ("*Community* Season 4 Premieres ... Someday").

Here, even in the extended space of *Community*, in a special episode of "Troy and Abed in the Morning," time is relative to network programming. A college's academic year can be organized according to fall and spring lineups, summer and winter breaks, and October 19th can be anytime. Changing their tune to "Troy and Abed airing someday," Troy and Abed — and the entire community — play with the "final authority" of studio executives until the very end. "The minds behind this ship know what they're doing" ("*Community* Season 4 Premieres ... Someday"), Abed says, and when the season airs, the last "Troy and Abed in the Morning," shot from another world and presenting multiple storylines that continue to proliferate and fork, resists closure.

Lacey Rose writes that *Community* has become "the most captivating behind-the-scenes soap opera on TV, with its leader exalted, then killed off and now resurrected for what likely is a final act." Rose's account of *Community* reads like the plot of *Buffy*, with its heroine's death in season five's finale "The Gift" (Episode 5.22) and resurrection on a new network, The WB, for a sixth and seventh season. The *Buffy*verse technically consists of seven seasons and a movie, although the movie predates the series. Whedon's other series, *Firefly* (2002–2003) is resuscitated beyond its limited run on network television as the film *Serenity* (here, recast as "one season and a movie").

While a future beyond Season 5 is uncertain, a truncated fifth season as a "final act" puts *Community* in good company, mirroring *Fringe* yet again. Offering "diverse futures" as well as "diverse times" at the end of its fourth season, *Community* continues to play with the "as-if." *Community* shows us "final authority," even that of the network, is illusory. In deferring the "deathlike ending," *Community* continues to suggest "a return, a new beginning: a rereading" for its fans, the network that sustains the series. *Community*, then, suggests not only a return to other genres and series, borrowings from those masterplots, but a redefinition of liminality itself, demonstrating how television exists and persists beyond studio offices to the other side of the screen.

Works Cited

"Abed's Uncontrollable Christmas." *Community*. NBC. 9 December 2010.
"Advanced Introduction to Finality." *Community*. NBC. 9 May 2013.

"All Good Things..." *Dawson's Creek*. The WB. 14 May 2003.
"Basic Lupine Urology." *Community*. NBC. 26 April 2012.
Borges, Julio Luis. "The Garden of Forking Paths." *The Norton Anthology of Western Literature*. 8th ed. Ed. Sarah Lawall. Vol. 2. New York: Norton, 2006. 2182–2189.
Brooks, Peter. *Reading for the Plot: Design and Intention in Narrative*. New York: Knopf, 1984.
"Chosen." *Buffy the Vampire Slayer*. The WB. 20 May 2003.
"*Community* Season 4 Premieres ... Someday." Online video clip. *YouTube*. 19 October 2012. Web. 23 September 2013.
Francis. "WonderCon 2012: 'Community' Panel and Roundtable." *Geeks Peeks*. WellThemes.com, 20 March 2012. Web. 24 September 2013.
"The Gift." *Buffy the Vampire Slayer*. The WB. 22 May 2001.
"History 101." *Community*. NBC. 7 February 2013.
"Intro to Felt Surrogacy." *Community*. NBC. 11 April 2013.
Jozic, Mike. "Interview with David Fury." *Meanwhile ... Interviews*. Web. 22 September 2013.
Kaveney, Roz. "A Sense of the Ending: Schrödinger's *Angel*." *Slayage: The Journal of the Whedon Studies Association* 4.4 [16] (2005): 37 pars. Web. 22 September 2013.
Lavery, David. "Apocalyptic Apocalypses: Toward a Narrative Eschatology of *Buffy the Vampire Slayer*." *Slayage: The Journal of the Whedon Studies Association* 3.1 [9] (2003): 43 pars. Web. 22 September 2013.
"Messianic Myths and Ancient Peoples *Community*. NBC. 21 October 2010.
"Mirror, Mirror." *Star Trek*. NBC. 6 October 1967.
"...Must Come to an End." *Dawson's Creek*. The WB. 14 May 2003.
Newman, Michael Z. "From Beats to Arcs: Toward a Poetics of Television Narrative." *The Velvet Light Trap* 58 (2006): 16–28. Project Muse. 17 September 2013.
"Not Fade Away." *Angel*. The WB. 19 May 2004.
"Paranormal Parentage." *Community*. NBC. 14 February 2013.
"Regional Holiday Music." *Community*. NBC. 8 December 2011.
"Remedial Chaos Theory." *Community*. NBC. 13 October 2011.
Rose, Lacey. "'Community's' Dan Harmon Reveals the Wild Story Behind His Firing and Rehiring." *The Hollywood Reporter*. 17 July 2013. Web. 20 September 2013.
"Smile Time." *Angel*. The WB. 18 February 2004.
"We're Syndicated!" Online video clip. *Comedy Central*. 5 September 2013. Web. 23 September 2013.

PART IV:
EXTRACURRICULAR ACTIVITIES

Community's Communities: Bringing the Fan to the (Study) Table
Joseph S. Walker

Dan Harmon's *Community*[1] is both a product of and a commentary on a television industry that has changed enormously in the last twenty years, particularly in its relationship to an audience that has grown more demanding, more sophisticated, and more deeply implicated in the structure of the television text itself. Building on the advances made by other recent, structurally innovative programs, the show destabilizes traditional notions of identity and distinction, making the act of watching the show part of the subject of the show itself. In essence, the stories of the seven-member study group at the heart of the show's narrative(s) invite the engaged viewer to occupy the vacant eighth chair at the study table that is the center of its universe, while at the same time insisting that it is impossible for any normative self to be maintained, in that position or any other.

To fully understand this, we must view *Community* in its proper context — the context provided by the flourishing of creativity and ambition in television today. It is difficult to resist the notion that we are currently experiencing something like a golden age of television production and reception, the maturation of a medium previously dismissed as unavoidably infantile. To a large extent, the improvement in quality seen in American television in recent years has been fostered and licensed by vast changes in the technology through which television is watched. Foreshadowed by the VCR, new technologies such as complete-season (or complete-series) DVD sets, DVR receivers, and internet streaming (begging the question, is it still a television show if you watch it on your computer, or even your iPod?) are buttressed by an increasingly vibrant and polyvalent entertainment media, including internet communities which allow, encourage, and preserve detailed, sophisticated critical discussions of programs and the people who make them.[2] Not so long ago, an individual episode of any given television series could be watched only at the moment of its broadcast, almost invariably within the isolating environment of the home and disrupted by commercial breaks, and retained only imperfectly in memory, rendering detailed consideration or sustained critical discussion difficult or impossible. Even a series like the original *Star Trek* (1966–1969), which inspired a devoted fan base that kept the series culturally "alive" for years after it went off the air, relied upon fan-generated materials, as well as published scripts and novelizations, to supplement syndication, the only way to see the actual program (however imperfectly, since syndicated episodes were often poorly maintained, carelessly edited, and shown out of sequence).

Today, an episode can be recorded by the home viewer and rewatched at leisure, purchased as part of a DVD set, or, more and more often, simply streamed online (through legitimate or illegitimate sites) as often as desired. It can (or, increasingly, must) thus be seen in the larger context of the series as a whole, not as an isolated text. Within hours of its airing, the episode will have produced a vigorous family of secondary texts in the form of reviews, summaries, criticisms, dissections, and annotations written by both professional critics and dedicated fans. It can be discussed not only with the viewer's immediate acquaintances, but with people around the world. It has become possible, in other words, for television series to stand alongside novels and movies as fully actualized texts, both available and appropriate for a variety of forms of detailed engagement and analysis. Simultaneously, the rise of cable and other alternate outlets, as well as the erosion of traditional limitations on subject matter and representation, have permitted the development of more adult, sophisticated subjects, plots, and characters. Naturally, a new kind of audience enables — indeed, demands — a new kind of text. A series such as David Chase's *The Sopranos* (1999–2007), David Simon's *The Wire* (2002–2008), or Mitch Hurwitz's *Arrested Development* (2003–2006, returning in 2013) simply could not have existed on American television prior to the late 1990s; no network would have broadcast it, and without the ability to revisit and reconsider earlier episodes, no audience would have been capable of fully appreciating it. To watch a single episode of *The Wire* is nearly meaningless; to watch the entire series is to experience a challenging artistic work of the highest order of complexity and ambition. Even the much-derided traditional three-camera sitcom has undergone similar leaps in quality and sophistication, with the lead in this arena being taken by *Seinfeld* (1990–1998).

Despite this flowering of structural, narrative, and topical creativity, however, most television series remain hidebound in their treatment of character as static, fixed, and unchanging. For much of television history, it was possible to attribute this thematic feature, at least in part, to the limitations on the audience's reception; the viewer would have access to only one episode of the show at a time, usually at least a week after having seen the show last. Even if a show made it into syndication, it was likely that episodes would be shown in essentially random sequence. Every episode of a traditional television series, in this context, had to be capable of functioning as a self-contained unit, presenting its characters in the kind of broad, unchanging strokes that created a comforting feeling of immediate familiarity. Thus, Hawkeye Pierce of *M*A*S*H* (1972–1983) must always and forever be the brilliant but rebellious surgeon, alternately joking about and railing against the obscenity of war; *Star Trek*'s original captain, James T. Kirk, must always and forever be the dashing, slightly arrogant hero; Lucy Ricardo, title character of *I Love Lucy* (1951–1957) must always and forever be the daffy, stage-obsessed wife. In a given episode, any one of these characters might seem to learn a lesson or undergo an experience which would fundamentally change their worldview, or at least have a lingering aftereffect, but only rarely would any reference to this be made in subsequent episodes. After all, there was no way of knowing if an audience member had seen the previous episode, and if they had not, they had no way to access it or even easily acquire information about it. In the language employed by Antonio Savorelli in his discussion of the recent evolution of the sitcom, such shows were "closed" ("actions developed in each episode hardly condition other episodes"), while the development of new technologies and a new audience has permitted shows to become increasingly "open" (which implies "a more complex story that overflows the boundaries of each single episode so far as to possibly cover the entire span of the series") (17).

Even in many of the most ambitiously open programs of recent years, however, characters remain remarkably and surprisingly consistent and unaltered from one year to the next. In many of the most highly acclaimed and eagerly watched series of the new mediascape, the inability of characters to grow or change is not a function of production, but rather a feature of a shared philosophical bleakness: true change or progress is difficult, if not impossible, to achieve in the worlds created by these shows. Again, here, *Seinfeld* and *The Sopranos* can serve as touchstones. *Seinfeld* was famously devoted to the rule that there would be "no learning, no hugs"; the four core characters remain fundamentally the same selfish, neurotic people throughout the entire run of the series as they are in the beginning, even as the show incorporates a growing universe of minor characters and running gags, which assumes a deep knowledge of previous episodes on the part of the audience. The audience's knowledge of Jerry's Manhattan grows with every episode, but there is no sign that the characters experience similar growth (the show acknowledges this in its closing episode, ending with the characters returning to the same meaningless conversation about shirts they had at the start of the pilot). Tony Soprano, more problematically, may well wish to change. *The Sopranos* begins with him consulting a psychiatrist, and when he is in a coma in the final season of the show, he dreams of a world where he is a completely different person, a harmless salesman rather than a fearsomely selfish and destructive gangster. Whatever his wishes, though, he is unable to escape the violent world that produced him or the violent self he has become. Again and again, over the course of the six seasons, Soprano tries to do things differently, only to end up returning to the world and the identity he has always known. Indeed, this is one of the major themes of the entire series: no matter how fervently they wish to change their identity or the circumstances which shape their lives, characters are unable to do so and usually pay high prices for the attempt (think, for example, of Carmela Soprano's doomed attempt to leave her domineering husband).

This idea is not unique to David Chase's universe; it has appeared again and again in television's most prestigious dramas and comedies of the twenty-first century. In *Mad Men* (2007–), the man who calls himself "Don Draper" must struggle continuously, and more and more often fruitlessly, to maintain the artificial self he has created in defiance of his past. In *Nurse Jackie* (2009–), Jackie Payton remains defined by addiction, even after going through rehab. Enoch Malachi "Nucky" Thompson of *Boardwalk Empire* (2010–) must abandon his pretense that he is only "half a gangster" and accept the full reality of his criminality. In *Dexter* (2006–2013), Dexter Morgan's "dark passenger" is so deeply embedded that he rarely even considers the possibility of change. *Seinfeld* writer and producer Larry David may long for real human contact on *Curb Your Enthusiasm* (2000–2011), but he is continually undermined by his own misanthropy, just as *The Office*'s (2005–) Michael Scott is by his irredeemable stupidity, the Bluths of *Arrested Development* (2003–2006, 2013–) by their oblivious greed, and Louis C.K. of *Louie* (2010–) by his inescapable weakness. All of these series have been enormous hits with both critics and popular audiences, and highly influential in the television industry.

Seen in their context, *Community* emerges as something strangely unusual in contemporary American television—a series which proceeds from the assumption that identity is not fixed, permanent and inescapable, but rather endlessly fluid and shifting in response to both internal desires and the influences of the external (and heavily mediated) world. Crucially, as we will see, this idea turns out to be no more positive than the more common notion that character cannot be altered or improved.

The characters of *Community* are threatened not by the iron bands of their identities, but rather by the suspicion that true identity no longer exists beneath the shifting sands of play and masquerade that define life at Greendale Community College — and, by the third season, in the world at large. As Tully Barnett and Ben Kooyman have pointed out, "The depiction of the fantastical and the real as intersecting states is at the heart of *Community*" (110). Indeed, the very world the characters occupy is characterized by its lack of solidity and stability. Greendale is less a school than a communal "Dreamatorium," seen in "Studies in Modern Movement (Episode 3.7); "Contemporary Impressionists" (Episode 3.11); "Virtual Systems Analysis" (Episode 3.16) endlessly reshaped by the whims, desires, and fears of its students and staff. The contemplation of the causes, benefits, and risks of this understanding of contemporary character and reality constitutes one of the central thematic concerns of the series as a whole, particularly in the third season and in the program's increasingly intense concern with the character of Abed.

The show's willingness to challenge the stability of its own characters is closely related to its awareness of the possibilities inherent in the new relationships between television and audience. It is certainly true that *Community* anticipates, as enthusiastically as any other show on the air, its consumption by a new audience which is not confined to singular viewings of individual episodes, and in so doing, shows how "the text's capacity to predict the ways audiences will comprehend it remains vital" (Savorelli 4). Phil Rosenthal, the creator of *Everybody Loves Raymond* (1996–2005), once famously said that he was making that show for CBS, "but in the back of my mind, it's for Nick at Nite."[3] *Everybody Loves Raymond*, in other words, deliberately looked backwards, aping classic tropes and storylines to reach an enormous audience through its nostalgia-tinged formula. Dan Harmon might say, with equal accuracy, that he was making *Community* for NBC, but in the back of his mind, he was thinking instead that it is for the Internet[4] — and for serving a devoted audience motivated not by nostalgia, but by an enthralling sense of discovery and privileged knowledge.

Consider, for example, "Cooperative Calligraphy" (Episode 2.8), which, despite confining the characters to a single room for its entire length, stands out as possibly one of the best episodes of the series and a key to the understanding of its metafictionalized world. The episode's plot hinges on the attempt to discover which member of the study group has stolen or lost Annie's missing purple pen; only at the end of the episode, unbeknownst to any of the characters, is it revealed that the pen was taken by the escaped lab monkey, Annie's Boobs, who has been living in the school's air ducts. In the opening seconds of the episode, however, as the characters are reacting to Dean Pelton's announcement of a Puppy Parade, the monkey's hand can, in fact, be seen in the background darting up from under the study table to grab the pen. The paw is in the indistinct background of a scene where focus is being drawn elsewhere, and is on screen for less than a second; it is exceptionally unlikely that most viewers watching the episode during its initial broadcast would notice it or understand its significance. It is far more likely that most of the show's fans learned about the paw in Internet postings and frame-by-frame videos which were available within hours of the episode being broadcast; it is likely that many went back to rewatch the episode, taking pleasure in the slightly shifted perspective provided by this revelation. It seems clear that the makers of the show relied upon precisely this happening, aiming at least this aspect of the episode not at their traditional NBC audience but rather at the far more devoted, analytical viewers they had learned to address. The episode is not just designed to be watched; it is designed to be rewatched.

A similar "bonus" for devoted fans unfolded not in half a second, but rather over the course of nearly three years. In both the first season and the second season, the movie character, Beetlejuice — a ghost who appears when his name is said three times — is mentioned in passing in dialogue ("Communication Studies," Episode 1.16 and "Cooperative Calligraphy," Episode 2.8). When Annie says the word "Beetlejuice" again in the opening moments of "Horror Fiction in Seven Spooky Steps" (Episode 3.5) an extra dressed as Beetlejuice can briefly be seen walking through the hallway behind her. Again, the joke is one that will make sense almost exclusively to fans devoted enough to regard online discussion and analysis of the show as an integral part of their spectatorship. What is being engaged here, in other words, is not merely a new way of receiving the show; someone merely watching the show on their iPod or on a computer through Hulu[5] would be as unlikely to recognize the joke as someone watching it in its Thursday night timeslot on a conventional television. Getting the joke here relies on not just watching the show, but actively engaging in a communal response to the show — that is, reading (and, likely, participating in) the reviews and commentary responding immediately to each episode in the online environment.

Simply watching the show is no longer assumed to be a complete experience. In a Twitter post made soon after this episode aired, Dan Harmon referred to this gag as an "Easter egg that took three years to hide. Our show is TOTALLY ACCESSIBLE." In the space of 140 characters, Harmon comments both on the content of the episode and on the well-documented tensions between *Community*'s creative team and a network, NBC, anxious for a wider viewership and higher ratings (with "viewership" and "ratings" both being understood here in highly traditional terms). Without deliberately alienating a mass audience watching the show in a traditional way (all three of the "Beetlejuice" episodes, after all, can be watched and enjoyed on their own merits, without deriving any particular import from fleeting lines of dialogue), Harmon and his team have instead made their show "TOTALLY ACCESSIBLE" to a smaller and more dedicated audience, one for which viewership is a mode of active engagement rather than passive voyeurism. For such viewers, watching *Community* is not merely an instance of passive voyeurism; it becomes an active, fundamental aspect of who one *is* and what one *does*.

Community does not merely acknowledge the existence of such an actively invested viewership; in its storylines and characters, it repeatedly represents such incorporation of media consumption into the construction of identity as a defining feature of the contemporary world. At first glance, this might seem to be true only for Abed, whose mastery of television trivia and desire to be a filmmaker in the early episodes have evolved into an obsession with film and television so strong that he is seemingly incapable of distinguishing between reality and the images on a screen. More precisely, he is incapable of interacting with the world in any way other than modeling his behavior on the characters and situations he has seen, to the degree that he frequently speaks of himself and his friends as being characters on a TV show (the fact that they are, in fact, characters on a TV show means that at moments Abed appears to genuinely pierce the fourth wall and make *Community* a legitimately metafictional, postmodern text). It is Abed who explicitly identifies the group's experience in "Cooperative Calligraphy" as a "bottle episode," a term for an episode confined to a single setting, usually for budgetary reasons. By contrast, when in the third-season episode "Origins of Vampire Mythology" (Episode 3.15) Abed is confronted with an encounter he has no immediate media analogue for, he can only turn to his friends and say "I need help reacting to something." The fact that the episode immediately cuts to a commercial at this point is perhaps an indication that none of the other characters in the scene can provide it — that is, that they have more in common with Abed in this respect than is immediately apparent.

The earliest episodes of *Community*— and particularly the show's pilot — suggested that the series would be structured around sexual tension between Jeff and Britta, a will-they-or-won't-they narrative hook that had already long since become a television cliché when the show first aired. The other characters were initially presented as the kind of familiar stock supporting characters who are similarly defined purely by a few distinctive traits — Shirley's decency and religious faith, Troy's stupidity and athletic skill, and Pierce's antiquated social attitudes. Abed's defining traits were his obsession with filmmaking, his desire to escape the restrictive control of his family, and his apparent location somewhere on the autistic spectrum. It is easy to conceive of a version of *Community*— and one which might have been more successful in reaching traditional viewers — in which these simple formulations of the characters never changed in any meaningful way.

Very quickly, however, the show began self-consciously inverting these expectations and defined roles, partly to accommodate the performers' actual abilities and partly out of an apparent desire to defy convention. The tension between Jeff and Britta was resolved — in a deliberately offhand manner — by the end of the first season, and Jeff himself, originally the clear central character of the show, became increasingly marginalized (watching the third season, it is startling to realize how often Jeff is uninvolved in the main plot of any given episode).

The "secondary" characters (including not only the study group, but also Dean Craig Pelton and Señor Chang) grew increasingly important and complex, often evolving considerably from their initial representations (the sensitive, concerned Troy of Season 3, for example, bears almost no resemblance to the meathead jock of the series' first few episodes). No character, however, has grown more or become more important to the series than Abed. To a certain degree, this might be seen as *Community* falling prey to yet another familiar sitcom convention, the hijacking of a series by a quirky secondary character. Think of *Happy Days* (1974–1984) becoming little more than the adventures of Fonzie, or *Family Matters* (1989–1998) becoming, in essence, *The Urkel Show*. Unlike those programs and casts, however, the world of *Community* was not being eclipsed by Abed; rather, it was becoming clearer that Abed's interests and inclinations were simply closely aligned with those of the show.

In other words, it is *Community*'s movement away from sitcom convention and toward a metafictional consideration of the contemporary destabilization of identity that makes Abed a more prominent character in the show's universe, simply because he is the character most capable of speaking to this theme. This was already occurring by the middle of the first season. Consider "Investigative Journalism" (Episode 1.13) in which Jeff becomes the editor of the Greendale paper. Abed dubs himself Jeff's assistant and, analyzing their respective characters and responsibilities, declares that Jeff is Hawkeye and he is Radar. Jeff (who has never actually seen *M*A*S*H*, but has only a general cultural knowledge of the program) initially treats this as a ridiculous idea which he simply humors. However, as the episode progresses, he adapts more and more of Hawkeye Pierce's appearance and demeanor, finally making Abed ecstatic by actually calling him "Radar." Despite his own initial disinterest in the comparison, Jeff — the character consistently most resistant to Greendale's shifts in reality — cannot help being caught up in Abed's media-fueled restructuring of reality.

As the series progresses this pattern is repeated time and again, with all of the characters falling, to varying degrees, into Abed-esque rewritings of their shared experience. This is most obviously true of Troy, of course. In the initial episodes of the series Troy's most significant role is as the former object of Annie's high school crush, but this quickly gives way to his identification as Abed's idealized best friend, partner, and sidekick. The key moment in this development — and a moment which foreshadowed much of what the series would become — is the brief sequence at the end of just the second episode, "Spanish 101" (Episode 1.2), when we see, under the show's credits, Abed and Troy improvising a nonsensical Spanish rap in the personae of gangster rappers. The sequence is less than a minute long, but it establishes a new relationship between the two and points to the direction the show would increasingly take, a direction premised on the performative appropriation of media identities and tropes. Indeed, the rap, initially intended as a moment of amusing filler, is far more representative of the show and far more important to its development than the remainder of the episode it is attached to. The improvised rap would grow into the "Troy and Abed in the Morning" segments, the show's various parodies and pastiches of various media forms, and ultimately into Troy and Abed's shared creation of the Dreamatorium.

Increasingly, other characters were drawn into the orbit of Abed's reframing of the Greendale experience as an ever-shifting series of movie and TV hyper-experiences. Annie, originally the most level-headed and serious-minded member of the study group, became a cohost of "Troy and Abed in the Morning." The "Morning" show itself, despite lacking cameras, somehow attracted a fan base, students who stood outside the study room window holding signs in the manner of *Today* or *Good Morning America*. Other characters, like Shirley and Pierce, were more resistant to this process — perhaps because their characters were older, or perhaps, more troublingly, because the Maternal Black Woman and the Addled Old Man are already media characters.

The growth of Dean Pelton as a significant character can also be traced to the show's increasing interest in the transformative possibilities of its characters; with his outrageous costumes and grandiose ambitions, Pelton seems hardly more connected to reality than Abed. The school he leads — the environment which provides the setting for *Community*— itself becomes increasingly unstable as the show develops. The prototype of its transformative abilities is on display in the key first paintball episode in Season 1, in which Jeff goes to sleep in his car and awakens to find that the campus has been transformed to a bleak, post-apocalyptic wasteland populated by roving gangs and defaced by hundreds of thousands of paintballs ("Modern Warfare," Episode 1.23). Later episodes will see the campus transformed into the world's largest blanket fort and into a Civil War battlefield ("Pillows and Blankets," Episode 3.14), into a film set ("Messianic Myths and Ancient Peoples," Episode 2.5), and so on.

The various transformations of the characters and the school are framed by a more complex transformation — that of the show itself. *Community*, of course, is not the first television show to do episodes in formats which differ from its norms. Among the most fondly remembered episodes of *M*A*S*H* is "The Interview," which presents itself as a black-and-white newsreel compilation of interviews of the characters, conducted by an actual newsman. *The Simpsons* similarly aired an episode in the format of "Behind the Music," presenting the family as a show-business institution rather than "real." Such disruptions of a program's normative form have only become more common; as Savorelli writes, "new comedy does not fear exposing its own device, but rather confirms its existence over and over again through its multiplication" (183).

No program, however, has experimented as often and as freely with such devices as *Community*. Examples abound: "Modern Warfare" apes *Die Hard* (1988) and other contemporary action films; "A Fistful of Paintballs" is a Sergio Leone Western; "Intermediate Documentary Filmmaking" duplicates the style of *The Office* (2005–2013), *Modern Family* (2009–), *Parks and Recreation* (2009–) and other "confessional" programs; "Basic Lupine Urology" is identical, in tone, format, and framing, to an episode of *Law and Order*. Even brief sequences within episodes can assume this function, such as the anime sequence in "Foosball and Nocturnal Vigilantism" (Episode 3.9) or the musical numbers in "Regional Holiday Music" (Episode 3.10) closely modeled after those in *Glee*. Frequently, Abed is central to these transformations; it is he who is first seen modifying his behavior into action-film mode in "Modern Warfare" ("Come with me if you don't want paint all over your clothes," an homage to *Terminator*), he who first gives in to the choir director's musical seduction in "Regional Holiday Music," he who reimagines the entire cast as Claymation figures in "Abed's Uncontrollable Christmas" (Episode 2.11).

Not infrequently, Abed is actually behind the camera, providing the diegetic rationale for the show's transformation; the third-season episode "Documentary Filmmaking: Redux" (Episode 3.8) is presented as his documentary about the Dean's attempt to film a new commercial for Greendale, and as the Dean's film spirals out of control, Abed's is compared more than once to *Hearts of Darkness*, the documentary that showed the similar collapses on the set of *Apocalypse Now*. Significantly, however, Abed chooses to end his project differently; rather than simply showing the Dean sliding into madness and failure, he steps in at the last moment to save the commercial and provide a happy ending. Addressing the camera to explain this decision, he refutes the common assumption that documentarians have no effect on the stories they tell: "We have more effect than anyone because we decide to tell it, and we decide how it ends. Will your story be just another sad one, of yet another man who just wanted to be happy, or will your story acknowledge the very nature of stories, and embrace the fact that sharing the sad ones can sometimes make them happy?" As Abed asks this question, we cut to the rest of the study group watching his film, hearing his question, and being able, because of it, to forgive the Dean for his excesses.

The moment is a remarkable one, both for Abed and for *Community* as a whole, because here Abed does not merely reenact a story or follow film conventions mindlessly; while still seeing the world through a screen, he takes control of the form he is using and turns it to constructive and redemptive purposes. Here, we have a demonstration that Abed's seeming insanity constitutes, in fact, a positive way to view and engage the world; it is a moment that valorizes and vindicates the character. The show frequently offers such moments; at the end of "Horror Fiction in Seven Spooky Steps" (Episode 3.5), for example, we learn that the psychological tests taken by the group reveal Abed to be the only sane one. In the conceptually and structurally daring "Remedial Chaos Theory" (Episode 3.3), which explores what happens in several alternate timelines when different members of the group leave to fetch pizza, it is Abed's absence that leads to the "darkest timeline," in which Jeff loses an arm, Pierce dies, and so on; the strong suggestion is that it is Abed who keeps the group whole and intact. While Jeff's "classic Winger" speeches often resolve conflicts to produce happy endings, to the degree that other characters come to anticipate them and on occasion mock them, it is Abed who frequently indicates that the moment for the speech has arrived and suggests how to frame it.

For all the show's approval of Abed, however, it also devotes a considerable amount of time in its third season to questioning him, challenging the idea that his approach to the world is one that can ultimately be sustained. Since, as we have seen, Abed's near-complete surrendering of his identity to popular culture has become emblematic of that taken by *Community* and its viewers, this challenge is a serious one. In "Contemporary Impressionists" (Episode 3.11), Abed spends so much money hiring celebrity impersonators to reenact movies with him that he risks both his own and his friends' lives. Even after Troy explains the problem to him, he wants to continue and agrees to stop only at Troy's insistence, although he fails to understand why he must; the episode strongly suggests that his inability to relate directly to reality is dangerous, and this drives the first wedge between him and Troy. Even after the rift between them is apparently healed at the end of "Pillows and Blankets" (Episode 3.14), Troy continues throughout the rest of the third season to express almost parental concern for Abed, suggesting that he needs to be cared for and watched over continuously. His concern is apparently justified; in "Introduction to Finality," the final episode of Season 3 (and also the last episode before Harmon was forced out of the show, and an episode which seems to have been designed as a workable finale to the series), Abed's forced separation from Troy drives him to assume the persona of "evil Abed" from the "darkest timeline," and he turns his energies to trying to destroy, rather than support, his friends.

He is ultimately redeemed by one more Winger speech, one which suggests that we can choose to act in the best interest of others rather than ourselves. While this does cause evil Abed's felt goatee (the visual sign of his evil) to fall off, it is worth noting that, even here, the show suggests that character is a matter of choice and action, not inherent identity. Abed's arc in the third season ultimately once again endorses, if tentatively, his playful, channel-surfing approach to reality; the last thing we see in the episode (aside from the traditional gag run with the closing credits) is him getting into his new, closet-sized Dreamatorium, having given the larger one up as a bedroom for Britta. Abed may be growing up, but he—and *Community*—still suggest that life is a matter of the stories we choose to tell and the masks we choose to wear.

This is all, of course, great fun. As the patterns of play and masquerade have spiraled outward from Abed to take in first his friends, then the rest of the school, and finally the series itself, it has provided smart, funny entertainment for legions of devoted fans. It has done so while self-consciously addressing the importance of fandom both within and beyond its fictional world; as Barnett and Kooyman note, the show "is both a work *of* fandom and a work *about* fandom, advocating for the crucial role of fandom and its communities in everyday life" (111). I would suggest, however, that there is also a darker side to this dynamic, and that it is too simple to see Harmon's show as simply and uncritically valorizing the fan. *Community* must be understood in the context of contemporary television—but it must also be understood in the context of contemporary America, a place of extreme economic uncertainty, the disenfranchisement of the working class, and the potential downfall of the middle class. Seen in this context, *Community* is perhaps less a joke than a dirge.

Consider this question: what do any of the central characters actually do for a living? Jeff was a lawyer, but has not been allowed to practice for years. Pierce was rich, but has been essentially disinherited by his father and his father's family. Shirley initially said she wanted to start a business, though she seemed startled when the possibility of this actually happening came up in the third season. None of the others appear to have regular employment of any kind, and none appear to be making any kind of significant progress toward their degrees. Nor can the members of the group be seen as finding meaning or identity in their families; aside from Shirley's ex-husband Andre and Pierce's abusive father, their family members have been virtually invisible since the first few episodes of the series. To all appearances, these characters find happiness and fulfillment only in the continual renegotiation of their identities through the tropes and affirmation offered by pop culture. The emptiness and darkness of such a world occasionally become visible in the show, perhaps most obviously in the second-season episode, "Mixology Certification" (Episode 2.10), in which alcohol reveals the loneliness and sadness the characters all carry with them. As fans, we love these characters, but it is not clear that any of them are capable of loving themselves.

For a previous generation, the classroom itself might have offered an alternative to fandom as a realm where identity could be forged. Greendale, however — with its minuscule budget, its incompetent Dean, its classes in Ladders and Baby Talk — is little more than a mockery of the old idea that education was a key to advancement or empowerment. What we have seen over the three years of the series are seven characters (and ourselves, the audience, the watchers in the eighth chair) retreating further and further into lives constructed of fantasy, play, and imagination even as their real lives recede from them. Life in the Dreamatorium is a great deal of fun — but would we really choose to live there?

To judge from our online discussions — from our eagerness to take up the eighth seat at the table — the answer is a resounding yes. Consider, for example, the treatment of *Community* at *The AV Club*, an online entertainment news and review site (and offshoot of the popular satirical "newspaper," *The Onion*). Early in the show's first season, *Community* was embraced as a favorite of the staff and readers of *The AV Club*, with frequent news stories about the program's ratings, cast, plans, and so on, and detailed, in-depth review essays of every episode posted soon after it aired. These reviews are mostly written by Todd VanDerWerff, whose detailed, thoughtful reflections frequently run to several thousand words. The commentary sections devoted to these reviews are perhaps even more impressive, often constituting thousands of comments by hundreds of individual commentators. While some of these comments are wastes of bandwidth (obvious trolls, ads for work-at-home services, leering comments about Alison Brie's breasts, and so on), many are themselves as detailed and reflective as the original reviews, and surely represent significant investments in time and thought. This audience's devoted investment in the show was also clear in the comments sections on the many news stories about *Community*, many of which discussed its troubled ratings and possible cancellation (which has seemed immanent at many points in the show's history). Indeed, a significant portion of *The AV Club*'s staff and readers essentially function as the online world's primary *Community* fan club, with the relationship between the two being close enough that, immediately after the fourth season, Dan Harmon himself participated in the site's detailed, episode-by-episode (and at moments, scene-by-scene) breakdown of the entire season's plots, themes, and character developments.

It is not difficult to see, in this degree of engagement and investment, some echo of Abed's relationship with *Inspector Spacetime* — but we must also see the challenges and limits of such a relationship. *Inspector Spacetime*, a note-for-note parody of *Doctor Who*, is initially introduced into the world of *Community* in "Biology 101" (Episode 3.1) when Britta tries to give Abed a new television show to watch to replace his beloved *Cougar Town* (perhaps the least convincing moment ever presented on *Community* is the idea that a television expert of Abed's magnitude would not already be well aware of such a show). Abed's obsessive interest in the program grows throughout the remainder of the third season and continues into the first several episodes of the fourth; he and Troy dress increasingly often as the Inspector and his sidekick, Constable Reggie, and the Dreamatorium is most often pressed into service to enact "Inspector Spacetime" adventures.

While this is frequently amusing, it is also troubling; it is not coincidental that Abed's Spacetime obsession occurs concurrently with the darkening and questioning of his character which dominates the third season. The Spacetime trope undermines the greatest strengths and appeals of Abed's character by reducing him from a self-aware savant who employs an encyclopedic knowledge of film and television to navigate the challenges of life to a monomaniacal fan incapable of distinguishing role-playing from reality. Throughout the first two seasons, Abed's knowledge of media tropes and production was empowering for him, providing a lexicon of ideas and identities he could employ to comprehend and negotiate the world. Crucially, this often involved referring to and drawing upon multiple programs and movies, not just one, and Abed's central motivation at all times remained his ambition to ultimately become a filmmaker himself. This version of fandom, as embodied in Abed, may be excessive or abnormal, but it is also enriching and productive, providing him with a clearer goal and a sharper understanding than most of the other characters enjoyed. None of this is true, however, of Abed's engagement with *Inspector Spacetime*. Here, Abed becomes increasingly preoccupied with a single media text, not with the possibilities and multiplicity of the media as a whole. He increasingly identifies himself as Inspector Spacetime in ways which reduce, rather than enhance, his ability to meaningfully interact with and know the world around him. Nor does the Spacetime obsession provide any meaningful path forward. In "Spacetime" mode, Abed demonstrates no interest in writing or directing; he merely plays the Inspector, giving every appearance of being satisfied with this and this alone. Through the *Spacetime* plot, *Community* demonstrates the crucial distinction between drawing upon the media to enrich our lives and becoming enthralled by the media to such a degree that we risk sacrificing our lives.

In essence, *Community*'s fans have, in *The AV Club* and elsewhere, constructed a communal space (not unlike Greendale) within which they can continually enact the central narrative of their involvement with the favored text. *Community* itself becomes a character in this narrative, a heroic presence jeopardized by the base forces of low ratings and corporate demands for "accessibility." The fan, in this reading, is the loyal ally, the faithful companion — the eighth friend, taking his or her place at the study table. The show does not suggest that fandom in and of itself is a negative thing; in a world utterly saturated with media texts, we all must, at least at moments, define ourselves through reference to them. In Abed's third-season arc, however, and particularly in his growing investment in *Inspector Spacetime*, the show does challenge its own fans to examine what motivates and defines their own potentially obsessive relationship with what is, when all is said and done, still just a television show. Even as we celebrate *Community* as a superb contribution to the television landscape, we must acknowledge its warnings about expressing ourselves exclusively in such a way.

Notes

1. NBC's removal of Dan Harmon from the show he created at the end of its third season, and the subsequent nine-month delay before the debut of the shortened fourth season, invites us to treat the first three seasons of *Community* as a distinct, self-contained narrative text. The fact that "Introduction to Finality," the final episode of the third season, concludes with a number of scenes clearly intended to provide closure to ongoing storylines and character arcs deepens this impression. In his review of the second episode of the fourth season, *The AV Club*'s Todd VanDerWerff, far and away the most dedicated and insightful commentator on *Community*, decides "that I needed to start treating *Community*, season four, as basically a new show." I follow his lead in this essay, confining my attentions entirely to *Community* as a program that lasted three seasons. The decision to do so is made all the easier by the fact that the fourth season is a sad shadow of the original *Community*, reducing the characters to their most cartoonish forms and recycling plots and themes the show should be past.

2. Virtual cults have developed around television *auteurs* like Joss Whedon and J.J. Abrams.

3. Rosenthal made this claim, in essentially these words, in a large number of interviews; one example can be found in Sepinwall.

4. The show also has its own webisodes, featuring Harmon himself.

5. Hulu is a website and streaming video service that allows viewers, either online or through special devices connected to televisions, to watch a large catalog of classic and new television series, movies, and other entertainment. At present, for example, paid subscribers to Hulu can watch any episode of *Community* at any time; viewers without subscriptions can watch the five most recently broadcast episodes. The world of streaming video changes frequently, however, and a series available on Hulu today might well be on Netflix or Amazon Prime tomorrow.

Works Cited

"Abed's Uncontrollable Christmas." *Community*. NBC. 9 December 2010.
Barnett, Tully, and Ben Kooyman. "Repackaging Popular Culture: Commentary and Critique In *Community*." *Networking Knowledge: Journal of the Media, Communication and Cultural Studies Association Postgraduate Network* 5.3 (2012): 109–134.
"Basic Lupine Urology." *Community*. NBC. 26 April 2012.
"Biology 101." *Community*. NBC. 22 September 2011.
"Communication Studies." *Community*. NBC. 11 February 2010.
"Contemporary Impressionists." *Community*. NBC. 22 March 2012.
"Cooperative Calligraphy." *Community*. NBC. 11 November 2010.
"Documentary Filmmaking: Redux." *Community*. NBC. 17 November 2011.
"A Fistful of Paintballs." *Community*. NBC. 5 May 2011.
"Foosball and Nocturnal Vigilantism." *Community*. NBC. 1 December 2011.
Harmon, Dan (danharmon). "The Easter egg that took three years to hide. Our show is TOTALLY ACCESSIBLE. RT." 22 November 2011, 9:16 p.m. Tweet.
"Horror Fiction in Seven Spooky Steps." *Community*. NBC. 27 October 2011.
"Intermediate Documentary Filmmaking." *Community*. NBC. 17 February 2011.
"Investigative Journalism." *Community*. NBC. 14 January 2010.
"Messianic Myths and Ancient Peoples." *Community*. NBC. 21 October 2010.

"Mixology Certification." *Community*. NBC. 2 December 2010.
"Modern Warfare." *Community*. NBC. 6 May 2010.
"Origins of Vampire Mythology." *Community*. NBC. 12 April 2012.
"Pillows and Blankets." *Community*. NBC. 5 April 2012.
"Regional Holiday Music." *Community*. NBC. 8 December 2011.
"Remedial Chaos Theory." *Community*. NBC. 13 October 2011.
Savorelli, Antonio. *Beyond Sitcom: New Directions in American Television Comedy*. Jefferson, NC: McFarland, 2010.
Sepinwall, Alan. "From the Archives: 'Raymond' Writers' Recipe for Comedy." *NJ.Com*. The Star-Ledger, 22 August 2008. Web. 18 March 2013.
"Spanish 101." *Community*. NBC. 24 September 2009.
"Studies in Modern Movement." *Community*. NBC. 10 November 2011.
"Virtual Systems Analysis." *Community*. NBC. 19 April 2012.

"Cool, Cool, Cool":
New Media Rhetorics of *Community*
G. Bret Bowers

> Announcement number one: All announcements will be cool starting right now.
> —ABED NADIR, "Football, Feminism and You" (Episode 1.6)

Beating out such comedy and television stalwarts as *30 Rock* (2006–2013), *Modern Family* (2009–), *Game of Thrones* (2011–), and *The Walking Dead* (2010–), *Community* received Hulu's "Best in Show" award in the first two years of the award. This award represents the best and most popular shows on the internet. Though critically acclaimed, *Community*'s ratings have remained relatively low compared to the other shows that were in contention for this award. Regardless of its low ratings, the show gained cult status through sites like Hulu and through other new media and social networking forms. The internet has been instrumental for *Community*'s popularity, using new media as a catalyst for growth and wide-spread appeal.

Because of its successful use of new media and social networking, defining the text of *Community* is difficult. The lines and boundaries of the shows narrative are blurred and obfuscated. Regarding those lines that delineate a text, many argue that they have always been blurry. However, the new media age makes the associations between texts and other texts (and authors) much more difficult to trace and navigate, since these texts now exist in world where those associations can be produced and distributed between entities at a near instantaneous rate. The speeds of which associated texts are developed and distributed form a dense jungle of interwoven and webbed relationships. Though the boundaries of a text are a proverbial demilitarized zone, successful texts such as *Community* rely on effectively using new media rhetorics to foster fan participation and engagement in the larger narrative.

In order to analyze the rhetoric of *Community*, I utilize what Jeff Rice describes as, the "Rhetoric of Cool." Using this as a framework, as well as pulling on the works of Henry Jenkins, Marshall McLuhan, and others, I examine the rhetorical activities and devices that the cast, writers, and fans of *Community* participate in which are behind *Community*'s popularity. Specifically, I interrogate the show's use of chora, appropriation, and commutation, framing them in Jenkins' concept of the participatory culture. By situating the rhetorical activities of *Community* in the context of a participatory culture, I suggest that in order to successfully appeal to audiences in a digital age and creating a successful cultural text, a new understanding of rhetoric and narrative needs to be adopted to meet new textual and rhetorical exigencies. As such, the Rhetoric of Cool serves as a framework for both designing and interpreting texts and narratives in the new media age.

Rice's rhetoric provides a glimpse inside successful new media texts. The complexity of his rhetoric echoes the emerging complexity of texts — all texts (textual, visual, viral, etc...). *Community*, though not considered a complex work of literature, is not simply a text that is passively consumed; it is, as Steven Johnson would suggest, a complex narrative that is cognitively demanding of its viewer. In *Everything Bad is Good for You*, Johnson writes that some television narratives "force [the viewer] to do work to make sense of them, while others just let [the viewer] settle into the couch and zone out. Part of the cognitive work comes from following multiple threads, keeping often densely interwoven plotlines distinct in [the viewers] head as [they] watch" (63).

The cognitive demands of television, noted by Johnson, narrowly focus on the text as episode and do not account for the greater complexity at work because of participatory media and new media. In this light, *Community* can be described as a cybertext, a text that requires more than a "non-trivial" and passive textual experience (Asareth). Likewise, Nick Marx contends in his article "'The Missing Link Moment': Web Comedy in New Media Industries," web comedies "[offer] additional content online that extended their respective diegeses and kept their loyal viewers engaged beyond the moment of television exhibition" (17). The show's use of new media expands the cognitive dimension of "the text," requiring the viewers to not only fill-in-narrative gaps, but also to collectively participate in a dynamic network of creation and participation between viewers and the cast, writers, and network.

The cognitive dimension of television is complex. According to Jay David Bolter, television demands constant surveillance. Television cameras continuously monitor the scene as the action takes place (93). For Bolter, the attention demands placed on viewers are much the same as those as a person playing a video game. Television narratives, however demanding attention, are much more complex than that of television even ten years ago. Cost, access, wi-fi, and, more generally speaking, ubiquitous computing have complicated television narratives. Television comedies, dramas, and whatever-reality-television-is considered are narratively much more complex because of media convergence and participatory culture. Instead of media and television that is simply a one-way street from producer to consumer, ubiquitous computing transforms the producer/consumer binary.

Critiquing and conceptualizing textual dynamics within new media and network culture requires a "calculus," as Kenneth Burke would call it, that accounts for the expanded cognitive, textual, and participatory narrative elements; elements, each of which, are responsible for forming the constellation of the "text" in the new media age. *Community*'s success is constituted by each individual node within the constellation of texts.

Central to my argument is the notion that the text that is not simply the show — *Community*. The show, however, is the textual prime mover, or hub. Encompassed with the show is a variety of other core texts. Since the concept of text in the postmodern age is one rife with vagaries, ambiguities, and absurdities, I categorize the various texts based on conceptual distance and person/persona of production.

Intrinsic Texts

Intrinsic texts are the texts which are constituted by the show — only. This includes cultural allusions and intertextual references. The various iterations of the intrinsic text include corporate sponsored texts, including the episodes, webisodes, interviews, the show website, and cast Twitter accounts.

"Spanish Videos"

Part 1: The webisode begins in Spanish class with the Spanish students showing their video homework assignments to the class. Abed and Star-Burns ("My name is Alex") present their assignment titled "Star-Burns: El Star Prince." The video depicts a hero "born of a beautiful mortal mother but fathered by the burning stars." This hero, Star-Burns El Star Prince, leaves his home and his wife, Amanda, to save the Spanish Princess from the evil wizard, Lord Diablo (played by Leonard). El Star Prince does so with his side kick, Star Brows (played by Abed). After a "Spanish" battle between El Star Prince and Lord Diablo in which they fling opposite words at each other, El Star Prince wins and manages to frees the princess, who actually goes back to Lord Diablo who has apologized for imprisoning her. Upon his "victorious" return home, El Star Prince finds that his wife has left him. Once the video ends, to glorious applause, Chang gives the group an F, telling they could redo it for a better grade if they included him in their revision, which leads to Part 2.

Part 2: The second part begins like the first, in the Spanish class. Señor Chang has allowed Alex and Abed to redo their previous video for a higher grade. In the video, El Star Prince and Star-Brows are chatting when they meet Señor Tigre (played by Chang), who has come back from a successful sexual conquest. The video goes to Lord Diablo and the Spanish Princess' wedding during which Señor Tigre has stolen El Star Prince's wife and begins attacking the wedding party. El Star Prince becomes jealous and then says that he will use his power of violence. El Star Prince and Señor Tigre battle, and Amanda realizes Señor Tigre is not a nice guy, throwing her drink onto him. This causes Señor Tigre to miss when he tries to shoot El Star Prince and Star-Brows. El Star Prince wins when he points out that the only reason Señor Tigre is successful with women is because he chooses ones who hate themselves. When they hate Señor Tigre, his self-esteem is negatively affected. Señor Tigre begins shooting fire from his eyes, burning people and the entire building. The video, clearly not as engaging as the first, receives lackluster applause, mostly from Abed and Chang. One student comments about how awful it is, causing Chang to give the entire class a C.

"Old White Man Says"

Old White Man Says (@oldwhitemansays) is Troy Barnes' Twitter account, who reposts racists sayings that Pierce says in his day-to-day life. The Twitter account makes its appearance in the first episode of season two, "Anthropology 101." The tagline describes the purpose of the Twitter site, stating, "I'm roommates with an old white dude. He's grumpy and racist. I just write down shit that he says." Though the episode first appeared on September 23, 2010, the Twitter account includes posts predating the episode. The posts are mostly one or two sentence racist jokes, which were used, both, on the show and solely on the Twitter account.

Paintball Assassin *(and* Paintball Assassin II*)*

These games — both based of the paint ball episodes from season one and two — place the player in the role of a Greendale student trying to shoot the cast members from *Community*. These games, and others, are available on the NBC site for *Community*.

Greendale Community College Website

The website — set up through NBC — at first glance is set-up much like a traditional college website, giving the viewer links to faculty, admission policies, and the library. It also has links to the campus newspaper: *Greendale Weekly*.

The site provides profiles of the Greendale faculty, links (fake of course) to financial aid, and admission procedures.

Inspector Spacetime

This is a popular sci-fi TV show that exists in the *Community* universe and has been running since 1962. The show, *Inspector Spacetime*, was first introduced in *Community* during the first episode of Season 3, "Biology 101." The show follows the Inspector and his constable throughout space and time. *Inspector Spacetime* is shared fascination of Troy and Abed and there are a large number of references to *Inspector Spacetime* throughout the show. *Inspector Spacetime* is homage to *Dr. Who*.

Extracurricular Texts

This set of texts are ones associated and sponsored by those related to the show, but are not sponsored at the behest of a corporate entity. In the case of *Community*, these texts include actor Twitter, social networking accounts, and professional web pages.

@alisonbrie

Alison Brie, who portrays Annie Edison, is one of the more active cast members on Twitter. Though her account is used generally for personal use, Brie's Twitter acts as nexus for *Community* texts, both show and fan created. The popularity *of Journey to the Center of Hawkthorne* came from her retweeting it from fan posts to her Twitter.

Danny Pudi's Facebook Page

Pudi is known for playing Abed. Pudi's Facebook page, unlike Brie's Twitter, mostly centers around status updates relating to *Community*. His page include updates thanking fans and mentioning episodes. However, like Brie's Twitter account, Pudi's page has links that are associated with *Community*, including links to a "Streets Ahead Remix" and Buzzfeed's "*Community* Relationships 101," which is a genealogy map that catalogs the relationships of characters.

Extrinsic Texts

When it comes to forms and media this is the most diverse category of texts. Extrinsic texts are text created that relate to the show, but are produced outside of the corporate structure. For instance fan fiction or other fan creations.

Journey to the Center of Hawkthorne

Journey to the Center of Hawkthrone is an open source two-dimension platformer video game based on the episode, "Digital Estate Planning," from Season 3. The game is fan designed game hosted by projecthawkthorne.com. The game is designed to mirror the game, the show, while also expanding the game through levels that exist, but are not shown during the episode.

Community: Texts and the New Narrative Economy

In his article, "The Language of New Media," Lev Manovich notes the emergence of new media as a "new cultural economy that transcends[s] the usual relationship between producers and consumers" (244). Manovich's notion of the changing cultural economy echoes Henry Jenkins' concept of a convergence cultural. Convergence, as Jenkins notes, refers to the "flow of content across multiple media platforms, the cooperation between multiple media industries, and the migratory behavior of media audiences who would go almost anywhere in search of the kinds of entertainment experiences they wanted" (3). Convergence, demands a relationship that distorts the lines between producer and consumer, highlighting the breakdown of the traditional producer/consumer dynamic. However, unlike Jenkins, Manovich suggests that there are two dominant elements of new media texts, categorizing them as "databases" and "algorithms." Unlike traditional texts, which rely on the traditionally closed narrative, new media texts act as a database, relying on associations between artifacts and texts, where those artifacts become part of an unending repository for the original and new texts. Bolter suggests,

> Convergence is the mutual remediation of at least three important technologies — telephone, television, and computer.[...] The telephone offers the immediacy of the voice or the interchange of voices in real time. Television is a point-of-view technology that promises immediacy through its insistent real-time monitoring of the world. The computer's promise of immediacy comes through the combination of three-dimensional graphics, automatic (programmed) action, and an interactivity that television cannot match [224].

The demonstrated success of *Community* is largely a reflection of its ability to move beyond traditional notions of the linear and closed narrative, transforming itself into a new form of new media database. The "database" concept is more than an electronic space where data is collected and organized; it "appear[s] as a collections of items on which the user can perform various operations — view, navigate, search" (Manovich 240). The database, unlike the narrative, creates an experience distinctly different than that of reading a narrative or watching a film. This experience of all texts, not just new media, is filtered through the lens of the dominant cultural form, which is no longer that of the linear narrative. Much like the traditional narrative, the database, as Manovich writes, is the "symbolic form of the computer age" (240). The appeal — the rhetoric — of new media hinges upon an associative network of elements and other narratives, as opposed to linear construction of narration.

Community, containing essential elements of the narrative, hinges on the new media conception of the database for its cultural appeal. *Community* has built cultural appeal by appropriating cultural form and logic of new media into its narrative, dovetailing the historically dominant cultural form with that of the digital. Like the show, the database, utilizes the logic of the web, where the story continually mutates and expands. Databases, unlike narratives, continually accumulate elements over time, transforming it from a simple story into a collection. The inclusion and expansion of intrinsic, extrinsic, and extra-curricular texts surrounding *Community* form something quite more than a story — they form a collection. The webisodes, games (NBC and fan sponsored), and so on, expand the available fan interactions with the show, mirroring the shift from narrative to the database as the dominant cultural form. The movement from the narrative paradigm to the database creates an exigency for an apparatus — a lens — to examine texts in the new media paradigm.

Jeff Rice's book *The Rhetoric of Cool* presents a way of understanding the rhetoric of new media texts. Rice offers a set of criteria that examines the rhetorical strategies of new media texts, adapting rhetorical strategies for texts that operate in a medium that fosters high participation with users. *Community's* textual landscape grants its viewers various nodes to enter, engage, and participate with the shows narrative. It is these nodes that need explicated, and Rice's rhetoric gives us a tool at analyzing the textual and rhetorical operation of *Community*.

Rhetorical Cool

Rhetorical Cool, as Rice conceives, refers to a set of rhetorical tools or devices used in new media texts, including chora, appropriation, and commutation. This section examines 'cool' rhetoric and the textual constellation of new media associated with *Community*. Specifically, rhetorical cool is used to analyze social media, fan-created, and show created games and webisodes.

Chora

One of chora's "essential properties," Edward Casey writes, "it its connectivity — its power to link up, from within, diversely situated entities or events" (qtd. in Rice 35). *Community*'s, as with other texts, success largely depends on the links it creates with other texts and events. At a textual or narrative level, all texts have choral attributes that include literary allusion and other intertextual elements. However, chora is more than the intertextual elements of a given text, as Rice notes. In contrast to traditional texts "readers respond to chora in a participatory manner" (Rice 35). Further explaining the concept of chora, Gregory Ulmer writes "chora evokes an image of cosmological creation for a park of creativity" (63). Chora, simply understood, is the place of links — intellectual, theoretical, creative, etc; links that spawn action and creation.

Looking back at the three types of texts I outline earlier — the extracurricular texts — best represent *Community*'s use of chora. The best example of chora, as noted by Rice, is the hypertext link. However, most importantly is not the specific example that matters, but the foundations of what make a hypertext link choral. There are specific features of the hyperlink that best represent chora including:

- Users (viewers, writers, etc....) can develop threads around words and ideas, requiring users to engage with a text in a variety of ways, media, and technologies.
- Chora obfuscates how a particular topos represents "one idea for one situation."

@alisonbrie, Alison Brie's and DannyPudi's Facebook page are choral centers for *Community*. Each of these texts in tandem with show *Community* works toward giving nodes that link together moments of invention.

The differences between Brie and Pudi's use of social networking are quite divergent. The core purpose of each is to further their own popularity amongst their fan base. However, Brie's number of posts are much greater than Pudi's, and the number of posts that are not strictly about *Community* are also much greater than his. However, there is some overlap in that they both do post news about the show. Further analysis of the content shows that much of the content is self-promotion and promotion for the show. However, the large number of posts not related to *Community* breaks down the distance between the actress and her fans, making Brie seem more accessible. The posts create a profile of Brie as a person — not just the character or the actress. The posts give a sense of her hobbies, likes, dislikes.

An examination of Danny Pudi's Facebook page demonstrates *Community* choral content. The page serves to connect and distribute the shows content, as well as other work of Pudi's. Though there are non–*Community* posts, the majority of content is related to the show. Within the past year, a majority of the posts related directly to the show. On his page are links to a radio interview with Pudi and Brie, episode posts that include photographs from the show, and updates about filming. Furthermore, because of the functionality of Facebook, Pudi's followers can post and add onto the content created (or posted) on the page.

When we compare Brie's Twitter feed to Pudi's Facebook account, we see both texts relate to viewers in two different ways. Brie's utilizes social networking to flesh out her own persona, with little regard to self-promotion, while Pudi's Facebook largely is promotional in nature. The medium of the content presented by each is largely varied. Each incorporates text, image, audio, and video in their posts. However, text is Brie's medium of choice; text is more immediate and more personal. The large amount of video content on Pudi's page reinforces his persona as actor and character. Though there is a wide gap between the mediums and purposes, each has its own audience appeal, allowing the show, working through other means, to appeal in multiple ways to its audience, which would not have been possible before the pervasive use of new media.

New media also provides those audiences the means to participate in *Community*. The interactivity present throughout Facebook brings together the producer and consumer. Producers get feedback and comments at light-speed. Audience reactions and feelings are instantaneous. The shortening of the feedback loop between producer and consumer in social networking spaces mutates these spaces. Instead of simple social spaces, these spaces now become sandboxes of invention. However, those spaces are not just a space solely to inform the producer, but also nodes where consumers interact with overall narrative of *Community*.

Appropriation

Appropriation is a common rhetorical strategy in post-modern literature. As a rhetorical strategy, appropriation is the theft of language, text, image, and ideas. For Rice, appropriation is central to new media texts: "All writing involves some degree of theft, particularly when writing is introduced in to the digital, an area that relies to a great extent on the 'borrowing' logic associated with appropriation" (57). Though it is assumed the purpose of appropriation is largely connected to social and/or ideological critique, appropriation produces new portals for engagement and participation. The concept of appropriation dovetails with Bolter's concept of remediation. Remediation, simply understood, describes the representation of one medium in another. For Bolter, "remediation is a defining characteristic of the new digital media" (45). Though remediation is a term germane to digital media, remediation and the appropriation of genres is not a process that is singularly exhibited in digital texts. Furthermore, media convergence further complicates textual genres, in that media and medium of texts — sitcoms, novels, films, etc.— are not singularly one genre. In this vein, *Community* is not just a television show.

In new media, text appropriation occurs largely in the intrinsic and extrinsic spheres. *Community* uses appropriation to foster a more engaged viewer experience through its use intrinsic and extrinsic texts. Since both spheres of new media texts use appropriation, it is essential to note that the types of appropriation that both spheres have similarities and differences. In the case of *Community's* intrinsic texts, appropriation is largely based on the use of literary, cultural, and textual, as opposed to the extrinsic texts which are largely user appropriations of the shows stories, characters, and other shows elements. More simply understood intrinsic texts appropriate from the social and cultural domains; thus, extrinsic texts are fan appropriations of the show extending, recreating, and remediating the narrative of the show.

Intrinsic Texts and Appropriation

Cultural appropriation is a key to *Community*'s audience appeal. Some of the appropriations occur as allusions, parody and homage, and through genre repurposing. Introduced in the episode, "Biology 101" (Episode 3.1), Inspector Spacetime is one of the more popular parodies that the show has used. Inspector Spacetime is homage to the British television show *Dr. Who*. The plot, the characters, and the technology used in *Inspector Spacetime* are similar to those in the original *Dr. Who*. Throughout the show, Inspector Spacetime is used in various plots—both major and minor. The show's appropriation of Dr. Who has given it another avenue to connect with its fans. During the cast interview during the 2012 Comic Con, a large number of fans in attendance were dressed as either the Inspector or his constable, Reggie. Because of the fans familiarity with the original *Dr. Who*, *Community* is able to situate itself in both reality and its own narrative reality. By appropriating cultural phenomena, the show is able to weave a narrative that is more dynamic and "real" than one that did draw on cultural parody. In addition to allusion and parody and homage, the intrinsic texts of *Community* also appropriate genres and style from other television and film series. Generally, the show's format is centered on the study table and follows a generic sitcom formula week-in-and-week-out. However, a number of episodes have appropriated the genre and form of other television series and film. Two specific instances of this type of appropriation have been used as episode formats.

As examples, *Community* has used the documentary genre that has been stylized by Ken Burns in the episode, "Pillows and Blankets" (Episode 3.14). The episode uses Burns' narrative style as voice over, as well as pulling on "historical" artifacts such as "text messages" and "emails" to fill in the narrative. Another example of the shows appropriation of popular genre is in the episode, "Basic Lupine Urology" (Episode 3.17). The episode models itself after *Law and Order*.

The plot of the episode plays out much like a police procedural. After the study group's yam is smashed, Troy and Abed are tasked to play detectives to track down suspects by "Chief" Shirley. After tracking down the suspect, Annie and Jeff play the roles of prosecutors, who eventually prove that the yam was intentionally smashed, saving their grade. In addition to appropriating the form of the narrative, this episode also appropriates the introduction of *Law and Order*, with the sullen music and iconic gavel bang.

The use of appropriation by the intrinsic texts reflects the common move associated with new media texts. Though these types of appropriations are geared toward a more "culturally" literate viewer, the content of appropriation is general enough for most viewers to get the references.

Extrinsic Texts and Appropriation

Extrinsic texts appropriate material not from culture, as intrinsic texts do, but from the material original to the show. In the case of *Community*, as with many television shows and films, fan fiction is the center of appropriation; the characters and the story are continued and altered in a variety of new stories. However, one particular extrinsic text downright steals the entire concept from the show. *Journey to the Center of Hawkthrone* is a fan created videogame inspired by the video game of the same title in the episode, "Digital Estate Planning" (Episode 3.20). The video game began as crowd source fan inspired project on reddit.com. The game pulls its graphics, plot, and design straight from what is seen the episode where the original was featured. Even though Journey to the Center of Hawkthorne was not directly licensed by NBC, the video game gained its popularity and recognition through Alison Brie's use of Twitter and the Comic-Con interviews where she mentioned it.

The game is representative of the larger work happening in participatory culture. Fans were able to get together and design the game with the help of other fans. Directly appropriating the content and design, the game expands the canon of *Community* texts to include those which are not created by the corporation, writers, or actors associated with the show.

Commutation

"Commutation," as Rice defines, "is the exchange of signifiers without concern for referentiality" (93). Simply speaking, commutation is a change of the form of expression. In the case of the rhetorical strategies for new media, commutation exists at the level of interpretation; the plane of the medium. Underlying the significance of commutation is McLuhan's notion that "the medium is the message." As McLuhan puts forth, the medium is responsible for human action (85). For rhetoric the medium — the genre — of communication is imbricated with socio/political ideologies. The mediums of representation change the beliefs and assumptions of a given message by simply changing the medium of which that message is communicated. The most common example of commutation is that of the remix or sample.

As it is filmed with live actors, there are certain assumptions and beliefs that viewers of *Community* experience, which guides their habits and understanding of the show. Commutation is about manifestation of experience. The show, though a typical sitcom, takes its viewers into a realm unfamiliar to the typical sitcom. New media flips the narrative appeal. Instead of leading the viewer through the show, engaging viewers by identifying with character(s) in the show, new media alters the landscape of the narrative appeal of *Community*. Traditionally, sitcoms like *Community* rely on appealing to its audience by using the lead actors as the horse to which the audience hitches their perspective. However, new media takes the traditional narrative appeal that hitches the viewer's perspective to the Jeff Wingers of the world and places them at the study table as a fellow Greendale Student.

Like many shows, *Community* utilizes a variety of media and genres in order to interact with fans. For instance, during the episode, "Anthropology 101" (Episode 2.1), viewers are introduced to a plot device in the form of a Twitter account: @OldWhiteManSays. Throughout the episode, Troy, the owner of the account, tweets racist comments that Pierce says aloud during the episode. Though it seems as if the Twitter account was only being used a plot device, the account actually existed. The account contains jokes that were not said during the episode and tweets are continually posted even weeks after the episode aired. @OldWhiteManSays was utilizing cool in a number of ways. First, its form used new technology and social networking. However, and more importantly, it changed the medium of experience in which viewers interacted with the show.

More importantly than the form of expression — like the tweet — the show also utilized webisodes. The webisodes function a bit differently than the traditional sitcom episode. They are much shorter and occur over a number of days, weeks or months. In the context of commutation, webisodes alter the narrative lens. Instead of lens that is dominated by the study group, the webisodes allow other characters in the show a space to flesh out and develop their character. For instance, in the webisode titled "Spanish Videos" there are four primary characters and only one — Abed — who is from the study group. The others, Star-Burns, Leonard, and Chang are all minor characters. And when the webisode was published, Chang had yet to be given the larger role that he occupied by the end of season three.

While @OldWhiteManSays and "Spanish Videos" employ commutation, the configuration of that commutation is widely divergent. For the first of these, the rhetorical device of commutation is more about changing the medium of audience engagement, as opposed to "Spanish Videos," which not only changes the mode of distribution, but also changes the character focus.

Conclusion

Ultimately, the rhetorical purposes of "cool" and narrative moves of new media transform the viewer. Instead of the voyeur on the couch, the viewer becomes a student fully immersed in the story experience; a narrative virtual reality. Bolter contends, "the goal of virtual reality is to foster in the viewers a sense of presence" (22). It is this sense of presence that *Community*'s appeal is founded on, an appeal rooted in the title of the show. It is not without irony that even though the show's title echoes the setting, it also is about the joining of people. Though the actors give us a sense of this *Community*, it is the shows use of new media and the rhetorical moves of the "cool" that give fans a fully immersive experience.

Works Cited

@alisonbrie. *Twitter*. Retrieved from https://twitter.com/alisonbrie.
"Anthropology 101." *Community*. NBC. 23 September 2010.
"Basic Lupine Urology." *Community*. NBC. 26 April 2012.
"Biology 101." *Community*. NBC. 22 September 2011.
Bolter, J. David, and Richard A. Grusin. *Remediation: Understanding New Media*. Cambridge: MIT Press, 2000.
Burke, Kenneth. *The Philosophy of Literary Form: Studies in Symbolic Action*. Berkeley: University of California Press, 1974.
"Community: Journey to the Center of Hawkthorne." *Project Hawkthorne*. GitHub. n.d. Web. 24 September 2013.
"Danny Pudi." *Facebook*. Facebook. Retrieved from https://www.facebook.com/pages/Danny-Pudi/114382756768.
"Digital Estate Planning." *Community*. NBC. 17 May 2012.
Giddings, Seth, and Martin Lister, eds. *The New Media and Technocultures Reader*. Abingdon, Oxon: Routledge, 2011.
Greendale Community College. Greendale Community College. n.d. Web. 24 September 2013.
Jenkins, Henry. *Convergence Culture: Where Old and New Media Collide*. New York: New York University Press, 2008.
Johnson, Steven. *Everything Bad Is Good for You: How Today's Popular Culture Is Actually Making Us Smarter*. New York: Riverhead, 2006.
Manovich, Lev. "Selected Material from the Language of New Media: 'The Database,' 'Data and Algorithm' and 'Navigable Space.'" Giddings and Lister 239–247.
Marx, Nick. "'The Missing Link Moment': Web Comedy in New Media Industries." *The Velvet Light Trap* 68.1 (2011): 14–23.
McLuhan, Marshall. "Selected Material from Understanding Media: The Extensions of Man." Giddings and Lister 82–91.
@oldwhitemansays. *Twitter*. Retrieved from https://twitter.com/oldwhitemansays.
"Paintball Assassin." *NBC*. Universal Media. n.d. Web. 24 September 2013.

"Pillows and Blankets." *Community*. NBC. 5 April 2012.
Rice, Jeff. *The Rhetoric of Cool: Composition Studies and New Media*. Carbondale: Southern Illinois University Press, 2007.
"Star-Burns: El Star Prince — Part 1." Community Wiki. *Wikia.com*. Wikia Entertainment. n.d. Web. 24 September 2013.
"Star-Burns: El Star Prince — Part 2." Community Wiki. *Wikia.com*. Wikia Entertainment. n.d. Web. 24 September 2013.
Ulmer, Gregory L. *Heuretics: The Logic of Invention*. Baltimore: Johns Hopkins University Press, 1994.

"Six seasons and a movie!" *Community*, Creative Processes and Being Meta

Laura Tansley

> It lets me adjust really specific settings that most people don't notice or think about.—ABED NADIR, "Introduction to Film" (Episode 1.3)

In "Introduction to Film," Britta has taken it upon herself to give Abed the funds to take a film course at Greendale. Abed approaches Britta in the cafeteria wielding a new, expensive camera and explains why the purchase is important to his craft in the quote above. When I first saw this episode, I was convinced that the camera settings were briefly adjusted for a section of this scene where Abed begins to order a coffee, and then returned to the original settings as the angle changes and he continues his order. I laughed when I saw this: it seemed the show was deliberately drawing attention to the care and specifics of the creative process of filming. I liked how drawing attention to the production of fiction by referencing and demonstrating filming techniques was taken to another level. This was not just a comment about a disparate group of people resembling characters in *The Breakfast Club* (1985); it was about the production behind the creation of characters.

Since trying to confirm this visual joke is difficult, I have begun to wonder if I had imagined the change in camera settings. Being unfamiliar with filming techniques makes it difficult to recognize changes I might have seen, and analysis or discussion online by experts provides no returns. What I find instead is people using the line as a tag for their posts in photography and digital technology forums, an artist tweeting the line to his followers. It seems that others enjoy this nod to the creative process too, the passion for intricacies and details, and, often-times, the thanklessness of the tasks we take so much pride in. This kind of self-referentialism occurs throughout three seasons of *Community*. The experience for viewers is that we become suddenly aware, if we were not already, of plots, characters, TV sitcom and filmic devices employed to create story. However, the kind of meta-commentary that *Community* utilizes is not solely based on observations of the egos, money, and odd personalities of the creators behind the often shambolic production of television.[1]

Community's metanarrative is often provided by super-fan Abed and his closest allies in blurring the lines between reality and fantasy, Annie and Troy. Jeff, the nonchalant but frustrated protagonist, is also complicit; all three seek to deconstruct the production of TV shows and films, as a way to translate and understand life for the sheer pleasure and enjoyment of it, or to manipulate others. However, these meta-narratives also deconstruct the reception of TV shows by fans and demonstrate how individuals can take the rules of sitcoms, participate in them to create their own narratives, and question the ways in which fiction and non-fiction are separated.

Part One: Meta-Creative Processes

In a season two scenario, in the episode, "Cooperative Calligraphy" (Episode 2.8), Abed becomes distressed by the fact that the day seems to be turning in to a "bottle episode." Annie has had one too many of her stationery items pilfered, so when her "purple pen with the gel grip" goes missing, she insists no one leave the study room until someone admits to taking it. When no one comes forward and Jeff is accused, he demands the doors be locked and that nobody leaves 'til the pen shows up: they're "doing a bottle episode." The term bottle episode refers to the need for a TV series to reduce costs by scheduling an episode that requires minimal characters and sets; mentioning this convention draws attention to the value of episodes in terms of production, perhaps indicating that this episode will not have spectacular sequences, but will focus on something more internal than external. Abed voices his unease about the effect a lack of a variety of scenes and extended action has on the characters taking part in a bottle episode, suggesting that they are "wall-to-wall facial expressions and emotional nuance," and because of the difficulties he sometimes has interacting socially, he remarks, "I might as well sit in the corner with a bucket on my head."

Trapped in the study room, forcing increasingly extreme measures on one another to locate the missing pen but coming to no conclusions, the group's trust in each another waivers. Annie admits, "I wish I could just find it behind my ear. I'd rather be that stupid than have to think that any one of us could be this inconsiderate." Shirley suggests, after everything they have done to root out the pen and the culprit, it seems impossible any one of them would go to such lengths to disrupt the group's emotional ties. Jeff latches on to this and recalls a comment Troy had made earlier that a ghost may have taken the pen. Jeff notes, "If we have to choose between turning on each other or pinning it on some specter with unfinished pen-related business, then I'm sorry, my money's on ghost." Troy then begins to tell his story of the ghost and its motivations:

> So, I see it as a lot like the movie *Paranormal Activity*, except for more boring and fancy. And I think, in 1856, it is possible that a man was beheaded while he was writing in his diary to his long-lost love, and now, he roams the halls of Greendale screaming for his pen, so he can write her a love-letter. "I need her, I need her," he screams as he looks for a pen.

The conclusion they agree upon is that something improbable makes more sense than the twisted behavior they would have to admit about themselves and each other. It is more realistic, then, to collectively create a ghost than accept cruelty and sadism as an aspect of the group dynamic. This scene is illustrative of how fiction can sometimes be favorable, how fiction can become more real than reality. It holds more truths, drawing attention to the arbitrary ways fact and fiction can be separated, and perhaps even encouraging the viewer to question the lines between fiction and non-fiction. The group's decision to construct a solution to the mystery of the missing pen speaks to the creative process undertaken to construct narratives. Paul John Eakin introduces this idea in the opening chapter of *Living Autobiographically*: "We tell stories about ourselves every day. Sometimes we can get other people to listen to them, but even when we can't, at any given moment this process of self-narration is constantly unfolding in our heads, in however loose and disorderly a fashion" (1).

What he suggests in *Living Autobiographically* is that we are authors of our own lives; we create stories out of events, linking them to other events, seeing the significance and relationships between feelings and everything that happens to us to make sense of our memories, or to create an understanding how we got to where we are.[2] Here, the group chooses to use the conventions of ghost stories (plots of pained, separated lovers; restless spirits bound by their actions in life to disconsolate, desperate wanderings in death, repetitiously performing hollow recreations of their physical lives), to form a narrative that reveals an understanding of their situation. These fictional elements become non-fiction, not because they are factual, but because they allow for the creation of something true and self-actualized for the group. The story of the ghost allows them to know something deep and sincere about their relationships with one another, which is very real.[3]

In a later episode "Paradigms of Human Memory" (Episode 2.21), it is revealed that it was Annie's Boobs that stole the pen: Troy's escaped monkey has developed kleptomaniacal tendencies and has been hoarding objects all year which, when gathered by Ben Chang, trigger memories for the group of some of the many misadventures experienced over the course of the series. This episode nods towards sitcom production conventions, specifically clip-shows which, for budgetary reasons, employ a framing premise in order for characters to reminisce over their funniest moments in a sequence of decontextualized flashbacks. *Community* subverts this expectation by including flashbacks to events that viewers have not been privy to, suggesting that all the funniest moments happened in our absence. A traditional clip-show relies on the audience's feelings of warm familiarity with the scenes clipped from original episodes, but with this episode, the decontextualization becomes part of the humor, as the scenarios that are flashbacked to are never explained. Awareness of this sitcom trope and use of a form that traditionally reconstitutes previously produced moments to do the opposite, suggests a willingness to manipulate the boundaries of format and to explore how the constraints of procedure can lead to creative liberation; that part of a creative process can be about learning the rules and then breaking them. In other words, clichés can carry potential.

Creative process is not held static after creation. Once the creative piece is completed, the writers/creators' understandings or even memories of the process can change, waver, or even disintegrate altogether, needing to be reconstituted somehow. This process of re/consideration continues to shape the product despite the moments of creation being in the past. It is possible to continually reconsider how something was formed, allowing processes to trace the creative journey forward and backwards as well, an illustration of this being the homage to "shipping" videos in "Paradigms of Human Memory." While discussing intimacies and transgressions that have occurred within the group, Annie suggests to Jeff that his attempts to compartmentalize his libido for the good of the group have been unsuccessful due to the tension she feels exists between her and Jeff. When Jeff questions this, she cites, "the Annie of it all, the long looks, the stolen glances." The scene then cuts to a montage of innocuous clips of Annie and Jeff, heavily romanticized by the use of slow-motion, fades, black and white filters, and Sara Bareilles' ballad, "Gravity." Jeff is incredulous and suggests, "You could do the same thing with Pierce and Abed." A second montage begins in precisely the same vein as the first, creating tender moments between Pierce and Abed from indifferent-seeming incidents such as Abed letting Pierce know his fly is undone.

This episode reflects on the fan practice of "shipping," or the belief that fictional or non-fictional characters could be, should be, or are in a relationship. Shipping takes many forms: fan-created YouTube videos being one way of expressing this. One particular user, Veritas724, enamored by the developing relationship between Jeff and Annie in "Debate 109" (Episode 1.9), created a "shipvid," or shipping video, which was then adopted by the show for Season 2. The video became the inspiration behind the montages used in "Paradigms of Human Memory," with the *Community* team employing the same kind of editing and fades, as well as the song, "Gravity." Dan Harmon tweeted Veritas724 on the day the episode was due to air: "[I]t's a tip of the hat, and a sincere thank-you note, to the Van Halen of *Community* fans."

Shipping is just one of the many existing forms of fan-created narratives borne out of existing texts. Vertias724's shipvid is no different; it creates an alternative narrative for Jeff and Annie exploring their relationship. What is different however, is Annie's reappropriation of the fan-fiction to explain her feelings for Jeff. The creative processes at work here demonstrate not only how appreciators of creative works can develop their own narratives, but how these narratives can be reabsorbed by the initial creative work for creative expansion and contraction. A creative piece moves out into the world, willingly soaking up the reactions of those who view and scrutinize it, and is subsequently altered by this. By choosing to incorporate these reactions, the creators of the original piece make the experience of watching and creating *Community* incredibly collaborative. The metatextual reference to the making of TV shows is expanded beyond production, to how fans react and how shows incorporate this.

Fans are also somewhat responsible for the show being renewed for a fourth season, again becoming part of the process of production through creative initiatives. The extended mid-season break in 2011 to 2012 caused consternation in fans that saw the shadow of cancellation creeping over *Community* through the NBC network's lack of enthusiasm for Season Three. All of a sudden, lines like "it's all downhill from here" in reference to the first paintball episode from Season One ("Modern Warfare," Episode 1.23), casually thrown around on the back of a sloganed sweatshirt in Season Two ("Custody Law and Eastern European Diplomacy," Episode 2.18), take on prophetic significance. "Six seasons and a movie," a line voiced by Abed as a retort to Jeff's suggestion that *The Cape* (2011) would be cancelled after three weeks ("Paradigms of Human Memory," Episode 2.21), gained additional metatextual significance when it connected with fans about *Community*'s future. It became a battle cry and a campaign-slogan to encourage NBC to renew the show for a fourth season, as did the idea that the news of an extended mid-season break confirmed the fact that viewers were experiencing "the darkest timeline," a reference to "Remedial Chaos Theory" (Episode 3.3) in which several alternate realities play out following the roll of a dice to decide which member of the group should leave Troy and Abed's new apartment to collect the pizza that has been delivered downstairs. One of the alternate realities has disastrous consequences for all members of the study group including limb-loss, sectioning, alcoholism and death. In reaction to this,

Abed makes felt, black goatees for the remaining study group members to wear, so they can commit to being the evil versions of themselves. Fans at the Tumblr site, "We Love *Community*," took this statement from Abed and recontextualized it, posting pictures of themselves sporting black goatees and pleading for *Community* to be saved. Again, the narratives of the show were taken by viewers and altered, detached somewhat from their original place in a story and manipulated to reflect a different a story which then became reattached to the story of *Community* after the decision was made to renew the show for a fourth season.

In June 2012, artwork produced in tribute to *Community* was displayed at PixelDrip Art Gallery's "Six Seasons and a Movie" exhibit in Los Angeles. Artists, and presumably, fans, drew inspiration from the first three seasons of the show and produced work that celebrates the characters and episodes in ways that seem to demonstrate genuine fondness. The exhibition itself was described by Mark Batalla, curator and manager of PixelDrip Art Gallery, as a "heartfelt tribute to both *Community* and its fanbase" (Zalben). Batalla suggests "the cast and crew's close relationship with fans is one that separates *Community* from many television shows," perhaps revealing motivations behind the exhibition (Zalben).

When fans are able to become part of the creative process through their own creativity, not just through a disembodied mapping of demographics and viewing habits, their relationship with the show is bound to be altered. Brian Raftery notes, "*Community* is a series by, for, and about people for whom pop culture is both a near-divine presence and a lens through which to view the world." The lens through which fans can view *Community* is one which is aware of television conventions because the show itself teaches viewers about these conventions, their purposes and their performances. *Community* reveals ways in which pop culture reflects life through its metatextual references and the ways characters use these pop culture references to interpret, enjoy, and manipulate life. This simultaneously draws attention to the fictionality of fiction, its constructs and, at times, its falsities, but also how it provides frameworks for understandings.

Raftery's article details a particular framework essential to Harmon's creative process. "Embryos" is how Harmon refers to them; circles divided in to seven segments which chart what he feels constitutes a satisfying story:

1. A character is in a zone of comfort
2. But they want something
3. They enter an unfamiliar situation
4. Adapt to it
5. Get what they wanted
6. Pay a heavy price for it
7. Then return to their familiar situation
8. Having changed.

The embryo is adapted to track every element of writing from character development, episode arcs (or in this case circles), to season plots. "To this day," Raftery writes, "Harmon still studies each film and TV show he watches, searching for his algorithm underneath, checking to see if the theory is airtight." But might it also be possible to use this framework to understand events that occur around us, to us, producing one of many possible narratives that attempt to encapsulate a moment by creating a story from it? We might do this unconsciously already, or we might be very aware of how we manipulate the details of our lives to create a story which means something to us. Annie's appropriated shipvid from "Paradigms of Human Memory" is a poignant example of how, unconsciously, interpretation of events necessarily means creating narrative and story, as well as drawing attention to the purposefully creative aspects of viewing and interpreting a television show.

Part Two: Meta-Fans and Fans of Meta

Community unashamedly appeals to the geek in us, encouraging us to collect gags, recognize allusions, and seek out source materials. The line voiced by Abed and Luis Guzmán, "Ever seen *Hearts of Darkness*? Way better than *Apocalypse Now*," suggest source material that might enhance an appreciation of the episode, "Documentary Filmmaking: Redux" (Episode 3.8). This kind of reference allows for new understandings of texts through new or different narrative frames, creating a pleasurable kind of intertextual journey, tracing inspiration and gaining an awareness for the way each source can be reflected upon, used and molded by con/texts. However, *Community*'s representation of, and appeal to, geeks or geekery is not as straightforward as those who collect and recount references. It also seeks to complicate the notion of who we consider geeks to be, and what behavior may indicate this designation. As collaborators, the geeky fans of *Community* are tenacious, inspired, and inspiring, but what about their representations in the show itself?

Abed seems to confirm what we have come to expect of representations of fans in TV and film: he can be defined as a geek due to his love for popular culture and the minutiae within it, demonstrated by his passion and deep and extensive knowledge of film and TV. He also lacks an understanding of social cues, and his appearance indicates a lack of interest in robust activities such as team sports. Abed seems to be like the same kind of geek Henry Jenkins discusses in *Textual Poachers: Television Fans and Participatory Culture*, focusing particularly on representations of "Trekkies" from a *Saturday Night Live* sketch. They are "brainless consumers ... [who] devote their lives to the cultivation of worthless knowledge ... are social misfits ... are feminized and/or desexualized ... [and are unable to separate fantasy from reality" (10). There are moments when Abed behaves like this. For instance, he spends $300 on a *Dark Knight* (2008) DVD ("Foosball and Nocturnal Vigilantism," Episode 3.9) and he seeks out the original, Japanese version of the fictional film, *Kickpuncher*, even though he openly acknowledges how bad the film franchise is ("Remedial Chaos Theory," Episode 3.3). He misreads social cues, assuming that he might have gone deaf when those around him mouth a silent conversation ("Pilot," Episode 1.1), and he does not pursue sex from his romantic encounters, preferring to discuss an aspect of his pop culture obsession with anyone who shows an interest in him, sexual or otherwise, be it at a Valentine's dance ("Early 21st Century Romanticism," Episode 2.15) or being hit on in a bar ("Mixology Certification," Episode 2.10). He also often blurs the lines between fantasy and reality by using film and television frameworks as a way to interpret his life. In one episode, he reimagines *Community* in stop-motion animation as a way to maintain some of the traditional elements of Christmas for which he feels he is losing control ("Abed's Uncontrollable Christmas," Episode 2.11). But unlike the "Trekkies" of the 1980s and 1990s, and following a 21st century trend for the re-evaluation of fans, nerds, and geeks, Abed is not negatively associated with these characteristics.[4] He is a reflection of the pleasure to be had in getting the joke when an obscure reference is made. Being a super-fan of film and television sometimes causes problems for him but also makes him loved and appreciated by his friends. His fanaticism, his geekery, is a barrier as much as it is a means for personal progression. In one of the final scenes from "Critical Film Studies" (Episode 2.19), Jeff is angry and frustrated after being lured in to a homage of *My Dinner with Andre* by Abed and encouraged to reveal fragile aspects of himself only to find the situation was contrived, ruining the surprise birthday party Jeff had planned for Abed: "It turns out while I was wasting my time trying to make you happy you were making yourself happy all over everyone else doing yet another stupid movie spoof." Abed replies, "I prefer the term homage." He then goes on to explain his concerns over how they do not seem to be spending as much time together as they used to: "It wasn't about making me happy. I chose *My Dinner with Andre* because it's about a guy who has an unexpectedly enjoyable evening with the weird friend he's been avoiding lately." Abed attributes this development in their relationship to his inability to change and grow, suggesting he's "more of a fast-blinking, stoic, removed, uncomfortably self-aware type" such as Data or Johnny Five. Jeff replies that he does not need him to grow or change, and their friendship seems to be restored by the genuine conversation they have about the nature of friendship and theirs in particular. Abed's movie allusions and re-creations has both the desired and opposite effect, frustrating and pushing away a friend that he is subsequently able to regain closeness with. Perhaps this is not progress, inasmuch as it seems more like one step back and one step forward. However, maintaining balance requires action from Abed; he recognizes his traits and aims to pursue a path that will prevent his relationships from deteriorating.[5]

Abed also complicates the issue surrounding the seemingly mutual exclusiveness of pop culture obsession and social inadequacies in fans by possibly having a developmental disorder. Throughout all three seasons Abed's behavior is often attributed to, but never explicitly confirmed as, being somewhere on the autistic spectrum. In "Introduction to Film" (Episode 1.3), Abed's father comments on his challenging behavior, suggesting that "he's a special boy"; the film Abed subsequently creates for his course references the difficulties experienced by his family responding to this. In another episode, Abed cites his "developmental disorder" as a reason to break up with his assigned lab-partner, although Jeff's use of the same excuse and along with a parody of Abed ("Star-Wars-Star-Wars, cool-cool-cool" in "Introduction to Film") coupled with the context of the rest of the group using clichéd reasons to end their respective partnerships thus satirizing relationship conventions, creates questions around the veracity of his statement ("Remedial Chaos Theory," Episode 3.3). In the pilot, after his revelation that he is prone to fabricating things in order to manipulate others, Jeff's retort to a critical statement from Abed, "Yeah? Well, you have Asperger's [syndrome]," to which Abed responds, "What is that?" suggests that Abed might be undiagnosed. By choosing not to confirm this in the show, all these instances comment on the lingering issue that surrounds Abed and representations of fans. The "Trekkies" Jenkins describes in the *Saturday Night Live* sketch with William Shatner are told to "get a life," the assumption being that their obsession for *Star Trek* has foreclosed "other types of social experience" (Jenkins 10). With Abed, it is not clear whether his obsessions are a consequence of, or a reaction to a possible disorder. He is, at times, the outsider, but because of what we know and do not know about Abed, this disrupts his confirmation as stereotypical fan. In the search for the purple pen in "Cooperative Calligraphy," as previously discussed, Abed is forced to cope with the situation rather than participate in it. He frames his experience through a television reference, "a bottle episode," but he also recognizes the "emotional nuance" involved is going to make it difficult for him to read the situation. His interpretation is bound by his fanaticism and his possible disorder; neither one taking precedence, neither one presupposing the other.

In the context of a series so hyper-aware of stereotypes, tropes, and devices, and so willing to reference them, Abed also becomes a way to reinforce the show's metatextuality by making us aware of his fictionality through his use of film and TV to narrate episodes. Abed recognizes himself as character, or more bluntly, a device that understands how devices help convey a story. In the second part of the college-wide paintball contest in Season Two ("For a Few Paintballs More,"

Episode 2.24), the theme transitions from the Western motif of the previous episode to a *Star Wars* theme. This is dictated by Abed who recognizes that the change in plot demands Greendale students still in the game join together to create a band of rebels and foil the plot of their rivals at City College, who look a lot like storm-troopers. Abed dons a waistcoat and says, "I'm calling dibs on the Han Solo role before Jeff slips in to it by default." He makes a decision to take on this role, understanding how it will affect his experience. This does not seem to be because he wants to appear roguishly charming. His motivations seem to be about the pleasure of bringing a character he loves to life (before someone else does it without realizing), and about how the Han Solo character will drive the narrative forward. Once the character has served its purpose, he insists that the role be dropped, as demonstrated by his response to Annie who, despite being initially resistant to his role-playing, becomes so charmed by him that even after the game is over she refers to him as "Han." Abed quickly puts a stop to this, stating, "I was only Han Solo because the context demanded it," and now that the context has changed, there is no need for him to continue inhabiting this character.

The movement of other members of the study group in and out of the realms of fandom and geekdom also seek to complicate our understanding of fans and geeks. Troy and Annie are introduced in the pilot as a jock and a goody-two-shoes, respectively. When they appear in the study room for the first time, Troy is wearing a letterman jacket, looking for someone to do his homework; Annie is neatly dressed and concerned about Jeff's qualifications as a board-certified tutor. Very rapidly, this image changes: it is revealed Annie had a nervous breakdown in high school, and Troy lost a college football scholarship by deliberately injuring himself. Their futures are unclear, but this promotes re-evaluation and open-mindedness.

Annie too takes pleasure from opportunities to use fiction to explore reality, recreating motifs and themes and playing at re-creating television shows, but these moments reinforce her moral code in regards to studiousness, school pride, and supporting her friends. When the group takes Troy to a bar to celebrate his twenty-first birthday in "Mixology Certification (Episode 2.10), Annie becomes obsessed with memorizing the details of her fake ID, approaching the situation as she would academically, with diligence and persistence. Intuiting details from what she knows about "Caroline Decker" from her ID, she creates a back-story, fleshes out her personality, creating the character of Caroline. When a bar employee asks about her plans, she replies, "Plans just fall off like me chicken crap off an armadillo. Annie's the one that plans things not me. Annie's my friend; she goes to school here." Without intending to, Annie uses this character to explore her own personality, to reflect on her decisions and consider the way she approaches life. Derived from Annie's existing knowledge of fictional, carefree Texan women: an "ass-kicker," a drifter, a *Thelma and Louise*–type who has dropped all ties to places and people, "Caroline" allows Annie to understand more about herself in a similar way to how Abed appropriates characters or themes from fiction to explore his relationships.

Troy's geeky behavior is evidenced through his relationship with Abed. His boundless enthusiasm complements Abed's pop culture obsessions and together they dress up, recreate favorite scenes, and immerse themselves in franchises, genres, and themes. However, Troy resists when it conflicts with his desire to develop as an individual. In "Epidemiology" (Episode 2.6), wearing *Aliens*-inspired costumes, Troy and Abed recreate the fight between Ripley in an exosuit cargo-loader and an Alien queen to impress women at a Halloween party. It has the opposite effect: Jeff suggests that the reason their performance backfired was because it reminded the women they were trying to impress of "taking their little brother[s] to ComicCon." Troy's response to this is to change his costume to "a sexy Dracula" and calling Abed a "nerd." The use of the word is biting, cutting at the foundations of their relationship by disparaging their common interests. Troy wants to become an adult and engage in adult activities and sees Abed's interests as preventing this. However, Abed's sacrifice of himself in order for Troy to "be the first black man to make it to the end," and defy a typical horror-film trope allows Troy to become a hero, taking action to save the students who have been poisoned by a batch of infected taco-meat. Troy works his way through the zombie crowd, defeating individuals and narrating his actions by commenting on the fictional figures other students have dressed up as. When he encounters zombie Little-Red-Riding-Hooded Annie, he says "what big fists you have-in your face!" punches her, and gets closer to his goal. His knowledge of popular culture is his support to achieve what he needs to inspiring him to continue; he channels action heroes and their corny remarks as they defeat their enemies, and he is ultimately successful.

Similarly, Jeff uses popular culture to achieve his goals but often with more cynical motivations. In the pilot, Jeff is introduced as wily, untrustworthy, selfish, and acutely aware of what he wants and how he can go about getting it. Jeff's appreciation of pop culture comes from an understanding that it can be used to relate to people, and thus, manipulate them. He knows a great deal, as much as his contemporaries, but unlike the others his understanding is that this knowledge can be used to influence people due to their own understanding of film and television tropes. His speeches, which often help to rally the group, draw conclusions, to summarize and extemporize, have the desired effect on the group: they recognize and understand the meanings behind the trope of emotional speeches. His speeches are resolutions; those who experience them are caught in the moment where they can imagine the music, the camera zooming, and the performance of emotive words by a film's protagonist. Jeff's speeches do not even necessarily have to make sense or be original to succeed; the signifiers surrounding the trope are strong enough to be persuasive; they have the same effect on the group as logical and convincing statements. These speeches are a mixture of premeditated, composed with cynical motivations, and heartfelt, un-self-conscious sentiments, but because the trope is so well established its place as either cynical or un-self-conscious, real or contrived, is difficult to define, particularly in the context of *Community* which is so ready to question the definitions of "real." What undoubtedly occurs is Jeff's constant movement between kinds of protagonists. Annie, Jeff, Troy, and Abed move between created realities, using their interpretations of characters and knowledge of fiction to work through situations and understand relationships. As viewers, we understand this use of fiction as a way for characters to develop; to continue their narrative.

The experience of watching *Community* and it being reflective of, and reflecting on, what we know and have come to expect from television and film, becomes like peering through a window at *Community*'s workplace. Viewers are able to glimpse processes at work, the creation of story and the story itself, as well as seeing themselves reflected there. They are also able to knock on the window and pass through their own ideas, influencing the reflection they see and the story seen beyond this. A layering of fictional and non-fictional elements takes place, one over another, over another, until it becomes difficult to establish how we separate real and who the creators are and what is the created. Images and ideas and processes blur; we become aware of the fiction we create from our real lives, creating a meta-experience of a meta-show.

Notes

1. Shows like *30 Rock* and *The Larry Sanders Show* explicitly reference this. They are behind-the-scenes comedies tracking the lives of those that create television shows.

2. Eakin extends the idea of self-narration as part of how a person processes his life, to self-narration creating identity. He discusses how the "self inheres in a narrative of some kind," that "our life stories are not merely *about* us but in an inescapable way *are* us, at least insofar as we are players in the narrative identity system that structures our current social arrangements," linking this narration into self with the inescapable influences of socio-cultural elements (Eakin, xii, x, author's emphasis).

3. Metatextual references in fiction inevitably draw attention to the relationship between the fictional product and the non-fiction process, which is why it seems apt to look towards current theories of non-fiction writing and its interactions with fiction (narrative construction and creative processes, for instance), to draw out some of the issues present in *Community*. What occurs is a questioning of the line drawn between the non-fiction and fiction elements of creative process. Dr. Micaela Maftei's work on the interplay between fiction and non-fiction has been very influential on the formation of these ideas. Her work is *The Fiction of Autobiography: Reading and Writing Identity* (Bloomsbury, 2013).

4. Dr. Lincoln Geraghty's "Representations of Fans and Fandom in American Film and Television" addresses this change, discussing the differences, for instance, between illustrations of fans in the '90s as comic-book-guy-figures in shows like *The Simpsons*, to the fan protagonists of '00's sitcom, *The Big Bang Theory*. An astute scene from the recent remake of *21 Jump Street*

where the two protagonists, educated in the '90s, return to school in 2012 to find that concern for the environment, trying hard, and wearing both straps of a rucksack (as opposed to single-strapping and nonchalant, twisted-spine and sciatica chic) have become the norm, also picks up on this change.

5. Notable traits in other study group members have a similar effect, suggesting that pop culture obsessions are not automatically alienating. Annie's competiveness drives her to accomplish her goals, but it also causes obnoxious outbursts and tantrums when something occurs to prevent these goals from being achieved in the way she desires. She becomes alienated in social situations in a similar way to Abed, isolated at events because of her perceived rigidity when it comes to rules, but she's also interminably reliable and a committed friend.

Works Cited

"Abed's Uncontrollable Christmas." *Community*. NBC. 9 December 2010.
"Cooperative Calligraphy." *Community*. NBC. 11 November 2010.
"Critical Film Studies." *Community*. NBC. 24 March 2011.
"Custody Law and Eastern European Diplomacy." *Community*. NBC. 17 March 2011.
"Debate 109." *Community*. NBC. 12 November 2009.
"Documentary Filmmaking: Redux." *Community*. NBC. 17 November 2011.
Eakin, Paul John. *Living Autobiographically: How We Create Identity in Narrative*. London: Cornell University Press, 2008.
"Early 21st Century Romanticism." *Community*. NBC. 10 February 2011.
"Epidemiology." *Community*. NBC. 28 October 2010.
"Foosball and Nocturnal Vigilantism." *Community*. NBC. 1 December 2011.
"For a Few Paintballs More." *Community*. NBC. 12 May 2011.
Harmon, Dan (danharmon). "@TweetingKerry I prefer the term homage. And it's a tip of the hat, and a sincere thank-you note, to the Van Halen of Community fans." 21 April 2011, 3:41 p.m. Tweet.
"Introduction to Film." *Community*. NBC. 1 October 2009.
Jenkins, Henry. *Textual Poachers: Television Fans and Participatory Culture*. London: Routledge, 1992.
"Mixology Certification." *Community*. NBC. 2 December 2010.
"Modern Warfare." *Community*. NBC. 6 May 2010.
"Paradigms of Human Memory." *Community*. NBC. 21 April 2011.
"Pilot." *Community*. NBC. 17. September 2009.
Raftery, Brian. "How Dan Harmon Drives Himself Crazy Making *Community*." *Wired*, 22 September 2011. Web. 9 December 2012.
"Remedial Chaos Theory." *Community*. NBC. 13 October 2011.
"We Love *Community*." *Tumblr*, 9 December 2012. Web. 9 December 2012.
Zalben, Alex. "Six Seasons and a Movie Art Show Celebrates *Community* In Style." *MTV Geek*. 21 May 2012. Web. 9 December 2012.

About the Contributors

G. Bret **Bowers** is an assistant professor of English at the University of Arkansas–Fort Smith. His research focuses primarily on multimodal composition and digital rhetoric.

Nettie **Brock** is in the Ph.D. program in communication at the University of Missouri. She has taught courses in cinema history, film history, film and society, horror films, public speaking, as well as race, sex and identity online.

Melissa Vosen **Callens** is a senior lecturer and academic advisor in the College of University Studies and an adjunct lecturer of English at North Dakota State University. Her interests include distance education, collaborative writing and a variety of pop culture topics.

Jeremy W. **Cook** is a professor of social sciences at Northern Oklahoma College. His research interests include globalization, Americanization, media studies and pop culture studies. He has been involved with a U.S. State Department grant on food security in Kenya and Uganda.

Jessica **Ford** is a Ph.D. student, tutor, and research assistant at the University of New South Wales in the School of the Arts & Media. Her research interests lie in contemporary postnetwork television and television histories with a focus on gender and feminism.

Mina **Halling** received a bachelor's degree in English literature, language and theory from Augsburg College. Her research interests are literary theory, pop culture and feminism.

Bridget Julie **Hanna** is an education deliverer at the Australian Centre for the Moving Image. Her research includes television and film studies and screen literacy education.

Elizabeth Fleitz **Kuechenmeister** is an assistant professor of English at Lindenwood University in St. Charles, Missouri, and a reviews section editor for the journal *Kairos*. She has written on Art Spiegelman comics, Lois Lane, the rhetorical power of a Planned Parenthood T-shirt and cookbooks.

Lindsy **Lawrence** is an assistant professor of English at the University of Arkansas–Fort Smith. She helped establish a digital indexing project, *The Periodical Poetry Index: A Research Database of Poetry in Nineteenth-Century Periodicals*, including texts by British and American poets, poets from earlier periods and poems in English translation.

Ann-Gee **Lee** is an assistant professor of English at the University of Arkansas–Fort Smith. Her interests lie in composition studies, covert rhetoric, civic discourse, women's studies, disability studies, language pedagogy/theory, literacies, film, television, art and design.

Robin M. **Murphy** is an associate professor of English at East Central University in Ada, Oklahoma. Her main research interests are civic literacy, trauma rhetoric, pop culture studies and feminist theory, and she serves on the review board of the *Computers and Composition Online* journal.

Lisa K. **Perdigao** is an associate professor of English at the Florida Institute of Technology. She wrote *From Modernist Entombment to Postmodernist Exhumation: Dead Bodies in Twentieth-Century American Fiction* and is co-editor of *Death in American Texts and Performances: Corpses, Ghosts, and the Reanimated Dead*.

Sallie Maree **Pritchard** is in the Ph.D. program in film, media and theatre at the University of New South Wales. Her interests include genre, spectatorship, and their possible applications to the practice of screenwriting.

Amanda **Riter** is pursuing a master's degree in English literature at Weber State University in Ogden, Utah. Her interests include modern media and popular culture, with an emphasis on adaptation studies.

Noah E. **Schmidt** is an English as a Second Language and English composition instructor in Arkansas. His interests lie in applied and documentary linguistics.

Laura **Tansley** has a Ph.D. in creative writing from the University of Glasgow, where she is a postgraduate tutor. Her research interests include creative processes, the relationship between fiction and non-fiction, women's experiences in writing and short-short forms.

Joseph S. **Walker** is an independent scholar and a member of the Mystery Writers of America. He has published articles on subjects including *Mystery Science Theater 3000, The Sopranos, Blossom*, films of the Coen Brothers, *The Blair Witch Project*, and comic mystery novels.

Index

Abed's father 219; *see also* "Introduction to Film"
"Abed's Happy Community College Show" 171; *see also* "History 101"
"Abed's Uncontrollable Christmas" (episode) 15–17, 31, 40, 42, 125, 130, 158, 171, 177, 190, 218; *see also* Christmas
Abrams, J.J. 195*n*2
"Accounting for Lawyers" (episode) 52, 61
activism 82, 83, 88, 91–94, 95, 104; *see also* Perry, Britta
"Advanced Criminal Law" (episode) 55, 57, 76
"Advanced Dungeons and Dragons" (episode) 12–14, 32, 34, 78, 125, 147; *see also* Fat Neil
"Advanced Introduction to Finality" (episode) 170, 176–177
allusion 112, 125, 138–150, 162, 169, 199, 204, 206, 218
"Alternative History of the German Invasion" (episode) 62, 104; *see also* Kevin
Amber (Pierce's stepdaughter) 78; *see also* "Basic Genealogy"
American Dad! (series) 126
anachrony 17–18, 20
analepsis 17–18
Angel (series) 174–175
animation 31, 40, 52, 112, 169, 171, 190, 218; *see also* "Abed's Uncontrollable Christmas"
Annie's Boobs 60, 185, 214; *see also* "Cooperative Calligraphy"; "Paradigms of Human Memory"
"Anthropology 101" (episode) 24, 62, 154, 156, 200, 208; *see also* Old White Man Says
"Applied Anthropology and Culinary Arts" (episode) 107
appropriation 77, 86, 142, 147, 150, 172, 189, 198, 203, 205–207, 215, 217, 221
Archwood, Colonel 122; *see also* "Basic Lupine Urology"
Aristotle 54

Arrested Development (series) 182, 184
art 9, 11, 46, 127–128, 134, 141, 160, 151, 164, 211, 216
"The Art of Discourse" (episode) 76
"Asian Population Studies" (episode) 105
Austin, Buddy 78; *see also* "Investigative Journalism"
Ayoade, Richard 152

Babylon 5 (series) 148
Bakhtin, Mikhail 139–143, 147, 149
Barnes, Troy 11, 19–20, 21, 28, 30, 32–33, 38, 45, 52, 57, 73, 85, 90–91, 94–95, 117, 118–121, 123, 131, 142, 143, 149, 152, 157, 161–162, 169, 176–178, 187, 188, 189, 191, 193, 200, 207, 208, 212, 213, 220, 221–222
"Basic Genealogy" (episode) 78; *see also* Amber
"Basic Lupine Urology" (episode) 111–123, 172, 190, 206; *see also* Archwood, Colonel; Fat Neil; Jamison, Todd; Jenkins, Vicki; Kane, Marshall
Batman 134, 162
Baudrillard, Jean 39–40, 42, 47
Beetlejuice (film) 186
"Beginner Pottery" (episode) 60, 121
Bennett, Andre 96, 192
Bennett, Shirley 29, 30, 43, 45, 55, 56, 60, 62, 73, 78, 82, 83, 85, 88–94, 96, 107, 109, 117–119, 131, 132, 143, 146, 158, 161, 177, 187, 189, 192, 207, 213
Beverly Hills, 90210 (series) 172–173
The Big Bang Theory (series) 49, 222*n*4
"Biology 101" (episode) 60, 94, 193, 201, 206; *see also* Inspector Spacetime
Blue Mountain State (series) 37
Boardwalk Empire (series) 184
Bogner, Coach Herbert 74–76; *see also* "Physical Education"
Borges, Jorge Luis 168, 170, 176
bottle episode 12, 30, 46, 159, 187, 212, 219

Bourdieu, Pierre 161
The Breakfast Club (film) 125, 162, 211
bricolage 114, 116, 119, 122, 123, 126
Brie, Alison 193, 201, 207
Brown, Yvette Nicole 177
Buffy the Vampire Slayer (series) 44, 172, 174, 175, 178
Burke, Kenneth 199
burlesque 114, 116–117, 119–120, 123
Burns, Ken 40, 206
Butler, Judith 68, 69, 86–87, 91

Campbell, Joseph 24–28
The Cape (series) 162, 176, 215
"Celebrity Pharmacology" (episode) 55, 61, 77; *see also* drugs
Chang, Benjamin 51–63, 76, 77–78, 102–103, 117, 131, 132, 144–145, 157, 169, 173, 177, 188, 199–200, 208, 214
Chang's wife/ex 60, 78; *see also* "Environmental Science"
Chase, Chevy 80n4, 105, 135, 176
chora 203–204
Christmas 15–17, 31–32, 40, 42, 107; *see also* "Abed's Uncontrollable Christmas"; "Comparative Religion"; "Intro to Knots"; "Regional Holiday Music"
civic discourse 114, 117–118, 123
clip show 17–20, 36, 40–44, 142, 143, 214
"Communication Studies" (episode) 57, 186
commutation 207–209
"Comparative Religion" (episode) 78, 105, 107, 109; *see also* Christmas; Mike the bully
"Conspiracy Theories and Interior Design" (episode) 59, 121; *see also* Professor Professorson
"Contemporary American Poultry" (episode) 40, 131, 146, 149–150
"Contemporary Impressionists" (episode) 48, 185, 191; *see also* Dreamatorium
"Cooperative Calligraphy" (episode) 30, 46, 159, 185–186, 187, 212–213, 219; *see also* Annie's Boobs
Cougar Town (series) 37, 47–49, 94, 131, 134, 162, 163, 193
Cougarton Abbey (series) 47–48
"Critical Film Studies" (episode) 85, 125–137, 152–165, 218–219; *see also* My Dinner with Andre
Curb Your Enthusiasm (series) 184
"Curriculum Unavailable" (episode) 36, 38, 43–45, 46, 59
"Custody Law and Eastern European Diplomacy" (episode) 215

Dallas (series) 174
The Dark Knight (film) 218
Dawson's Creek (series) 172, 173–174
"Debate 109" (episode) 43, 215
De Beauvoir, Simone 84

Dexter (series) 184
Día de Los Muertos 57; *see also* "Introduction to Statistics"
Die Hard (film) 7, 8, 125, 143–144, 190
diegesis 13, 21, 84, 167, 173
"Digital Estate Planning" (episode) 32, 33, 40, 202, 207; *see also* Gilbert; video games
Doctor Who (series) 47, 170, 193, 201, 206
documentary 9–11, 22, 32, 34, 40, 51, 176, 190, 206, 217
"Documentary Filmmaking: Redux" (episode) 9–12, 32, 34, 190, 217; *see also* Guzmán, Luis
Dreamatorium 33, 185, 189, 192, 193, 194; *see also* "Contemporary Impressionists"; "Studies in Modern Movement"; "Virtual Systems Analysis"
drugs 61; *see also* "Celebrity Pharmacology"
Duncan, Professor Ian 58, 60–61, 66, 73, 76, 91, 94

"Early 21st Century Romanticism" (episode) 60, 218
Eco, Umberto 37
Edison, Annie 29, 33, 56, 57, 60, 73, 77, 78, 83, 85, 88, 90–94, 96, 108, 117, 120–123, 131, 143, 145–146, 149, 157, 158, 172, 186, 189, 207, 212–213, 214, 215, 217, 220–222, 223n5
"English as a Second Language" (episode) 60, 101, 102–103
"Environmental Science" (episode) 56
"Epidemiology" (episode) 32–33, 42, 55, 164, 221; *see also* Halloween; zombies
Everybody Loves Raymond (series) 185

Face/Off (film) 144
Facebook 201, 204–205
Faludi, Susan 87, 88
Family Guy (series) 125, 126
Family Matters (series) 188
fandom 42, 49, 112, 114–115, 120, 125, 133, 135, 136, 137, 148, 173, 178, 181, 182, 186, 189, 192, 193–194, 197, 198, 201–202, 203, 204, 206, 207, 208, 209, 212, 214–220, 222n4
fantasy 9, 12, 14, 38–39, 42, 44, 147, 169, 174, 185, 193, 212, 218
Farscape (series) 151
Fat Neil 12, 13–14, 32, 34, 78–79, 119, 123, 147–148; *see also* "Advanced Dungeons and Dragons"; "Basic Lupine Urology"
Felicity (series) 172, 177
feminism 68, 74, 82–96; *see also* Perry, Britta
"The First Chang Dynasty" (episode) 62
A Fistful of Dollars (film) 38, 145, 146
"A Fistful of Paintballs" (episode) 38, 46, 98, 145, 190; *see also* paintball
flashback 7, 17–20, 36, 41–45, 142, 214
"Foosball and Nocturnal Vigilantism" (episode) 190, 218

"Football, Feminism and You" (episode) 77, 82, 84, 85, 88–91, 96, 99, 104–105; *see also* Greendale Human Being
"For a Few Paintballs More" (episode) 38, 47–48, 98, 219–220; *see also* paintball
Friedan, Betty 84
Friends (series) 37, 42
Fringe (series) 167, 169, 173–174, 178

Game of Thrones (series) 197
"Geography of Global Conflict" (episode) 95
Gilbert (Pierce's half-brother) 33–34; *see also* "Digital Estate Planning"
Girls (series) 83
Glee (series) 172, 173, 177, 190
The Godfather (film) 149
The Golden Girls (series) 42
Goodfellas (film) 40, 149–150, 162
Greek (series) 37
Greendale Babies 171; *see also* "History 101"
Greendale Community College 9, 11, 12, 13, 28, 29, 34, 36–37, 38–39, 40, 44, 47, 49, 58, 59, 62, 63, 65, 66, 67, 73, 75, 76–77, 79, 99, 100, 101, 104, 116, 121, 148, 184–185, 190, 192, 194; web site 58, 200–201
Greendale Human Being 98, 101, 105–106; *see also* "Football, Feminism and You"
Guzmán, Luis 9, 217; *see also* "Documentary Filmmaking: Redux"

Halloween 32–33, 42, 55, 170, 221; *see also* "Epidemiology"; "Horror Fiction in Seven Spooky Steps"; "Introduction to Statistics"; "Paranormal Parentage"
Happy Days (series) 188
Harmon, Dan 24–28, 31, 32, 35, 38, 43, 58, 63, 67, 76, 80n4, 80n5, 82, 83, 112, 133, 146, 148–149, 150, 168, 171, 175–176, 181, 185, 186, 191, 193, 195n1, 195n4, 215, 216–217; *Dan Harmon Poops* (blog) 80n4; *Harmontown* (podcast) 76, 80n4
Hawthorne, Cornelius 52, 192
Hawthorne, Pierce 9, 12, 13–14, 21, 29, 30, 32, 33–34, 38, 43, 45, 55, 56, 61, 73, 77, 78–79, 80n4, 84, 85, 89, 90, 95, 96, 105, 118, 131, 132, 147–148, 149, 157, 161, 170, 173, 176, 177, 183, 187, 188, 189, 191, 192, 200, 208, 214
Hearts of Darkness (film) 9, 190, 217
hero 24–35, 51, 57, 221
heteroglossia 139, 145, 146, 148
"History 101" (episode) 59, 171, 177; *see also* Greendale Babies
"Home Economics" (episode) 85; *see also* Halloween; Miller, Vaughn
homosexuality 74, 89
The Honeymooners (series) 174
"Horror Fiction in Seven Spooky Steps" (episode) 95, 158, 186, 191; *see also* Halloween

Hughes, Thomas: *Tom Brown at Oxford* (book) 68, 70–71, 79
Hulu 186, 195n5, 197
hyperreality 36–49

I Love Lucy (series) 174, 183
Inception (film) 142
Inspector Spacetime (series) 47, 169–170, 193–194, 201, 206; *see also* "Biology 101"
"Intermediate Documentary Filmmaking" (episode) 9–10, 176, 190
"Interpretive Dance" (episode) 99
intertexuality 126, 128, 135, 139, 140, 141–142, 145–146, 148
"Intro to Felt Surrogacy" (episode) 174; *see also* puppets
"Intro to Knots" (episode) 45; *see also* Christmas
"Introduction to Film" (episode) 58, 84, 211, 219; *see also* Abed's father
"Introduction to Finality" (episode) 29, 191, 195n1
"Introduction to Statistics" (episode) 57, 77, 78; *see also* Día de Los Muertos; Halloween
"Investigative Journalism" (episode) 29, 78, 103, 108, 188; *see also* Austin, Buddy
Isakson, Professor Pat 58, 59; *see also* webisodes
It's Always Sunny in Philadelphia (series) 49
Ivy league university 65, 76

Jameson, Frederic 127–128, 129, 133, 134–135, 141
Jamison, Todd 120–122; *see also* "Basic Lupine Urology"
Jenkins, Vicki 122; *see also* "Basic Lupine Urology"
Jeong, Ken 177
Journey to the Center of Hawkthorne 202, 207
Jung, Carl G. 52

Kane, Professor Marshall 117; *see also* "Basic Lupine Urology"
The Karate Kid (film) 57
Kevin 51, 61, 62–63; *see also* "Alternative History of the German Invasion"; "Benjamin Chang"
Kickpuncher 162, 218
Kill Bill: Vol. 1 (film) 145–146
Kill Bill: Vol. 2 (film) 145–146
Kristeva, Julia 139, 148

Lambert, Garrett 140–141
The Larry Sanders Show (series) 222n1
law 28, 51–52, 73, 76, 98, 99, 101, 111–123
Law and Order (series) 111–123, 172, 190, 206–207
Locke, John 114–115
logic 15, 24, 89, 103, 123, 144, 147, 154, 203, 205, 222

The Lord of the Rings (book/film series) 16, 62
Louie (series) 184
Lyotard, Jean-François 126–128

Mad Men (series) 125, 184
Mao, Zedong 59
masculinity 65–80, 86; dandy 67, 69, 71, 72, 74; metrosexuality 67, 69, 73, 74–77, 80
M*A*S*H* (series) 37, 107, 174, 183, 188, 189
McHale, Joel 177
McLuhan, Marshall 198, 207–208
Mead, George Herbert 115, 116, 118, 120, 123; social behaviorism 115; symbolic interaction 115
media-literacy 140, 141, 145
meme 116, 118, 123
"Messianic Myths and Ancient Peoples" (episode) 58–59, 168, 189
metadiscourse 38, 112, 113, 114, 120, 125, 126–127, 128, 133, 135, 136, 137, 142, 154, 168, 170, 173, 185, 212, 215, 216, 217, 219
The Mighty Boosh (series) 154
Mike the bully 78; *see also* "Comparative Religion"
Miller, Vaughn 85; *see also* "Home Economics"
mimicry 46, 77, 116–121, 123, 133, 143, 146, 149
The Mindy Project (series) 83
"Mixology Certification" (episode) 192, 218, 220–221
mockumentary 7, 9–11, 16
Modern Family (series) 9, 190, 197
"Modern Warfare" (episode) 7–9, 29–30, 80, 98, 140–141, 143–144, 164, 189, 190, 215; *see also* paintball
Muppet Babies (series) 171
The Muppet Show (series) 170
My Dinner with Andre (film) 129, 133, 134, 157, 160, 162–163, 164, 165, 218; *see also* "Critical Film Studies"
mythology 25–26, 37, 51, 52, 62

Nadir, Abed 9, 10–11, 13, 15–17, 18–19, 21, 31–32, 33, 38, 40, 42, 43, 45, 46, 47–48, 52, 55, 57, 75, 84, 94, 117–123, 130–137, 141, 142, 143, 146, 149–150, 152, 154–155, 156, 157, 158–159, 160–162, 164–165, 167–169, 171, 176–177, 178, 185, 187, 188–189, 190–192, 193–195; Chad 131, 134, 135
narration 7, 9–22, 24, 26–27, 34–35, 43, 46, 51, 66–67, 69, 71–72, 77, 79, 80*n*1, 83, 84, 126–128, 132, 133, 134, 135–136, 138, 139, 140, 143, 146, 148, 150, 153–154, 155–158, 162–163, 167, 168–176, 181, 182, 187, 194, 195*n*1, 197, 198–199, 202–204, 206–209, 212, 213, 215–217, 219–222, 222*n*2
The New Girl (series) 74, 83
new media 197, 198, 199, 202–203, 206, 207–209

nihilism 76, 128, 133, 137
90210 (series) 172–173
Nurse Jackie (series) 184

O'Bagy, Elizabeth 53
The Office (series) 9, 37, 125, 184, 190
Old White Man Says 200; *see also* "Anthropology 101"
"Origins of Vampire Mythology" (episode) 187

paintball 7, 29–30, 38, 39, 43, 44, 46, 47, 98, 112, 140–145, 175, 177, 189, 190, 200, 215, 219–220; *see also* "A Fistful of Paintballs"; "For a Few Paintballs More"; "Modern Warfare"
"Paradigms of Human Memory" (episode) 17–20, 36, 42–43, 60, 142, 213–214, 215, 217; *see also* Annie's Boobs
"Paranormal Parentage" (episode) 170; *see also* Halloween
Parks and Recreation (series) 9, 83, 126, 190
parody 7, 9–10, 12–14, 37, 38, 40, 47, 112–115, 117, 119–123, 133–138, 140–150, 159, 163, 172–173, 193, 206, 219
"Pascal's Triangle Revisited" (episode) 38, 98
pastiche 116–117, 119, 122–123, 127, 133, 134, 141, 160, 189
Patterson, Val 53–54
pedagogy 56–59, 106
Pelton, Dean Craig 9, 10–11, 32, 34, 51, 60, 62, 72–73, 76, 90, 98–109, 121, 122, 123, 141, 143, 158, 175, 177, 185, 188, 189, 190, 193
Perry, Britta 9, 16, 21, 28, 38, 42, 55, 56–57, 73, 76–77, 80, 82–96, 119, 131, 142, 143–144, 146, 152, 156, 157, 158, 161, 162, 187, 188, 192, 193, 211; *see also* activism; feminism
"Physical Education" (episode) 74–75, 121; *see also* Bogner, Coach Herbert
"Pillows and Blankets" (episode) 40, 189, 191, 206
"Pilot" (episode) 24, 28, 39, 46, 65, 72, 73, 83, 130, 184, 187, 218, 219, 220, 221
Plato 46, 136
"The Politics of Human Sexuality" (episode) 98
postmodernism 39, 44, 87–88, 94, 126–129, 133–137, 139–141, 172, 187, 199
Predator (film) 145
Professor Professorson 59; *see also* "Conspiracy Theories and Interior Design"
"The Psychology of Letting Go" (episode) 60, 91–94
Pudi, Danny 47, 201, 204–205
Pulp Fiction (film) 129–135, 152, 156, 157–165
Punch (periodical) 67–68, 70, 71
puppets 92, 174–175; *see also* "Intro to Felt Surrogacy"

race 52–53, 55–56, 60, 79, 83, 98–109, 200, 208
Rashomon (film) 41, 45, 168
"Regional Holiday Music" (episode) 31–32, 44, 173, 190; *see also* Christmas
religion 25, 80n3, 98, 100, 105, 107, 109, 187
"Remedial Chaos Theory" (episode) 20–22, 36, 45–46, 167–170, 176, 191, 215, 218, 219
rhetoric of cool 198, 203, 208, 209
Rodriguez, Leonard 141, 173, 199, 208
Rose, Mike 73, 79
Roswell (series) 177
Rowan and Martin's Laugh-In (series) 125
Run Lola Run (film) 168

Saturday Night Live (series) 125, 217, 219
Saved by the Bell (series) 173
Scarface (film) 144
"The Science of Illusion" (episode) 84, 85, 158
Scrubs (series) 37, 48, 75, 126
Seinfeld (series) 37, 126, 174, 182, 183, 184
sexism 91, 93–94, 95
sexuality 9, 28, 71, 77, 78, 83, 85, 90, 91–94, 98, 123, 143, 157, 187, 200, 214, 218, 221
The Simpsons (series) 125, 126, 143, 150, 189–190, 222n4
simulacrum 36–37, 39, 40, 43, 44–49
simulation 33, 37, 39, 40
sitcom 7, 9–10, 18, 20, 37–40, 44, 46–49, 66, 112, 114, 115, 117, 121, 123, 125, 132, 150, 154, 157, 176, 182–183, 188, 205, 206, 208, 212, 214, 222n4
"Six seasons and a movie" 215, 216
Slater, Prof. Michelle 38, 77
The Sopranos (series) 182, 183–184
"Spanish 101" (episode) 28, 52, 54–56; *see also* "Benjamin Chang"
Star Burns/Alex Osbourne 57, 118, 119, 120, 122, 123, 199–200, 208
Star Trek (series) 40, 45, 168, 176, 182, 183, 219
Star Wars (film) 38, 163, 219, 220
"Studies in Modern Movement" (episode) 185; *see also* Dreamatorium
Superman 176

Tarantino, Quentin 135, 145, 146, 159–160, 161, 162, 163, 164
Terminator (film) 141, 190
Terminator 2: Judgment Day (film) 141

text 8, 21, 44, 126–130, 133, 134–136, 138–150, 153–158, 160–161, 164, 168, 170, 171, 173, 177, 181, 182, 185, 187, 194, 195n1, 197, 198, 199, 201–207, 215, 217
30 Rock (series) 83–84, 125, 197, 222n1
tiger 53, 56, 59, 62
trickster 51–63
Troy and Abed in the Morning 43, 177, 178, 189
28 Days Later... (film) 7, 140
21 Jump Street (film) 222–223n4
Twin Peaks (series) 174
Twitter 49, 125, 133, 163, 186, 199, 200, 201, 205, 207, 208, 211, 215

the unconscious 24–35, 52, 217
"Urban Matrimony and the Sandwich Arts" (episode) 96

video games 33, 40, 111, 125, 162, 198, 202, 207; *see also* "Digital Estate Planning"
"Virtual Systems Analysis" (episode) 32, 33, 40, 185; *see also* Dreamatorium

The Walking Dead (series) 197
Wanted (film) 144
The Warriors (film) 7, 143
webisodes 57, 58, 59, 195n4, 203, 208; "Dean Pelton's Office Hours" 99; "The 5 A's" 58, 59; "Spanish Videos" 57, 199, 208–209; "Star Burns El Star Prince" 57, 199–200
Whedon, Joss 44, 174, 175, 178, 195n2
Who's the Boss? (series) 162
Winger, Jeff 9, 12, 17, 19, 20, 21–22, 24, 28–30, 33, 34, 36, 38, 39, 42, 43, 44, 45, 51, 54, 55, 56, 58–60, 62, 65, 66, 67, 69, 72, 73, 74–80, 80n1, 80n4, 83, 85, 86, 90, 94, 95, 96, 102, 103, 106, 112, 117, 120–122, 123, 130–137, 140–141, 142, 143, 144, 146, 149, 150, 152, 154, 156, 157–165, 171, 172, 173, 176–177, 187–188, 189, 191, 192, 207, 208, 212–214, 215, 218, 219, 220, 221, 222; speech 19, 20, 29, 43, 45, 76–77, 191, 221–222
The Wire (series) 182

The X-Files (series) 169, 174

YouTube 59, 214

zombies 32, 221; *see also* "Epidemiology"

www.ingramcontent.com/pod-product-compliance
Ingram Content Group UK Ltd.
Pitfield, Milton Keynes, MK11 3LW, UK
UKHW041944140426
5217IPUK00014B/651